Freedom and Time

Freedom and Time

A Theory of Constitutional Self-Government

JED RUBENFELD

Yale University Press
New Haven and London

Designed by Mary Valencia
Set in Stone type by Binghamton Valley Composition
Printed in the United States of America by Sheridan Books, Chelsea, Michigan

Library of Congress Cataloging-in-Publication Data

Rubenfeld, Jed, 1959–
Freedom and time : a theory of constitutional self-government / Jed Rubenfeld.
p. cm.
Includes bibliographical references and index.
ISBN 0–300–08048–4 (cloth : alk. paper)
1. Liberty. 2. Time. 3. Democracy. 4. Constitutional history—United States. I. Title.
JC585.R82 2001
320'.01'1—dc21 00—044914

A catalog record for this book is available from the British Library.

The paper in this book meets the guidelines for permanence and durability of the Committee on Production Guidelines for Book Longevity of the Council on Library Resources.

10 9 8 7 6 5 4 3 2 1

Contents

Part I

LIVING IN THE PRESENT

One

THE MOMENT AND THE MILLENNIUM

On the first page of one of his novels, the author of *The Book of Laughter and Forgetting* has a wife ask her husband a question. How can it be that Western Europeans, generally so anxious for their safety, drive at breakneck speed on the highway? The husband's answer:

> What could I say? Maybe this: the man hunched over his motorcycle can focus only on the present instant of his flight; he is caught in a fragment of time cut off from both the past and the future; he is wrenched from the continuity of time; he is outside time; in other words, he is in a state of ecstasy; in that state he is unaware of his age, his wife, his children, his worries, and so he has no fear, because . . . a person freed of the future has nothing to fear.[1]

This man is exemplary. For a long time, we have called on ourselves, in the name of freedom, to live—in the present.

The demand to live in the present has taken many forms. One repeated trope is casting off the dead hand of past law: "The earth belongs to the living," wrote Jefferson.[2] Another is waking from a sleep: "J'ai hiverné dans mon passé," said Apollinaire.[3] Another: bringing a repressed past to present consciousness and thereby escaping its grip. The "neurotic," Freud discovered, "suffer from reminiscences"; "they cannot get free of the past."[4]

None of this is hedonism. Living in the present is a matter, in the first instance, not of pleasure but of freedom. And of *speaking*. Kundera's motor-

1. Milan Kundera, Slowness 1–2 (1996).

2. *See infra* Chapter 2.

3. Literally, "I have hibernated [or wintered] in my past." Guillaume Apollinaire, *La Chanson du Mal-Aimé,* in Alcools 20 (William Meredith trans., 1964) (1913).

4. Sigmund Freud, *Five Lectures on Psychoanalysis,* in 11 The Standard Edition of the Complete Psychological Works of Sigmund Freud 16–17 (James Strachey trans. & ed., 1962) [hereinafter Standard Edition].

cyclist, for example, who wants to be free of past and future, also wants to talk. He has an "impatience to speak." He has the "stubborn urge to speak." Why? Because he too suffers from reminiscences, which he wishes he could forget. But why speak about such events? Not to dwell on them, or dwell in them. No: exactly as Freud would have had it, by speaking in the present, he would expurgate the past. Only speaking, he imagines, "can make him forget."[5]

This connection between freedom and speech is not fortuitous. It is as deeply established in the language of constitutional liberty as in that of modern psychology. It arises wherever freedom has been idealized as living in the present. For in this ideal, freedom consists of following nothing other than the self's own will, its own voice. This voice, the one that speaks for the present and must be followed if freedom is to be had, appears and reappears in modern thought, expressing itself under a wide variety of names: the "voice of the people"; the "inner voice" or "true voice" of the individual; the "free speech" that is the primary right of democratic liberty.

And when it is experienced this way, as a matter of listening to our own *present voice,* freedom wars with all the texts, large and small, written and unwritten, that govern us.

In political life, the conjunction of liberty with present will puts democracy at war with constitutional law. In personal life, it puts freedom at war with character and with all the commitments, professional or intimate, in which we find ourselves engaged. It leaves us mystified, in other words, by the people we are, the monuments we have built, and the aspirations we pursue.

The desire to live in the present has a history. As we will see, it originates in an imperative of political liberty at the dawn of the modern age and proliferates thereafter—but only after having transmuted itself, obeying a logic we will explore, into an imperative of individual liberty—throughout modern culture. We are used to thinking of modernity as defined in part by future-oriented ideals of progress, increasing technological control, and so on. But modernity achieved its break with the past only by according the present the most profound normative and ontological privileges, and this privileging of the present eventually gave to modern man—who becomes modern man through just this progression—as little reason to think of his society's future as he has to think of its past.

Why are we not more familiar with this history? Because it is constantly obliged to conceal itself. Endlessly repeated, the demand to live in the present must endlessly present itself as something radically new. For the novel is what

5. *Id.* at 39, 152, 144, 149.

this desire desires, which means that it can never admit the extent to which it is itself so repetitious, so historical, so old.

To give just one example, consider "post-modernism." In the words of one of its most lucid proponents, the post-modern "life strategy" is:

> a determination to live one day at a time. . . .To forbid the past to bear on the present. In short, to cut the present off at both ends, to sever the present from history. To abolish time in any other form but of a loose assembly, or an arbitrary sequence, of present moments; to flatten the flow of time into a *continuous present.*[6]

If this "life strategy" seems bold and new to its proponents today, so perhaps did this one forty years ago:

> In short, . . . the decision is . . . to explore that domain of experience where security is boredom . . . and one exists in the present, in that enormous present which is without past or future, memory or planned intention. . . .[7]

What is extraordinary about the post-modern "life strategy" is only that it does not recognize how old-hat it is, how existentialist, how its image has been reflected forever in the smiling face ("live one day at a time!") of the heartbroken, dreamless consumerism that we fortunate Westerners know and love so well.

One especially far-reaching expression of the demand to live in the present can be found in modern economics. The freedom to gratify present preferences here becomes the primary term in understanding rationality, individual liberty, and indeed the very function of the individual in society. "The individual serves," as Galbraith puts it, "not by supplying," and not by "saving[ ]," but "by consuming." Leaving behind visions of man as maker or citizen or dreamer, we now have this: man as consumer. Modern economic rationality is far from hedonistic, but it remains wholly consistent with a society that does not save; a society that borrows uncountable sums against the credit of succeeding generations; a society whose stupefyingly gigantic productive apparatus is organized around the ideal of more and more immediate gratification.

6. Zygmunt Bauman, Postmodernity and Its Discontents 89 (1997) (emphasis in original).

7. Norman Mailer, *The White Negro: Superficial Reflections on the Hipster,* 4 Dissent 276, 277 (Summer 1957).

"A certain emancipation from slavery to time is essential to philosophic thought," wrote Russell. "To realize the unimportance of time is the gate of wisdom."[8]

But the truth is that every effort to "emancipate" ourselves from time, no matter how successful, must, in order to *be* successful, entrench itself in time. It must *hold;* an "emancipation from slavery to time," if it is to emancipate, must at a minimum be remembered, carried forward, projected into the future. The urge to emancipate the present from history is in this sense self-canceling. As a result, it has never commanded, and can never command, the sovereign position to which it aspires.

An example: the revolutions of the eighteenth century proclaimed the right of the living to govern themselves, but these revolutions in fact sought and won historical entrenchment of a certain constitutional transformation. If this transformation expressed the "voice of the people" then, it also projected its governance on generations to come. In America at least, the institutions of liberal constitutional democracy that emerged from this revolution have remained remarkably stable, paradoxically producing a powerful impetus in modern politics to conserve, to preserve, to be faithful to the past.

Modernity's psychological revolution is even more explicit in its contradictory relationship to the claims of the present. Psychoanalysis, ostensibly calling on individuals to free themselves from, to let go of, to "forget about" their past, also obliges its subjects to relive their past. Freud was well aware of this seeming contradiction. Having told his pupils that the neurotic lives too much in the past, he also told them this: "You will perhaps be surprised to learn" that "the task of a psycho-analytic treatment" is "to fill up all the gaps in the patient's memory, to remove his amnesias."[9] Remembering to forget: in order that individuals can forget their past, in order that they live more fully in the present, psychoanalysis asks them to dwell in their past more than any psychology ever had.

Which is to say: the distinctively modern voice, the voice that speaks in the name of the present and hence of freedom, has always been equivocal. Proclaiming a freedom to be in the here and now, a freedom that was supposed to consist of living in the present, this voice turns out to require an interminable engagement with the past and with the future. The self and the society that were supposed ideally to live in the present turn out to have

8. Bertrand Russell, Our Knowledge of the External World 171 (rev. ed. 1961).

9. Sigmund Freud, *Introductory Lectures on Psycho-Analysis,* 16 Standard Edition at 282.

temporal commitments wholly exceeding, wholly ungraspable within, this ideal.

Nietzsche's call to live in such a way as to be able to will, at each moment, the eternal recurrence of the whole, was an attempt to respond to this predicament. If a self cannot live in the present without also projecting itself backward and forward in time, then a way would have to be found to bring the entirety of past and future within the scope, within the commanding but joyful affirmation, of present will. Of all the modern efforts to idealize freedom as perfect conformity between life and will, Nietzsche's is unsurpassable, because he calls on man both to live in the moment and, simultaneously, to live for all time.

But modernity sundered the moment from the millennium. Modernity *created* the present moment—created it as the exclusive site of being, and hence as the exclusive site of will and freedom—precisely by wrenching it from Christian cosmology and hence from eternity's machinery. The present moment *cannot* be what Nietzsche wants it to be—the ontologically and normatively privileged site of will, which alone can make us free—and yet be reunited with eternity. The willing-of-eternal-return remains joyfully skewered by a characteristically modern equivocation: between the desire to live in the present and—the search for lost time.

The call to live in the present portrays freedom as something that we ought to have, or at least aspire to have, here and now. If modern man wants what he wants here and now, what he wants first of all here and now is freedom.

But suppose freedom can never be had in the here and now.

In a sense, this thought is obvious. Of course it takes time to become free. But suppose it takes time, perhaps a long time, to *be* free. If so, it would follow that there could never be a present moment at which we are free. That even if freedom were possible for us, indeed even if it were actual, still it would never be possible for us to be *actually* free—here and now.

And suppose this difficult truth holds because it also takes time, perhaps a long time, to—*be*. Not that time is necessary to all Being-as-such, whatever that might mean, but that time is necessary in a special way to the being of things human: of human being and hence of human freedom. Every page of this book is an elaboration of this proposition.

What might be the significance of this thought? Here are four implications, to be elaborated in subsequent chapters. The first concerns the nature of the self and the mystery of the I. What is this thing, this I, the I whom I think I know when, aware of my own thinking, I think I am?

In the effort to know ourselves, two opposing temptations beguile us: toward what Merleau-Ponty called "full" and "empty" subjectivity. ("There are at bottom only two ideas of subjectivity—that of empty, unfettered and universal subjectivity, and that of full subjectivity sucked down into the world.")[10] Sometimes we say who we are in the following way: by reference to our nationality, race or ethnicity, sex, religion, job, and so on. Here the I is filled up with the attributes and engagements that most centrally define me as the person I am. From this perspective, someone may say of himself that he would be "a totally different person" if he had, for example, a different belief about God.

Yet at other times we feel the absolute insufficiency of this perspective to capture the being of the I. Every belief we hold, every feature of our body, seems suddenly contingent and inessential to the I, which presents itself to us as the unheld holder of our beliefs, the incorporeal possessor of our bodies. Here we seem to know that the I *is,* but we are unable to predicate it except by saying, by repeating, that it is—I. And in this empty Cartesian predication, which ought to mean nothing, we may glimpse, with Yeats, the shivering singularity of humanness, the infinity of creation in ourselves:

I am I, am I . . .
All creation shivers
With that sweet cry.[11]

The full subject is rooted. He knows who he is. The empty subject knows no limits. He is free. As a result, in the play between these subjectivities—and this play plays itself out throughout modern thought—an opposition is created between self-knowledge and freedom.

This opposition is perfectly reproduced, for example, in Rawls. His individuals, whose subjectivity is empty in exactly Merleau-Ponty's sense, attain autonomy only by surrendering all particular knowledge of who they are. An idiosyncracy of the "original position"? Hardly. The same opposition is reproduced in the "thicker," "situated," or "encumbered" selves of Rawls's communitarian critics. These selves own a much fuller subjectivity, but the result is that they find themselves obliged to honor communal obligations that are

10. Maurice Merleau-Ponty, *Everywhere and Nowhere,* in Signs 126, 154 (John Wild ed. & Richard C. McCleary trans., 1964). MacIntyre makes a very similar point. *See* Alasdair MacIntyre, After Virtue 32 (2d ed. 1984).

11. William B. Yeats, *He and She,* in The Collected Poems of W.B. Yeats 286, 287 (Richard J. Finneran ed., 1989).

"antecedent to choice"—for instance, defending slavery.[12] These "involuntary obligations" of membership exert their claims on a communitarian self not by virtue of any choice he has made but by virtue of his being and his knowing who he is.[13] The communitarian self knows himself much better than does the Rawlsian subject, but he attains self-knowledge only at a substantial price to his autonomy.

Whenever social science or cultural criticism seizes on one of these two tendencies in self-understanding—the tendency toward full or empty subjectivity—it produces stick figures instead of persons. Today such stick figures trick about in great numbers, peopling the regiments of "identity politics" on one side, where each individual is more or less consigned (even if only "strategically") to a racialized, sexualized, or intersectionalized identity that society has constructed for him, and the models of economic analysis or "rational choice" on the other, where empty subjectivity prevails and the social construction of individuals and their preferences is more or less ignored.

Merleau-Ponty not only remarked on the existence of these two opposing subjectivities. He went on to observe that they in fact arise from the "same idea."[14] What idea? We might put it this way: both are committed to the idea of a subject constituted as what it is here and now. This is obviously true of the "empty" I, "universal" and "unfettered," which is fully itself in a present moment of apperception, disentangled from all the connections it has had or will have to the world. Something similar holds for "full subjectivity," which, while understanding its historical situation to be central to what it is, is also fully existent here and now. The full I, "sucked down into the world," defined by its memberships, its beliefs or desires, and the social constructions that it inhabits, is consigned to being the person that the world has made it today (obliged, for example, to honor the "involuntary" duties that derive from its being who it is). As a result, both these selves are thrown into question by the thought that human being takes time.

The place of time in the being of persons is at once obvious and obscure. Most of us understand, although we might not use Derrida's words to express the thought, that "the being of what we are is first of all inheritance."[15] We

12. *See* Michael J. Sandel, Democracy's Discontent 13–17 (1996). Sandel invokes the figure of "Robert E. Lee on the eve of the Civil War," feeling a paramount obligation to defend Virginia, to illustrate the kind of "involuntary" obligation of membership that may be incumbent upon "thickly constituted" individuals.

13. *Id.* at 14. *See infra* at 97–98.

14. Merleau-Ponty, *supra* note 10, at 154.

15. Jacques Derrida, Spectres of Marx 54 (Peggy Kamuf trans., 1994).

are what we are in virtue of what has been given to us. But really to think through the extended temporality of human being would require us to break from a certain assumption we almost always hold concerning the relation of being to time. It would require us to break from the idea, in the case of human being, that what is is what it is here and now.

To say that I am what I am only *over time* is to say something very different from the proposition that what I am is decisively shaped by what I have been, or that I will continue to be the person I am over time. If I am I only over time, then there is never a present moment at which I can say, *I am.* I do not *now* exist. At any given moment, there will have been an I only by virtue of my having led a human life.

Recognizing temporal extension in the I dissolves the conflict between self-knowledge and autonomy. For if "the being of what we are is first of all inheritance," it is also—and also first of all—*will:* not in the sense of a present mental state, which would ideally be given voice and effect in the here and now, but in the testamentary sense of that word, the sense of projecting one's governance into the future by making provision for the future. We constantly devise; we *will* ourselves to and into the future. The temporally extended I is not unfettered, and it is therefore able to know itself in its real particularity, but neither is it consigned to being what it is. Temporality roots the I in a historically determined life-world, but it also ensures that the I can never be defined by reference to its position in the world at any particular time. Its identity is infinite within the limits of the possibilities open to it in its actual temporal trajectory.

Such a self does not exist prior to or apart from its worldly embodiment at any given time, but it is never reducible to its nationality, its race, or any other series of attributes or relationships. Hence its freedom is not sacrificed at the altar of self-knowledge. It achieves freedom not by severing itself from its past, nor by following the call of its own present will or voice, nor by "inhabiting" the identity constructed for it by its community, but by giving itself texts, bequests, commitments that it lives out over time.

The second implication of restoring time to freedom concerns the theory of constitutional self-government. The term "counter-majoritarian difficulty" refers to the notorious problem of constitutional law's evident anti-democratic nature. To quote Alexander Bickel, who coined the term in one of the most influential books written on constitutional law in the past fifty years:

> [W]hen the Supreme Court declares unconstitutional a legislative act or the action of the executive, it thwarts the will of representatives of the

> actual people of the here and now; it exercises control, not in behalf of the prevailing majority, but against it. That, without mystic overtones, is what actually happens.[16]

And that is why it can be said that "judicial review is undemocratic." Conclusion: constitutional law is "a deviant institution" in "American democracy."[17]

Observe how this "difficulty" works itself out entirely within the present-tense ideal of freedom described above. Democratic freedom is conceived essentially as governance by the will of the "actual people of the here and now." As a result, a text that resists this present will becomes a deviance, a democratic scandal, a problem forever demanding and forever escaping explanation. Eliminating the "mystic overtones" from constitutionalism leaves constitutional law—a mystery.

There is a host of conventional answers to constitutional law's "countermajoritarian difficulty." For example: constitutional law is consistent with democratic freedom only to the extent that it is ultimately responsive to contemporary popular will. Or: constitutional law is consistent with democratic freedom if it does no more than create and safeguard a set of procedural conditions for the formation and effectuation of informed majority will. Or: constitutional law is consistent with democratic freedom to the extent that it enforces the a-temporal postulates of free and equal individuality on which democracy rests. None of these answers answer, because they either embrace the basic premise that democratic freedom is ideally a matter of achieving governance by the present will of the governed, or else they reject the ideal of democratic self-government altogether, sailing off into realms of a-temporal truth in which the fundamental law of the nation is to be derived from the work of one or another moral philosopher.

Now suppose that democratic freedom, if such a thing is possible at all, is never possible at any present moment. The thought, once again, is not the trivial point that it might take centuries to transform a monarchy into a democracy. The thought is that democratic self-government is itself something that exists, if it exists at all, only over time. Suppose, in other words, that democracy consists not in governance by the present will of the governed, or in governance by the a-temporal truths posited by one or another moral philosopher, but rather in a people's living out its own self-given political and legal commitments over time—apart from or even contrary to popular will at any given moment.

16. Alexander Bickel, The Least Dangerous Branch 16–17 (1962).
17. *Id.* at 17–18.

Restoring time to democracy in this way solves the "counter-majoritarian difficulty." For constitutional law is "essentially" "undemocratic" only when democratic self-government is conceived within an ideal of governance by the will of the governed "here and now." Restore time to self-government, and constitutionalism would no longer stand in a mysterious, presumptively oppositional relationship to democracy. Constitutionalism would *be* democracy—or rather it would promise to be democracy—over time. Constitutional law would be the institution through which a people struggles to memorialize and hold itself to its own fundamental political and legal commitments over time.

Taking this promise seriously requires us to take seriously the idea of a generation-spanning people acting as a political subject. Therefore the subject of peoples, of their commitments, of their reality, and of the conditions of their existence will occupy central chapters of this book. The temptation today is to call peoples imaginary—dangerous fictions. But here too we will find that, in conceiving what it means for persons to be a people, modern political thought has remained trapped within an ideal of voice, common will, and presence.

To make credible the idea of national peoples, it will be necessary radically to reduce what it means for a set of persons to be a people. To reduce it *to writing* (but I do not mean a literal writing), and thereby to extend it, without "mystic overtones," over time. If this anti-republican republicanism, stripped of the ideals of popular voice and popular will, can be worked through, then all the seeming paradoxes of constitutional democracy will fall away.

Third implication: at the same time, there will come into view a conception of individual freedom that cannot be identified with any of the old liberal formulations. This freedom would consist not of a right to engage in self-regarding conduct, nor to pursue happiness after one's own fashion, nor to act on one's own will consistent with a like liberty for others, nor to self-determination, nor to act on the basis of reasons justifiable to all. It would consist of a right not to be written upon, not to have one's life scripted or conscripted by law, not to be made the instrument of dictation. In this anti-liberal liberalism, we will find written constitutionalism's unwritten law: a right of privacy, of inviolable individual freedom, that no democracy can do without.

Fourth implication: the aggressive "globalization" today of a certain political-legal order—essentially free-market democracy, backed up by a written constitution modeled on or even copied from the United States Constitution—

is a process about whose embarrassments we Americans, among its most earnest purveyors, cannot afford to keep silent.

The problem is not that elements from one political-legal culture can never be successfully transplanted to another. This often-cited problem is often overstated. Transplants can be done, and the expected rejection of foreign tissue does not always occur.

The problem, rather, has to do with the relation between the constitutional order and time. One ideal of today's exporters of written constitutionalism is to give developing countries the priceless gift of democratic self-government. They say, in effect, "Here are the institutions of democracy. If you follow them, you are self-governing."

But this ideal fails to understand what was genuinely revolutionary in the democracy initiated by American written constitutionalism. Breaking from a two-thousand-year-old tradition, in which a democratic constitution meant a constitution establishing a democratic politics, America understood a democratic constitution to mean, in addition, a constitution *democratically made.* America made *democratic constitution-writing* part of democracy itself.

That is why there is an unbridgeable difference between the United States Constitution in the United States and a carbon copy of that constitution for the Yap in Micronesia. It is not merely that there will always be gaps between "what's on paper" and "what's real." The point is that the commitments embodied in the United States Constitution are not universal truths for all peoples. They owe their authority and meaning to acts of American democratic constitution-writing and to the way in which this nation has lived under these acts for two hundred years. The authority, the legitimacy, and the value of American constitutional law, for us, all depend in important part on its claim to being law that embodies this nation's *self-given* fundamental political and legal commitments.

Genuinely to export American written constitutionalism to another country would not, therefore, be a matter of transplanting the American Constitution. It would be to transplant the idea and practice of a nation living out commitments of its own authorship over time.

This ideal is not served when professors and students draft basic legal provisions for countries they have barely heard of—even if the provisions they draft are good ones. A written constitution may seem democratic in content, but if this constitution is imposed or maintained undemocratically, something other than democratic constitutionalism will be brought about. Such a constitution will never lose the taint of fundamental illegitimacy, of subjection, of imposition from without. All this is visible in the case of Japan and its restless dissatisfaction with its "peace constitution."

In other words, the "end of history" supposedly brought about by the globalization of the free-market-democratic-constitutional order would require there to be and to *have been* a particular history in the nations to which this order is exported. There must have been a certain history, a provenance in popular struggle and democratic authorship, in order for this order to have for them the value and meaning it has for us. To export this order without this history is to betray it.

And exporting this order without a certain *future* is also to betray it. The legitimacy of a constitution is never secured through a single founding moment, even a moment of perfect popular will. The way a constitution is lived under is equally essential, and this living-under has to include the continuing possibility of a democratic *re*-writing of fundamental law. Democratic provenance is never enough, because a people cannot be supposed to be living under its own commitments if its constitutional order embodies commitments that are no longer the people's own. Hence the most perfect "founding moment" could never be enough.

To be sure, a nation that lives under a constitution imposed from without—imposed, say, by an occupying army or a colonial government now departed—might come to accept the document, to embrace its authority, perhaps even to revere it. But the inhabitants of such a nation will at best be obliged to indulge in a kind of constitutional sacralization. They will see their form of government and their basic law as not changeable, not derived from and hence not subject to their own authorship. At best they will not trust themselves to change their constitution; at worst they will see in it the end of history. But of course the democratic enactment of a constitution is no guarantee against this pathology either.

Part I of this book explores the emergence of the desire to live in the present, describing its origins in modern political thought and its extensive proliferation in contemporary culture. In particular, it describes how a *speech-modeled* conception of self-government came to take pride of place in modern political and constitutional theory, a conception organized around the freedom of speech and the ideal of governance by the present will or voice of the governed.

Part II elaborates a counter-ideal: the ideal of temporally extended freedom. Here the freedom of speech yields its central place to the freedom to write, and the speech-modeled conception of self-government is replaced by a conception of self-government as living out, over time, commitments of one's own authorship. Crucial to this discussion will be the task of finding a way to think about human identity—both personal and political—that incorporates temporal extension into the very structure of the subject.

Part III works out the understanding of American written constitutionalism that follows from this temporally extended conception of self-government. This understanding I call constitutionalism as democracy. Here the counter-majoritarian difficulty is solved, and an account is given of how the Constitution would be interpreted if it were read as written—as an exercise in temporally extended self-government. This account will conclude by elaborating the reconception of fundamental individual liberty—of the right to privacy—that constitutionalism as democracy makes possible.

The demand to live in the present presupposes that it is possible *not* to live in the present. (We would hardly need to be exhorted to do what it is impossible for us not to do.) But what does it mean to live elsewhere than in the present?

For Freud, it was a question of monuments. "[N]ot far from London Bridge, you will find a towering . . . column, which is simply known as 'The Monument'," "designed as a memorial of the Great Fire" of 1666. Such "monuments," wrote Freud, "resemble hysterical symptoms in being mnemic symbols." Of course "there is certainly nothing pathological" in "mourning" for "a short time." "But what should we think of a Londoner who paused to-day in deep melancholy" or "shed tears before the Monument," "instead of going about his business in the hurry that modern working conditions demand?" "Yet every single hysteric and neurotic behaves like these two unpractical Londoners. Not only do they remember painful experiences of the remote past," but "they cling to them," "neglect[ing] what is real and immediate."[18]

A logic is set in motion here, a logic of de-monumentalization. But this logic cannot be consummated. What sort of life could be lived without monuments? Without "mnemic symbols" (which is to say, without writing)? Freud's passage is of course itself a monument.

The logic this passage puts in play correlates the security of one's grasp on "the real and immediate" with increasing or maintaining one's speed (the "hurry" of "modern working conditions") and, conversely, correlates this "hurry" with freeing oneself from the past. Kundera also observes this logic. He offers us this "equation" of "existential mathematics": "a person who wants to forget starts unconsciously to speed up his pace . . . the degree of speed is directly proportional to the intensity of forgetting."[19]

But once this logic is set in motion, we are obliged to see that Freud's "practical Londoner," his man of "business," is not moving nearly fast

18. Freud, *supra* note 4, at 16–17.
19. Kundera, *supra* note 1, at 39.

enough. After all, he has a great deal on his mind—his debts, his fears about the future, his mistress—other than the "real and immediate." Only Kundera's man, "hunched over on his motorcycle," living in "the present instant of his flight," has achieved escape velocity. Only he "has nothing to fear."

This man, however, is in "flight." As it turns out, he is flying from embarrassment at what he has done and will have to do. Having "nothing to fear," he is in fact nothing but afraid—of his past, of his future. The desire to live in the present presents itself as the cure, but it is in fact a symptom. Of a fear. Of a smallness.

The present is small. Living in it is the refuge of those who cannot bear the large responsibility for living over time, the responsibility for what they have been and will be. We are all familiar with this smallness. It is what we feel when, "going about our business" in the "hurry that modern working conditions demand," we have the sense of having filled our lives pursuing the most minuscule and shallow of objects. But today this smallness infects, much more, our political aspirations. It underlies the public sense discernible today of having reached the end of an era, the end of our era, and of having nowhere now to go.

Our politics grows ever more insipid as it grows ever more attentive to what we want, or say we want, here and now. We have today a productive capacity enabling us to realize our dreams to an extent beyond the wildest dreams of those who lived before us—if only we had dreams!

What are our ambitions, here in America, what plans do we have with respect to our unprecedented technological power? What ambitions do we have for the next fifty years? The next five? Other than enhancing the usual economic indicators, none. At this moment, at this millennium, it would seem we have no future. Let us live to see that change.

Two

THE AGE OF THE NEW

One day we woke up to find that the defining event of our millennium had turned into—a bug. A computer bug. Naturally, the predictions of global darkness proved to be the usual millenarian fantasies, but the bug itself was real enough. How much did we spend to exterminate it? According to one estimate, about $600,000,000,000—and that for the United States alone.

This is a book about freedom: more specifically, about democratic freedom under a written constitution. Hard to believe, but there is a connection between this subject and the so-called Year 2000 problem. In this chiliastic coding fiasco lay a secret truth about our democratic culture, a truth even about the United States Constitution. (I said it was hard to believe.) To see this, however, requires the unearthing of a certain historical moment, a Rousseauian or Jeffersonian moment, in which the constitutional texts of the 1780s and the computer codes of the year 2000 have their common root.

Rousseau, composing a draft of what would become *The Social Contract,* had this to say of true sovereignty:

> Now the general will that should direct the State is not that of a past time but of the present moment, and the true characteristic of sovereignty is that there is always agreement on time, place and effect between the direction of the general will and the use of public force.[1]

Contemporary readers of Rousseau are likely to be arrested by the "general will," or perhaps by the apparent intrusion here, into French political philosophy, of a principle from French dramatic poetry. I want to emphasize a different point, the point that to modern eyes might seem self-evident. If there were such a thing as the "general will," and if one sought governance

1. Jean-Jacques Rousseau, *On the Social Contract or Essay About the Form of the Republic (Geneva Manuscript),* in On the Social Contract 157, 168 (R.D. Masters ed. & J.R. Masters trans., 1978) (1762).

by this will, then the "general will" that ought to govern, says Rousseau, is in principle that *"of the present moment."*

With this thought, Rousseau expresses—although in a characteristically more exact and exacting fashion—an idea that fairly bursts from the pages of eighteenth-century radical thought. As Sheldon Wolin puts it, the idea was that "each generation was free to reconstitute political society" as it saw fit, when it saw fit.[2] This thought appears again and again in texts written by men on both sides of the Atlantic, and on both sides of the Channel, throughout the mid- to late 1700s: Webster[3] and Paine,[4] for example, in America, Smith in England,[5] Turgot and Condorcet in France.[6] But perhaps most famously, for us, this idea appears in a Jeffersonian text. This text is worth rereading: it is Jefferson's second declaration of independence—this time from time itself.

The text in question is a letter, written in Paris, addressed to James Madison, and dated September 6, 1789.[7] Speculation has it that this letter was not really

2. Sheldon Wolin, Politics and Vision 311 (1960).

3. *See* Noah Webster [writing as "Giles Hickory"], *On Bills of Rights,* 1 Am. Mag. 13, 14 (Dec. 1787) ("[T]he very attempt to make *perpetual* constitutions, is the assumption of the right to control the opinions of future generations; and to legislate for those over whom we have as little authority as we have over a nation in Asia."). For more on Webster's views, see Gordon Wood, The Creation of the American Republic: 1776–1787, at 376–83 (1969).

4. *See* Thomas Paine, *Rights of Man,* in The Life and Major Writings of Thomas Paine 251, 254 (Philip S. Foner ed., 1961) ("Every age and generation must be as free to act for itself, *in all cases,* as the ages and generations which preceded it. . . . [A]s government is for the living, and for the dead, it is the living only that has any right to it.").

5. *See* Adam Smith, *Private Law,* in Lectures on Jurisprudence 459, 468 (R.L. Meek et al. eds., 1978) ("The earth and the fulness of it belongs to every generation, and the preceeding [sic] one can have no right to bind it up from posterity.").

6. *See, e.g.,* Jacques Turgot, *Endowments,* in The Life and Writings of Turgot, Comptroller General of France 1774–76, at 219, 221–28 (W. Walker Stephens ed., 1895); M. de Condorcet, IX Oeuvres de Condorcet 415–16 (A. Condorcet O'Connor & M. François Arago eds., 1847) ("Les bornes de la durée des lois constitutionelles ne doivent pas s'étendre au delà d'une génération." [The limits of the duration of constitutional laws must not extend beyond one generation.])

7. Letter from Thomas Jefferson to James Madison (Sept. 6, 1789), in 15 Thomas Jefferson, The Papers of Thomas Jefferson 392 (Julian Boyd ed., 1958) [hereinafter Letter to Madison]. Of the many discussions of this letter, particularly interesting treatments may be found in Hannah Arendt, On Revolution ch. 6 (1963); Garry

a letter at all, but rather a kind of manifesto for the use of Jefferson's French friends, with the address to Madison serving as cover in case the document came to light.[8] But whether written for America, France, or both, the letter unquestionably testifies to some of Jefferson's deepest political convictions, to which he recurred throughout the rest of his life.[9]

Jefferson begins by asserting that he is going to treat a proposition that, although heretofore undiscussed "either on this or on our side of the water," deserves a "place . . . among the fundamental principles of every government."[10] What is this new fundamental principle? "I set out on this ground, which I suppose to be self evident"—and this phrase, "to be self evident," cannot fail to echo, at least for American readers, the original Declaration of Independence—*"that the earth belongs in usufruct to the living."*[11] Not to "the dead," nor yet to "the unborn," but only to us, to those alive here and now.[12] The archaic "in usufruct," to which we will return presently, drops out from

---

Wills, Inventing America: Jefferson's Declaration of Independence 123–48 (1978); and Herbert Sloan, *The Earth Belongs to the Living,* in Jeffersonian Legacies 281 (Peter S. Onuf ed., 1993).

8. This is Professor Boyd's hypothesis. *See* 15 Thomas Jefferson, *supra* note 7, at 390. For a contrary view, see Sloan, *supra* note 7, at 305 n.18. Jefferson did eventually deliver the letter to Madison. For Madison's reply, see Letter to Thomas Jefferson (Feb. 4, 1790) in 13 James Madison, The Papers of James Madison 22 (Charles Hobson & Robert Rutland eds., 1981).

9. Jefferson's continuing reliance on the letter's thesis is visible in his Second Inaugural Address, March 4, 1805, and in various other letters. *See, e.g.,* Letter to John W. Eppes (June 24, 1813), in 11 The Works of Thomas Jefferson 297, 298–301 (Paul Leicester Ford ed., 1905); Letter to Samuel Kercheval (July 12, 1816), in 12 *id.* at 3, 11–14; Letter from Thomas Jefferson to Joseph C. Cabell (July 14, 1816), in Early History of the University of Virginia, as Contained in the Letters of Thomas Jefferson and Joseph C. Cabell 67 (Nathaniel F. Cabell ed., 1856).

10. Letter to Madison, *supra* note 7, at 392.

11. *Id.* (emphasis in original).

12. For an argument that Paine was the source of this "fundamental principle," see Alfred O. Aldridge, Thomas Paine's American Ideology 265 (1984). For an argument that Jefferson inspired Paine, see Adrienne Koch, Jefferson and Madison: the Great Collaboration 75–88 (1950). For an argument that Jefferson's principal source was his physician, the somewhat mysterious Dr. Gem, see Boyd's editorial notes in 15 Thomas Jefferson, *supra* note 7, at 384–87, 391–92. The best conclusion may be Lynd's: "we are clearly dealing with an idea which was in the air among an international circle of intellectual friends and cannot, without misplaced concreteness, be attributed to any single author, time and place." Staughton Lynd, Intellectual Origins of American Radicalism 79 (1968).

subsequent statements of the thesis, both in this letter and in future, so that the proposition becomes, in all simplicity, "that the earth belongs to the living."[13]

There is a hint of religion here, as there often is when Jefferson speaks of "the earth" or of those who labor in it. ("Those who labor in the earth are the chosen people of God, if ever he had a chosen people, whose breasts He has made His peculear deposit for substantial and genuine virtue.")[14] In the letter to Madison, Jefferson will say that "the living" hold their rights to the earth by "the law of nature," a law that for Jefferson, as for so many others, was affiliated with divinity ("the laws of nature and of nature's God" is the phrase used in the Declaration). Staughton Lynd is not wrong, therefore, to link Jefferson's thesis to "the ancient conception that the earth was given by God, its ultimate owner, to mankind in common."[15]

But if there remains a Christian root in Jefferson's "earth," his "fundamental principle" is also a repudiation, an almost point-by-point refutation, of a central Christian tenet: that the "meek" "shall inherit the earth."[16] Forget the meek, Jefferson says: it is the living who shall inherit the earth. And forget inheritance: the living "derive these rights not from their predecessors, but from nature."[17] But above all, forget *shall:* it is not that the earth *shall* go to the living, tomorrow, or in some millennial future. The earth *belongs* to the living, it does so in the present tense, it does so as a matter of right right here and now, a matter of the right *of* the here and now *to* the here and now. The earth belongs to us today, if only we are not meek but rather bold enough to seize what nature makes ours.

Thus Jefferson's thesis rejects the *shall* of a millenary future. It also rejects the *shall* that comes from the past, the governance of old law, the authority of the dead. A corollary of the living's sovereignty over the earth is that "the dead have neither powers nor rights over it."[18] Repeatedly the letter disclaims inheritances that putatively impose obligations on the legatees. Jefferson is

13. Letter to Madison, *supra* note 7, at 396.

14. Thomas Jefferson, *Notes on Virginia* (1787), in Basic Writings of Thomas Jefferson (Philip S. Foner ed., 1944).

15. Lynd, *supra* note 12, at 69. Professor Sloan goes further, saying that Jefferson's letter on this point merely repeats the "cliché" that "God, after all, gave the earth to mankind." Sloan, *supra* note 7, at 293.

16. *See Matthew* 5:5 (King James [1611]) ("Blessed are the meek: for they shall inherit the earth."). The gospel here quotes from more ancient scripture. *See Psalms* 37: 11.

17. Letter to Madison, *supra* note 7, at 394–95.

18. *Id.* at 392.

particularly incensed at the idea of the dead passing down debt,[19] a problem with which he had personal acquaintance.[20] If "Louis XV and his contemporary generation" have run up debts to "eat, drink and be merry," is the "present generation" "obliged" to pay for their "dissipations"? The answer: "Not at all." It follows that inherited *laws* are equally non-obliging. As the living are "masters" of "their own persons" along with the earth, they are not bound by any part of the previous generation's legacy, financial or legal.[21] How long, then, can one "generation" maintain its own laws? Calculating generational longevity at eighteen years and eight months—"or say 19. years as the nearest integral number"[22]—Jefferson famously concludes that no law, not even a constitution, can hold for longer than that period. "Every constitution, then, and every law, naturally expires at the end of 19 years."[23]

If we recall that Jefferson was writing in 1789, a year of some small significance in the history of democracy and of constitution-writing, and that the addressee of his letter was James Madison, who at that time was overseeing the enactment of a Bill of Rights not slated to expire after nineteen years, we will better appreciate the irony of Jefferson's position. To say in 1789 that "the earth belongs to the living" was not only to justify the American and French Revolutions, freeing the present, indeed urging the present, to cast off the dead hand of the past. It was also to impugn the tremendous efforts of those who, in the name of those revolutions, on "either . . . side of the water," were seeking to reach their hands, through law, into the future. To Jefferson in 1789, who could not participate in America's constitutional conventions because he was in France, and who could not participate in France's constitutional conventions because he was American, the very principle that gave legitimacy to those conventions condemned their work as illegitimate.

19. *See id.* at 393 ("For if the 1st. [generation] could charge [the next generation] with a debt, then the earth would belong to the dead and not the living generation."); *id.* at 394–95.

20. For an account of the letter stressing its genesis in Jefferson's personal financial position, and particularly in his inherited encumbrances, see Sloan, *supra* note 7, at 288–91.

21. See Letter to Madison, *supra* note 7, at 394.

22. *Id.* at 394. The reasoning was as follows. "[G]enerations, changing daily by daily deaths and births, have one constant term, beginning at the date of their contract, and ending when a majority of those of full age at that date shall be dead." *Id.* According to the mortality tables that Jefferson consulted, "the half of those of 21. years and upwards living at any one instant of time will be dead in 18. years 8. months." *Id.*

23. *Id.* at 396.

Jefferson is not to be understood as counseling pure selfishness on the part of the living. The right of the living is usufructuary; we hold the earth in a kind of trusteeship for those who will be alive tomorrow ("in usufruct" means roughly "in trust"). Hence the living have duties. We must not saddle the future with debt, nor damage the earth that will belong to future generations tomorrow just as it belongs to us today. As Herbert Sloan observes, there is an affiliation here between Jefferson and, of all people, Edmund Burke, who two years later would write: "With respect to futurity, we are to treat it like a ward. We are not so to attempt an improvement of his [sic] fortune, as to put the capital of his estate to any hazard."[24]

But Jefferson's thesis has a corollary against which Burke would direct all his eloquence: the living, according to Jefferson, despite their usufructuary duties toward future citizens, must not *identify* themselves politically with those citizens. We alive today must not suppose that we stand in a special political relationship to past or future Americans—a relationship different, say, from the one we bear to the present inhabitants of China—such that we would be entitled or required to regard America's past or future as in some sense *our own.* To quote Noah Webster, whose thinking on these matters was similar to that of his contemporary Jefferson, we stand in the very same relation to "future generations" of Americans as we do to "a nation in Asia."[25] Past and future Americans are foreigners to us, and we to them. Jefferson is explicit. "We seem not to have perceived" it, he writes, but *"one generation is to another as one independant nation to another."*[26]

Thus does Jefferson declare independence a second time, thirteen years after the first. In the original Declaration, however, the entity declared independent was a *"people,"* implicitly distinguished from others *geographically* or *territorially.* Now, however, the sovereign entity is the *"generation,"* its independence *temporal.* As noted above, Jefferson was hardly alone in this line of thought. The sovereign, independent present was being revealed—the present was revealing itself to itself—in text after text written in the second half of the eighteenth century.

Indeed, for the *encyclopédiste* Turgot, impatience with inheritances was such that even the *charity* of the dead had to be excoriated. Jefferson was infuriated by inherited debt, but Turgot inveighed against testamentary be-

24. Edmund Burke, *An Appeal from the New to the Old Whigs* (1791), in Further Reflections on the Revolution in France 91 (Daniel E. Ritchie ed., 1992). *See* Sloan, *supra* note 7, at 298–300.

25. Webster, *supra* note 3, at 14.

26. Letter to Madison, *supra* note 7, at 395 (emphasis added).

neficence, which both "subsidise[d] idleness" and placed the living under the yoke of the dead, "as if ignorant and short-sighted individuals had the right to chain to their capricious wills the generations that had still to be born."[27] Mere *monuments* to the dead—and such "mnemic symbols" are regarded here from the very same perspective of practicality, of the "real and immediate," that Freud will adopt toward monuments 150 years later—are an affront to the living:

> If all the men who have lived had had a tombstone erected for them, it would have been necessary, in order to find ground to cultivate, to overthrow the sterile monuments and to stir up the ashes of the dead to nourish the living.[28]

It was necessary, in other words, for men to stop monumentalizing the past. It was necessary for them to learn to live in the present. The proposition that the earth "belongs to the living" was not new in 1789, but this revelation of the present, on behalf of which Jefferson, Rousseau, Turgot, and so many others spoke, this demand for government of the present, by the present, for the present, in its break with Christianity, in its break with the past, was new for Western thought.[29] It was the discovery—the self-discovery—of modernity itself.

This discovery has swept though our culture with astonishing reach. But as it spreads, in many of its manifestations, the demand that we live in the present undergoes a decisive transformation: from an imperative of *political* freedom or well-being to an imperative of *individual* freedom or well-being. If this transformation was contrary to Jefferson's or Rousseau's intentions, still it was in part dictated by the very logic of the position that they embraced. Politics and collective political entities like nations are almost unintelligible in the present moment. If we are to live in the present, we have neither reason

27. Jacques Turgot, *supra* note 6, at 228.

28. *Id.*

29. The social contractarians, including Locke and even Hobbes, had adumbrated Jefferson's thesis insofar as they conceded that present individuals could not be bound by the "original compact" without their consent. *See, e.g.,* Thomas Hobbes, Leviathan pt. 2 ch. 26 at 204 (Richard Tuck ed., 1996) (1651); John Locke, Two Treatises on Government, bk. 2, ch. 8, § 116, at 390 (Peter Laslett ed., 1965) (1690). Locke avoided Jefferson's revolutionary result by arguing that anyone who inherits property consents to the original contract. *See* Locke, *supra,* § 73, at 358. For an overview of the relevant pre-eighteenth-century intellectual history, see Stephen Holmes, *Precommitment and the Paradox of Democracy,* in Constitutionalism and Democracy 195, 207–15 (Jon Elster & Rune Slagstad eds., 1988).

nor time to invest importance in political entities like nations, which identify themselves by reaching far into both past and future.

That is why Jefferson and his contemporaries fastened their political rhetoric on the rights and needs of the "present generation." The "generation" would be the self-governing entity with which individuals who live in the present were to identify themselves politically. It would supply a window of time—nineteen years, said Jefferson—in which past-expressed political will could continue to bind. But it turns out to be quite difficult to say exactly what this "generation" is or how its will becomes an acceptable substitute for the inter-generational nation or people whose authority to impose obligations on the living, and indeed whose very existence, has been rejected.

Classical notions of kingdom and politics had envisioned an ancient, immutable body politic, in which all subjects, whether dead, alive, or yet to be, were equally bound up. Thus Hooker: "the act of a public society of men done five hundred years sithence standeth as theirs who presently are of the same societies, because corporations are immortal; we are alive in our predecessors, and they in their successors do live still."[30] Thus also Burke, who reacted to Jeffersonian radicalism by describing society as a "partnership not only between those who are living, but between those who are living, those who are dead, and those who are to be born."[31] But to Jefferson in 1789 (and after), we are emphatically *not* "alive in" the dead or those yet to born. The dead are dead: "the dead have no rights," he wrote; they "are nothing."[32]

At the same time, however, according to the letter of 1789, although we do not "live in" our "predecessors" or "successors," we are still to see ourselves as belonging to a "generation," conceived as a collective political agent with a definite life span and a binding will. The generation, then, was to occupy an intermediate political space between the older sovereign state and the modern sovereign individual, a being who had already appeared, if only embryonically, in eighteenth-century political philosophy.

By 1789, there was a growing realization that even the citizens of a flourishing republic would be animated by their own, conflicting self-interests: a realization we can call Madisonian, although, as Gordon Wood has shown, it was shared by many others of the period. In this way, the radical republi-

30. Richard Hooker, Of the Laws of Ecclesiastical Polity 194–95 (1969) (1593).

31. Edmund Burke, *Reflections on the French Revolution,* in 8 The Writings and Speeches of Edmund Burke: The French Revolution, 1790–1794, at 146–47 (L.G. Mitchell ed., 1989).

32. Letter to Samuel Kercheval (July 12, 1816), in 12 The Works of Thomas Jefferson, *supra* note 9, at 3.

canism of the American Revolution already hinted at the pluralist, individualist liberalism that was to come. Thus to name the "generation" as a subject of self-government was to hold out a stopping point between the ancient but disintegrating classical body politic, with the king at its head, and the modern individualistic world of factional, interest-group politics at which Madisonian thought hinted.

In other words, imagining the "generation" as the subject of democratic self-government had in the late eighteenth century a special virtue: it was to deliver the political unity that the Revolution simultaneously promised and threatened. While allowing for conflicts of interest between rich and poor, old and young, and so on, the generation would yet be a self-governing *whole,* of which individuals would remain but *parts.* Jefferson's letter to Madison continues: "Individuals are parts only of a society, subject to the laws of the whole." But "when a whole generation, that is, the whole society dies, . . . and another generation or society succeeds, this forms a whole, and there is no superior." The generation is one; it is "whole." It is society itself. It is supreme.

But this investment of the "generation" with wholeness, with agency, and with supremacy is deeply precarious. If the present moment cannot be bound by the past-enacted will of a nation, why is it bound by the past-enacted will of a "generation"? Indeed, what is this "generation" if not a generation *of a particular nation* (otherwise it would include the present inhabitants of "nations in Asia," who are supposed to be as foreign to us as is the next "generation")? But if the "present generation" is necessarily the present generation *of Americans, of Frenchmen,* and so on, then it would seem this "generation" cannot even be postulated without covert reliance on the intergenerational entity that was supposed to have been dismissed.

The difficulty at bottom is this. The idea of a binding "generational will" is not reconcilable with the "fundamental" and "self evident" principle from which it is supposed to be derived: that the earth "belongs to the living." It is this principle that motivates both the anti-millenarian and anti-old-law implications of Jefferson's letter. Both follow, for Jefferson, from recognizing the rights and needs of those alive in the here and now as against the claims of a worshiped past or a worshiped future. But the independence of the "living" is not the same as that of a "generation." Because individuals are born, come of age, and die every day, the thesis that "the earth belongs to the living" tends to work against the notion of a singular, unified generation, governing itself under a unitary generational will for nineteen years. (This was a difficulty that Jefferson's letter first acknowledges, but then works hard to suppress.)[33] Jefferson's own logic, taken to its conclusion, does not provide a stopping point at "generational will." On the contrary, if the earth genuinely belongs to the living, there is no stopping point other than Rousseau's: the governing will ought to be that "of the present moment."

In other words, even Jefferson's little nineteen-year period in which constitutions can hold and in which law can bind—even this small effort to save a little time for law and politics—is nineteen years too long. Once cormorant time begins to devour inherited law, once a superstitious reverence for the power of what is dead and gone has been exploded, then the law laid down yesterday is in principle as non-obliging as the law laid down twenty or two hundred years ago.

And then the question becomes: is there a place or a time for politics or for law *at all* once this process has begun? Rousseau's solution—that the law made at one popular assembly is good until the next—is certainly possible (or at least the difficulties raised by this solution need not concern us here), but this solution cannot paper over a certain profound ambivalence that the present-oriented conception of liberty bears to the entire project of law and politics. It is an ambivalence that Rousseau displays throughout his life and work. Rousseau may speak in the name of collective self-government, but his presentist logic presses inexorably toward the figure with which he begins and ends: a figure who, despite being initially or nostalgically imagined in a primitive state of nature, is gradually revealed for what he is—isolated, a-political man, modern man himself, living in the present, lacking a history or a future.

The proliferation of the imperative to live in the present, and its transformation into an imperative of *individual* welfare, can be seen in a wide variety of modern practices, institutions, styles, and literatures. I will illustrate by referring, in the briefest possible fashion, to three very different domains of contemporary thought and culture, each emblematic of modernity in its own way: rational-actor economics, Freudian psychology, and the concatenation of art forms characteristically called "modern" or "modernist."

33. *See* Wills, *supra* note 7, at 126–28. Jefferson initially asks Madison to indulge in a thought experiment. "[S]uppose a whole generation of men to be born on the same day, to attain mature age on the same day, and to die on the same day." Letter to Madison, *supra* note 7, at 393. This supposition is necessary to keep "our ideas clear"; in such circumstances, the "generation" could bind itself for 34 years. *Id.* When, thereafter, Jefferson confronts the fact that populations in fact "chang[e] daily by daily deaths and births," *id.* at 394, he says that the "only difference" this makes is to decrease the number of years that a generation may bind itself (from 34 to 19). *Id.*

The reappearance of Jefferson's fundamental principle in contemporary economics is unmistakable. As Kenneth Arrow has observed, economics has never quite been able to explain why present policymakers should take into account the interests of *future* generations at all.[34] A traditional utilitarian calculus, of the sort typically deployed in economic analysis, would, if taken seriously, show "the utilities of future generations enter[ing] equally with those of the present." But this view would require that, at any given moment, "virtually everything should be saved and very little consumed, a conclusion which seems offensive to common sense."[35] The "most usual" economic solution to this problem "assert[s] a criterion of maximizing a sum of *discounted* utilities," a solution "more in accordance with common sense and practice," but whose "foundations" are "arbitrary."[36] The only logical solution, Arrow suggests, is that the welfare of future individuals should *not* enter into today's policy-making analysis—not directly. Rather, "any justification for provision for the future" must rest only on *present* individuals' preferences, such as the inclination of parents to provide for the welfare of their progeny. If, as seems to Arrow likely, "fathers think more highly of themselves than of their sons," and "more highly of their sons than of subsequent generations," this approach will, happily, produce a result "very much the same as that of discounting future utilities,"[37] but it will do so without arbitrary or false pretenses.

Which is to say: the earth belongs to the living.

Arrow is not necessarily representative of contemporary economic thought in this line of reasoning; he may merely be more determined to take conventional economic premises to their logical conclusion. The economic conception of rational action, as I will discuss in detail later on, is remorselessly present-oriented. To be sure, *homo economicus* is not Kundera's motorcyclist. He invests; he is supposed to be trying to maximize expected *future* utility. But don't let appearances deceive: an individual's concern with his future is fortuitous, from an economic point of view. Rationality as understood in conventional economics is measured solely by reference to how well an agent's decisions instrumentally satisfy his *present* aims and preferences. If a rational economic actor forgoes present pleasures in favor of future wealth, it is only

34. *See* Kenneth J. Arrow, *Notes on Rawls's Theory of Justice,* in 1 Collected Papers of Kenneth J. Arrow: Social Choice and Justice 96 (1983).

35. *Id.* at 111.

36. *Id.* (emphasis in original).

37. *Id.* at 112. Of course it would also follow that "the burden of saving should fall only on those with children and perhaps in proportion to the number of children." *Id.*

because and to the extent that he happens currently to have a "taste" for his own future utility. If the agent does not have this taste, economics supplies no reason for him to do so. On the contrary, just as Arrow suggests, economic analysis regards the future as relevant to its calculations only if and to the extent that there exist present future-oriented preferences. The culmination of economic rationality is, therefore, the idea of *discounted present value,* through which everything we want from the future can be reduced to a present demand for—what else?—currency.

Economics, from this point of view, is already a kind of modern psychology, but if modern psychology proper begins in earnest with Freud, then it too begins with a declaration of temporal independence. The defining discovery of psychoanalysis is that mental ill-health consists of living in the "mnemic" grip of a certain traumatic past. This past, never having been made present to consciousness in its own time, is expungeable only through speech. Hence the obsession, in our very psychotherapeutic culture, with *talking,* with voice, with confessing. Behind the endless confessionalism of contemporary culture, the putative idea is always what Freud said it was: to get free of the past by speaking it here and now.

Being in the moment is the aspiration of all those cheap psychotherapies that proclaim their devotion to the now in flawless temporal tautologies. The past is past, they remind us. Or: however we got to this place, here is where we are. Or: live one day at a time. Or: today is the first day of the rest of your life. These profundities may at first blush seem to leave open a substantial measure of concern for the future, as if they seriously called on a person to think about "the rest of his life." But of course this future can never quite arrive. For if every day is the first day of the rest of your life, when and what is the "rest"?

The ennobling feature of psychoanalysis, as compared with the fatuities of contemporary therapeutic culture, is its relentless pursuit of truths about which we would prefer to deceive ourselves. But this means that the psychoanalytic subject who would learn to escape the past's grip has to dwell in that past. Triply so: he must remember it; he must find this past reenacted in every relationship and in every slip of the tongue of his daily life; and finally, he must relive it yet again through the transference relationship. As a result, psychoanalysis actually bears a deeply equivocal relationship toward the cult of the present. This is why contemporary psychotherapeutic culture is suspicious of too much Freudianism, which it regards as perversely obsessed with the past, bogged down in childhood and even in infanthood.

But tower though Freud does above the babble of today's self-help movements, he laid the ground for their presentism. It was he who proclaimed psychotherapy's goal as enabling its patients to "get free from the past."[38] The id was to be replaced by ego, and the id, as Freud said, knows nothing of time. It has no "recognition of the passage of time." Only the ego can recognize the id's impulses as "belonging to the past."[39] Only the ego recognizes the "reality principle," which, for Freud, is "the power of the present."[40] Hans Loewald is surely right to see the "ego's function" as that of "creating and recreating presence."[41] The entire point of the "talking cure" was and is nothing other than to replace the mnemic past with the living present: to allow the individual *to live in the present.*

The same desire for a fully lived present moment is visible in modern art forms too. Consider the novel. Everyone knows about the novel's "narrativity," but its astonishing presentism is no longer obvious to us. What made the novel novel was nothing other than its unprecedented ability to draw readers into a present lifeworld, into the interior present consciousness of its protagonists. To understand the novelty of this experience, one must bear in mind the distance between spectacle and audience typical of classical art forms. The novel succeeded as no other art form had in creating for its readers the experience of living in the (fiction's) present, even if this present was the present of a bygone time. Film is more novel still in this respect, producing the simulacrum of a fully lived moment with greater intensity than reality itself. And of course virtual cinema will be the most novel of all.

But again there is an equivocation, a complication or self-contradiction, of the kind observed a moment ago in connection with psychoanalysis. The basic element of *plot* has from the beginning been essential in literature and film, giving these media an extended temporality that complicates their dedication to presence. Indeed this extended temporality has been necessary to produce the experience of living in the fiction's present lifeworld. Novels gave their readers an unprecedented experience of a fully lived fictive present, but they achieved this experience of presence only through an unprecedented temporal extension, a tracing of human lives from childhood onward in a degree of detail unknown to other art forms. This equivocal effort to master the whole being of a person over time without sacrificing the priority of the present appears in the novel's very beginnings, for example in the impossible tale of conception with which *Tristram Shandy* begins.

In the scandalous opening pages of Sterne's novel, a sire is interrupted in

38. *See supra* at 3.

39. Sigmund Freud, *New Introductory Lectures on Psychoanalysis,* 22 Standard Edition, at 74.

40. Sigmund Freud, *An Outline of Psycho-Analysis,* in 23 Standard Edition, at 206.

41. Hans W. Loewald, Papers on Psychoanalysis 44 (1989).

flagrante delicto by his wife's reminder to wind his *clock*. This interruption, we are told by the first-person narrator, who is himself the offspring of the conjugal act being described, caused all the infirmities from which he, Tristram, suffers. Which is to say: a fully successful act of human creation was not possible where the creator was obliged to recall the necessity of time's going on. A moment of perfect creation would evidently have required an escape from time's clutches. Such a moment would at least have permitted, if it did not require, the clock to stop.

But at the same time, the novelist's *own* act of creation—and with Sterne we are dealing almost with the act of creating the Western novel itself—cannot be attained this way. On the contrary, the act of novelistic creation is attained only by a narrator who already knows and keeps in mind the temporally extended trajectory of the life here brought into being. The very grammar of narrative sentences, as Arthur Danto has pointed out, is made possible only by foreknowledge and only by placing the events being described in a relation with the actors' future temporal trajectory.[42] Thus an *author's* siring of a life cannot be done with the clock stopped. It can occur only in time, only over time, and with all the awareness of time's going on that, we were told, interfered with the proper siring of the life whose story is being recounted.

There is, then, a temporal aporia in play here, a struggle between the novel's remarkable capacity to grasp a whole life and its remarkable capacity to deliver an experience of a fully lived present. *Tristram Shandy* is hardly unique in displaying this aporetic struggle within the novel between temporal extension and presentism. The same struggle is named by the title of the greatest cycle of twentieth-century literature, although that name is all but lost when translated as *The Remembrance of Things Past*. Proust's theme: we precisely are not *here,* not *now.* We are not ourselves, we are never what we are, in a present moment. We are who we are only by virtue of a temporally extended identity that re-collects the past fragments of its being and projects them, as a single subject, through time and into the future—even if we are not quite in control of this process, even if it comes upon us in the access of memory provoked by a certain tune or smell. I will return to the equivocality

42. *See* Arthur C. Danto, Analytic Philosophy of History (1965). An "ideal chronicler" of events, as Danto puts it, might in principle transcribe every event as it happened in its own time. But only a narrator can write sentences of the form, "The author of *Principia Mathematica* was born at Woolethorpe on Christmas Day, 1642." Or: "Through the half-open window, he saw her for the last time." Such sentences "refer to at least two time-separated events even though they only *describe* (are only *about*) the earliest event to which they refer." *Id.* at 143.

of modernity's desire to live in the present later in this chapter; and I will discuss at length the relationship between personal identity and time in Chapter Seven. For now let me say only this: modernity's insistence of wrenching the present from the past can never be taken at face value. It is always defied by its own more fundamental, temporally extended commitments.

Nevertheless, as modern literature works out its own logic, it tries notoriously to break down plot, narrativity, and temporal extension in a variety of ways. This strategy produces, however, not freedom or exhilaration but—emptiness. Beckett knew this, and he provided the most powerful memorials: the painstaking description of the movement of a second hand in *Company;* the fragmentation of perspective and destruction of historical time in *How It Is;* the temporal involutions of the trilogy *Molloy, Malone Dies,* and *The Unnameable.* Even Beckett's most accessible works, *Waiting for Godot* and *Endgame,* are united on this point: both those who wait for that which will never arrive and those for whom everything is already over have only the present moment to live in—or escape from—or to come to a stop in. The present moment is all there is, and there is, therefore, nothing, nothing but a certain play of words or logic, a contentless verbal rigor without or almost without verbs—the rigor of death. "And now here, what now here, one enormous second, as in Paradise, and the mind slow, slow, nearly stopped. . . . The words too, slow, slow, the subject dies before it comes to the verb."[43]

So too, but without Beckett's uncompromising conscience, the non-verbal "modern" art forms—abstract expressionism, modernist architecture, modern dance, and so on—make the banishment of narrativity a defining feature. The anti-narrativity of abstract art may occasionally present itself as an almost pre-modern aspiration to timeless forms. Perhaps the strange balance of a Rodchenko gives this impression. But if we fix our gaze on the post-war style epitomized by Pollock, the color field painters, and so on, we find an abstract art seeking not to achieve timeless truth but rather to express, or so it would seem, a pure moment of creation or being, in its own presence, without past or future. "It is as though one's experience" of such works, said Michael Fried thirty years ago, "has no duration—not because one in fact experiences a picture by Noland or Olitsky or a sculpture by David Smith or Caro in no time at all, but because at every moment the work itself is wholly manifest." Of course this story isn't true: no work of art could be at "every moment," or indeed at *any* moment, "wholly manifest." Say rather that Fried expresses

43. Samuel Beckett, Texts for Nothing: Collected Shorter Prose 1945–1980 at 76 (J. Calder ed., 1984).

the unrealizable ambition of the modern abstract style: "Presentness is grace."[44]

Or think of the faceless functionalism of modernist architecture. Compare the traditional cliché of the house as castle with the modernist cliché of the house as *machine-à-habiter.*[45] A castle, however modest, is a historically laden place, providing a refuge, a sense of the subjecthood of the owner, a site where stories unfold. The house as machine cuts off this historicity and narrativity. It is an instrument in a functional network. It is like a dishwasher, existing to satisfy present needs. There is nothing but the present in modernist architecture; it was a style that could not imagine, and made no provision for, its own going out of date. Which is why it became dated so fast. And the moment a modernist building becomes dated, it has nothing left to offer. ("Post-modernist" architecture, scavenging history at will, actually escalates modernism's presentism, stripping historical references of their referents, treating all historical periods as substitutable, fungible commodities in a contemporary currency.) The *machine-à-habiter* would keep its inhabitants in this present that offers nothing but itself. Stories can still happen to such inhabitants, but only when they *get out of the house.* Hence the burgeoning psychic meaning of that very modern phenomenon, the vacation.

But these glimpses into modern economics, psychology, and aesthetics only hint at the breadth of the phenomenon I want to describe. Behold a society consumed with consumption, a society obsessed with currency, with speed, with being up-to-the-minute. Behold a society whose citizens bear not arms but—second hands.

Kundera's motorcyclist does not represent the only way to pursue a fully lived present moment. It is equally possible to seek flight from time while remaining entirely sedentary—in a movie theater, perhaps, or in one's own TV room. The sensational desire and violence that dominate our entertainment iconography vividly display the thirst for a fully lived present. This thirst is most sensible when violence is itself eroticized. Desire is always future-directed, but erotic violence finds its consummation in extinguishing the tomorrow of its object, thus extinguishing desire's own future at the same time. De Sade too, like Rousseau, wished to live in the present.

To be clear, among the many ideals of living in the present, some do not

44. Michael Fried, *Art and Objecthood,* in Minimal Art 136, 145, 147 (Gregory Battcock ed., 1968).

45. Le Corbusier [Charles Jeanneret], Towards a New Architecture 4 (Frederick Etchells trans., 1931) (1923).

belong to modern sensibilities at all. For example, it is possible to construct from New Testament materials, as Kierkegaard and Heidegger did, a distinctly "Christian insight into the momentous quality of every moment as a choice or decision where all eternity hangs in the balance."[46] This "insight" is usually traced to the Pauline emphasis on wakefulness and *kairos* ("moment," "decisive turning point," "crisis"). But Paul's admonition to be "wakeful" was in its own time and place entrenched firmly within a pre-modern millennial temporality: the temporality of judgment days, second comings, and afterlives. Hence the early Christian ideal of living in the present, if there was one, should not be confused with our own. On the other hand, when this Christian "wakefulness" wakes from its dreams of a millennial future and becomes a matter of "Dasein's being wakeful for itself," then it assumes a modern form.

Another instance of a non-modern ideal of living "in the moment" might be found in the parables and imagery of Zen Buddhism. The Zen ideal of emptying out, which has no truck with Western materialism, makes this conception of living in the present worlds apart from our own. Of course there will be plenty of Western consumers of such Eastern spirits, experiencing satori in their twenty minutes at a Kyoto rock garden (marveled about that evening in the comfort of the *ryokan*). But think of the figures of gnarled men or trees in Eastern painting, represented alongside the quivering wing or blossom, and then think of the place of age in Western iconography. As the Western imperative to live in the present works itself out, old age becomes increasingly anathematized. Rembrandt's self-portraits proceed to Wilde's *Picture* and then to the non-age of commercial television; in this progression, the public appearance of old age comes to be seen as inappropriate, frightening, or even a little disgusting, useful only, if at all, to suck time's ravages upon itself, letting us see by contrast how relatively unwrinkled we still are.

Behold, then, a culture juvenescent, forever growing young. We would erase time's mark, if only we could, from the very face of our being. Why do we adore youth? It is not solely because of our fear of death. We fear engagement in time. Fear of death may be universal, but the modern adoration of youth is not; it expresses something more. Figured so long as callow or feckless, Alain Finkielkraut observes, being young today has become the only

46. Charles R. Bambach, Heidegger, Dilthey, and the Crisis of Historicism 212, 214, 237 (1995). For Kierkegaard's use of early Christian thinking, *see* Søren Kierkegaard, The Concept of Anxiety 87–90 (Princeton Univ. Press 1980), and John Caputo, Radical Hermeneutics 15–21 (1987). On Heidegger's translation of the Pauline *kairos,* see both Professor Bambach's book, cited immediately above, and Thomas Sheehan, *Heidegger's "Introduction to the Phenomenology of Religion," 1920–21,* 55 Personalist 312 (1979–80).

"categorical imperative."[47] Finkielkraut quotes Fellini describing the spell of youth on modern culture:

> I wonder what . . . kind of evil spell could have fallen upon our generation, to explain how we started, all of a sudden, to look at the young as the messengers of who knows what absolute truth. The young, the young, the young . . . you would have thought that they had just arrived from outer space. . . . Only some form of collective madness could have made us consider children of fifteen . . . the master guardians of all truths.[48]

It is not so much truth, however, to which the young hold the key. It is being alive, being free. Modernity adores youth because it imagines youth as exquisitely unburdened by temporal engagements, unencumbered by a life-in-progress, fully present as subject and object of desire. *To be young is to live in the present.* That is why youth—in both its sexuality and its self-destructiveness, in both its self-confidence and its alienation, in short in all its *uncommittedness*—is desired above all things. How do we know that this cultivation of youth does not merely reflect the fear of death? Because even as the marriage age goes up, there is one form of commitment—one act always described, at least, in terms of a "committing"—on the part of the young that actually increases in modern society. Now if youth were valued for its distance from death, then the young person who committed this act would be seen as merely stupid, absurd, utterly unyouthful. But on the contrary, the committing of this act, which today for the first time almost claims the status of inalienable right, presents itself as specially alluring for the young, strangely confirming what they are supposed to be. It is the means by which a young person incomprehensibly and yet so understandably does what so many of us wish we could do: escape time altogether.

That the modern era puts into play a new temporality—a new relationship to time—is a theme common to a number of modernity's most acute observers, among them Hans Blumenberg, Jürgen Habermas, Anthony Giddens, and, perhaps influencing all of them, Walter Benjamin.[49] But against this

47. Alain Finkielkraut, The Defeat of the Mind 130 (Judith Friedlander trans., 1995).

48. *Id.* (quoting Federico Fellini, Fellini par Fellini 163 [Paris: Calmann-Lévy 1984]).

49. *See, e.g.,* Walter Benjamin, Illuminations 263–65 (Hannah Arendt ed. & Harry Zohn trans., 1973); Hans Blumenberg, The Legitimacy of the Modern Age 457–62 (Massachusetts Institute of Technology trans., 1983); Anthony Giddens, The Consequences of Modernity 17–18 (1990); Jürgen Habermas, The New Conservatism: Cul-

claim, or against the living-in-the-present variation of it that I have been describing, a number of doubts might be raised.

It might be wondered, for example, whether pre-modern individuals really experienced time in a manner significantly different from the way we do. It might be denied, moreover, that anything useful can be gained from an effort to define the "essence" of "modernity." Finally, to the extent that there is a modern temporality, it might be objected that this temporality is not present-oriented but profoundly historical and futural. After all, modernity is famously the era of "historical consciousness" as well as of progress, and these terms suggest relationships to time considerably richer than a bare desire to live in the present. I will address these doubts in turn.

To say that a new temporality emerges in the modern age is not to suggest that modern persons have some wholly new "experience of time" or of the passage of time. This suggestion is sometimes made. Benedict Anderson, for example, seems to think that the "pre-modern mind" "had no conception" of "radical distinctions between past and present."[50] Of the existence of such categorically different temporal schemas, we should remain dubious, just as we should when anthropologists tell us of Indian tribes who do not distinguish among past, present, and future. (How happy, how hopeful they must be, unable to experience loss.)[51] When I refer to a temporality definitive of the modern age, I mean not a new conception of time, or a new ability to conceive the past or future, but a new devotion to the present, a new investment of the present with tremendous ontological and normative privileges, so that wrenching the moment from time's grip and living in the present somehow become imperatives of freedom, of authenticity, of well-being.

It is true, of course, that any attempt today to define modernity, to capture the "spirit" of the modern epoch, seems—well, naively modern. Blumenberg tells us that the very use of the word "epoch" to denote a particular historical

---

tural Criticism and the Historians' Debate 48, 175–76 (Shierry W. Nicholsen trans. & ed., 1992).

50. Benedict Anderson, Imagined Communities 22–23 (rev. ed. 1983).

51. *Compare* Douglas W. Ackerman, *Kennewick Man: The Meaning of "Cultural Affiliation" and "Major Scientific Benefit" in the Native American Graves Protection and Repatriation Act,* 33 Tulsa L.J. 359, 374 (1997) ("Anglo-Americans conceive of time linearly," whereas "Native Americans" have a "cyclical" or "spatial" "conception of time"), with Glen Stohr, *The Repercussions of Orality in Federal Indian Law,* 31 Ariz. St. L.J. 679, 685 (1999) ("Anthropologists are fond of citing the example of the Hopi language, which lacks words indicating past and future. The casual listener—and first-year anthropology student—often mistakes this to mean that Hopis cannot identify temporal experience, which is patently absurd.").

period, possessed of its own "character and individuality," is itself modern, with significant examples dating to the same late-eighteenth-century period discussed above.[52] One might be tempted to conclude, therefore, with Lyotard and so many others, that the first step toward a less naive history must be to abandon the defunct modern project of telling grand historical narratives about the distinctive character of the modern era.[53] "Modernity ends when it is no longer possible to treat history as linear."[54]

The difficulty with this "post-modern" stance, as Bernard Yack points out, is that there are few historical narratives grander and more linear than the story in which a modern era of "linear" history or of grand historical narrative "ends" and is superseded by a post-modernity that has overcome such historical naivete.[55] If, Yack goes on, we really wanted to end our grand-narrative ways, we would not proclaim the end of modernity, but would instead stop trying to install any single "master-concept" (including that of telling grand historical narratives) as the key to modern life. Hasn't every one of these master-concepts—enlightenment, rationality, secularization, historicity, individuality, equality, capitalism, alienation, sexual liberation—proven hollow? Don't we know by now that all of modernity's self-definitions, whether self-aggrandizing or self-accusatory or both at once, are at best half-truths? "Accepting [the post-modern] critique should spell the end of our *illusions* about the coherence and integrity of modern experience, rather than the end of modernity itself."[56]

This conclusion is surely correct, so long as we recall that "illusions" of "coherence and integrity" can themselves provide coherence and integrity. Grant that modern thought deludes itself in imagining the totality and coherence of its break with the past. Yet there remains, as Yack himself repeatedly demonstrates, throughout a surprisingly wide range of modern thought and practices—political, sociological, philosophical, aesthetic—the insistent pursuit of a single directive: "breaking with the past."[57] This imperative, this declaration of the present's independence, however naive, however illusory or self-aggrandizing, already entails the distinctive modern temporality that I have tried to describe—the desire to live in the present.

52. *See* Blumenberg, *supra* note 49, at 457–62.

53. *See, e.g.*, Jean-François Lyotard, The Post-Modern Condition xxiii–xxiv (G. Bennington & B. Massum trans., 1984).

54. Gianni Vattimo, The Transparent Society 2 (David Webb trans., 1992).

55. Bernard Yack, The Fetishism of Modernities 74–75 (1997). Giddens makes the same point. *See* Giddens, *supra* note 49, at 47.

56. Yack, *supra* note 55, at 5.

57. *Id.* at 29, 35.

Hence a fundamental equivocation: the modern insistence on the present's independence from the past genuinely calls into play a new relationship to time, but the reality remains that there is no such thing as the present's independence from the past. "[I]f the 'modern age' itself explicitly wanted to be a new age," Blumenberg observes, "historical cognition does not require that there be a reality corresponding to such a pretension."[58] Except in one respect: "if the 'modern age' itself explicitly wanted to be a new age," then "historical cognition" *does* require one "reality" corresponding to this pretension—the reality of this wanting and of the belief that this want had been or could be realized.

Modernity's declaration of the present's independence is, therefore, not so much false as fundamentally equivocal. Modernity does possess a "master-idea" differentiating it from the past—the idea precisely of the present's independence from the past—but this idea can never be concretized, never realized in any institution. Institutions are what persist from one day to the next; they are what hold the present to the past. Hence the wish to escape time's grip must never be materialized, never rendered into a form of life, never concretized, memorialized or institutionalized; it cannot be, without reentrenching the present into history and thereby reestablishing time's grip.

In other words, as modernity unfolds into an "age," the age of the new cannot be what it wants to be because the new is no longer new when it is *aged* in this way. Constantly desiring to have the new, to be new, modernity inescapably betrays its age, its repetitiveness, its historical determinedness. The culmination of this self-demolishing desire is the embarrassing celebration, every decade or so, of a "new age," a "new man" or "new woman," a "new world order."

The novel is so old a desideratum of modernity that the very term "novel" has suffered a cleavage in its meaning. Today the word signifies not only that which is new but also something that has come to seem slow and old-fashioned by comparison to the far more sensational arts and entertainments that have followed. The novel has lost its novelty; that is the plight of the age of the new. "Nothing new under the sun" is a pre-modern sentiment; only in the modern era does being new itself become old, opening up an ennui unknown to prior times. "The youth of America is their oldest tradition," said Wilde. "It has been going on now for three hundred years."[59]

I stress this equivocation, this self-demolition, in order to situate the desire

58. Blumenberg, *supra* note 49, at 463.

59. Oscar F. O'F. W. Wilde, *A Woman of No Importance* (1893), in 7 The Complete Works of Oscar Wilde 159, 275 (1923).

to live in the present in relation to those more familiar facets of modern thought that might at first blush be supposed to run counter to it: modernity's famed "historicity" and its equally famous utopian ideals of progress. There can be no doubt that the imperative to live in the present announces itself at the same time as, and indeed as a result of, the emergence of the "epochal" historical consciousness—differentiating the modern "epoch" from others of the past—that Blumenberg describes so well. In one sense, the interdependence of presentism and historicism is merely another instance of the equivocations within the desire to live the present that I have already emphasized. Let me re-emphasize it now: there is no such thing as living in the present. Every self that seeks its freedom—individually or politically—by living in the present fools itself, either denying or flying from its real, inevitable engagements with past and future. So I do not mean to deny the familiar thesis that "modern man" is "historical man" or that modernity introduces a new "historicism" into Western thought.[60]

But the moment it declares itself free and sovereign, the present turns ungratefully on the historical consciousness that helped to set it free. To the newly independent present, history quickly comes to seem deadening, useless, the rusting ladder that should have been heaved away after its use. If modernity "discovered" history, if modern man is "historical man," it is also true that only for modern man can history be—bunk.

It is not only the modern industrialist (not to mention consumer and scientist) for whom history becomes bunk. All across modern thought, too good a memory quickly becomes a thing condemned. History, Renan wrote in 1882, is the enemy of nations.[61] Too great an interest in one's past is neurosis, Freud announced (even as he also announced that the neurotic's cure demands an interminable analysis and recathecting of that past). Nineteenth-century "historical theology," Rosenzweig said, necessarily failed in its object, which was "to heave the past overboard," and thereby "bring the ship of belief . . . safely across the ocean of the present."[62]

60. *See, e.g.*, Mircea Eliade, The Myth of the Eternal Return 141 (W.R. Trask trans., 1954).

61. "L'oubli, et je dirai même l'erreur historique, sont un facteur essentiel de la création d'une nation, et c'est ainsi que le progrès des études historiques est souvent pour la nationalité un danger." 1 Ernest Renan, *Qu'est-ce qu'une nation?* in Oeuvres Complètes de Ernest Renan 887, 891 (Calmann-Lévy eds., 1947). ("Forgetting, and I will even say historical error, are essential factors in the creation of a nation; thus is the progress of historical studies often a danger for nationality.")

62. Franz Rosenzweig, The Star of Redemption 100–01 (W.W. Hallo trans., 1971).

But on the "malady of history," the "historical disease" afflicting modern "individuals as well as nations," Nietzsche is clearest. Consider, says Nietzsche, the "extreme case": "the man without any power to forget." Such a man could not be happy. Happiness depends on "forgetting the past," on "feeling 'unhistorically,' " on leaping into "the moment." "One who cannot leave himself behind on the threshold of the moment and forget the past . . . will never know what happiness is."[63] But above all, such a man cannot be *young* and therefore cannot be really *alive*. Nietzsche protests against "modern historical education," which has produced "the premature grayness of our present youth." "[T]here is a degree of sleeplessness . . . , of 'historical sense,' that injures and finally destroys the living thing, be it a man or a people or a system of culture." The world needs to be "redeemed" from history and from the "graybeards" who study and teach it; the young must rule. "I trust in *youth* that has . . . forc[ed] from me a protest against the modern historical education." When a "new generation" cries, "Give me life," "then will come the reign of youth."[64]

Nietzsche's "man without any power to forget" comes to life in a story by Jorge Luis Borges, *Funes el memorioso*.[65] After a fall from a horse, a young man named Funes attains a memory so "perfect" that he has constantly before him in vivid detail everything he has ever seen or read. He claims to be fortunate in this, but his life is not enviable. The same fall left him crippled. He is insomniac, confined to his dark bedroom, overwhelmed by an "inexhaustible reality." He is "not very good at thinking": he feels a need to give every number its own proper name. "Instead of seven thousand thirteen (7013), he would say, for instance, 'Máximo Pérez'; other numbers were . . . 'the whale,' 'gas,' 'a stewpot'. . . . Instead of five hundred (500), he said 'nine.' " His mind is so "teeming" with "particulars" that he can no longer grasp "abstract" terms such as "dog."[66]

And he cannot be young. He "saw—he *noticed*—the progress of death." He cannot help "continually perceiv[ing] the quiet advances of corruption, of

63. Friedrich Nietzsche, The Use and Abuse of History 14–15, 75, 77 (A. Collins trans., 1949).

64. *Id.* at 15, 71–75.

65. Jorge Luis Borges, *Funes, His Memory,* in Collected Fictions 131 (A. Hurley trans. 1998). A *memorioso* is a person of prodigious memory. Borges does not expressly refer to Nietzsche in *Funes,* but there are obvious implicit references. *See, e.g., id.* at 131 (describing Funes as "a precursor of a race of supermen—'a maverick and vernacular Zarathustra' ").

66. *Id.* at 136–37.

tooth decay, of weariness." At the age of nineteen, he looks as if he himself had become a memorial—"older than Egypt," "monumental like bronze." Funes dies at twenty-one from congestion of the lungs.[67]

But if there is irony when Nietzsche, the classicist, inveighs against history, the irony in Borges's story is almost overpowering. The narrator of *Funes* is recounting events "half a century" after they happened. He remembers Funes vividly, even though he saw him no more than three times. His memory, in other words, is remarkable. (He is himself a "memorioso.") His first words are "I recall"; he adds, however, that he has "no right to speak that *sacred* verb." And he is speaking, it turns out, or rather writing, as a contribution to a volume memorializing Funes's life. Thus the story not only depends on memory but is itself an act of memory and monumentalization, even as it describes the fatality of memory and monumentalization.

Such is the ambiguous fate of modernity's vaunted historical consciousness: modern man cannot be without it, but before long he wants to disown it, because it encumbers his happiness, his youthfulness, his life in the present. Nor is this history's only threat to modern man: more insidiously, history undermines his beliefs and values. Historical knowledge makes us see the contingency, the constructedness, the historical givenness, of everything we believe, and in this way too it drives us inexorably into the present moment. Even science, in which modern man takes most pride, comes under historical attack when historians discover that science's "truth" is merely the product of the current "scientific paradigm," which can claim no special privilege over previous "paradigms." But the historians of science who make this last-ditch effort to reclaim for history science's epistemic supremacy tend to leave out the fact that their reasoning applies against themselves. The historical critique of scientific truth applies a fortiori to history itself, whose validity claims are either modeled on those of science or, at a minimum, are assuredly governed no less than those of science by ruling "paradigms," shifting methodologies, conceptual "revolutions," and so on.[68] If, therefore, history undermines what modern man thinks he knows about the world, it undermines what he thinks he knows about history as well, leaving him more than ever to stand on the

67. *Id.* at 137.

68. On science's "paradigms," see Thomas Kuhn, The Structure of Scientific Revolutions (3d ed. 1996). Kuhn's history (of science) is usually understood, ironically, as if it were making covering-law truth-claims like those of science itself, just as Hempel famously said history should. *See* Karl Hempel, *The Function of General Laws in History,* 39 J. Phil. 35 (1942). On history as narrative, see, for example, Paul Ricoeur, Time and Narrative (K. McLaughlin & D. Pellauer trans., 1984); Paul Veyne, Comment on écrit l'histoire (Paris: Seuil, 1971).

here and now—to stand on what works, to stand on his currency, his consumer goods, his present preferences, his present will. Thus does modern historicity ultimately erase itself.

But what of the future-orientation, the utopianism and progressivism, so well-known in modern thought? The truth is that modernity does not have much of a future. It never did.

To be sure, the modern age begins by proclaiming a new tomorrow, a vision of boundless scientific advance and utopian teleologies. Today we even feel nostalgia for these new tomorrows. In fact, together with its utopianism, modernity has always been nostalgic too, longing for forsaken traditions, for the old, unselfconscious ways. These twin longings—for a past that never was, and for a future that never will be—are inevitable reactions in a subject severed from its real past and its real future. Modern utopianism and nostalgia arise precisely from the admonition increasingly delivered by modernity to its inhabitants—on pain of being inauthentic, unhappy, superstitious, or, worst of all, out of date—to live in the present.

It will be said that I am not doing justice to the forward-looking dimensions of Hegelianism and the other historical teleologies that made progress and human betterment central to modern thought. But just think how many of these grand teleologies, notwithstanding their seeming forward-lookingness, either were fantasies, not genuinely looking to a real future at all, or, if not that, tended to terminate just about where the writer was at the moment of his writing. Hegel is exemplary: modernity's ultimate valorization of the present is to find itself always just arriving at the *end of history*.

When Habermas speaks of a "new time consciousness" developing "in Western culture" since the late eighteenth century, he describes it in the following terms: "the present moment is understood at each moment" as repeating the "epochal new beginning that marked the modern world's break" with the past. *At each moment:* this is what undoes modernity's future. For if each moment must itself be an "epochal" beginning, if each moment must be the dawn, then there is never time for the epoch that was to begin, for the day that was to dawn.[69]

69. Habermas, *supra* note 49, at 48. *See also id.* at 175–76 (describing modernity's present as "a present that is concentrated in the significance of the contemporary moment"); François Ost, Le Temps du Droit 15, 24 (Montreal 1999) (describing modern culture as so "saturé d'instantané" [saturated with instantaneity] that "les projections d'avenir ne procèdent plus que de la science-fiction ou d'utopies incapables de concrétisation" [projections of the future can no longer proceed except in the form of science fiction or of utopias incapable of realization]).

Modernity is the era of the fresh start, where every day is a fresh start. It is the product on the supermarket shelf that "stays fresh for months." In this deathless freshness, in this endless starting, the present is called upon to bear a new relationship to time: to seize itself, to wrench itself from time's grip, to be for itself, to be for the moment, rather than the millennium.

Where did modernity's devotion to the present come from? Perhaps from the Enlightenment, with its relentless critique of tradition. (Newton is worth more than all antiquity, said Voltaire.)[70] Or perhaps from capitalism. Or from the breakdown of religious eschatologies. Or from the industrial revolution, with its upheaval of established social institutions. Or from the collapse of sexual taboos. All these thoughts—I will not call them explanations—may help with the question of origins, or they may beg it. But however we got to this place, here is where we are.

Except that we are not here, at all.

To break with the past is not to live in the present. The revolutions of the 1780s are incomprehensible as efforts to live in the present, because one of their primary objects was to lay down enduring commitments, written in blood, for the time to come. The enterprise of constitutional self-government, commencing in America at the very moment when Jefferson was writing his letter to Madison, and as central to the modern era as any institution or technological development, exceeds and defies modernity's present-tense temporality. The project of memorializing national commitments and living up to them over time is not conceivable in terms of governance of, by, and for the present. But then the nation itself, as Jefferson well understood, defies the temporality of the here and now in the name of which he spoke. And while ideas of nationhood predate the modern era, there can be no doubt that the nation-state is the dominant form of modern political organization, forming in earnest at the very moment—the Jeffersonian or Rousseauian moment—when the present was waking up to itself.

A vast temporal struggle or aporia is, therefore, instinct within modern political thought (just as such an aporia can be seen in modern psychology, in Borges's story of excessive memory, in the novel, and so on). Its own temporally extended commitments, its own being-over-time, exceeds the grasp of its obsession with currency. Modernity can never quite understand itself.

70. Voltaire [François-Marie Arouet], Voltaire's Notebooks 409 (T. Besterman ed., 1952) ("Boerhave utilior Hippocrate, Newton totà antiquitate, Tassus Homero"). But he added, "sed gloria primis" (but glory to the first). *Id.* Professor Gay makes this epigram the epigraph of the first volume of his study of the Enlightenment and dates it to around 1750. *See* Peter Gay, The Enlightenment: An Interpretation—The Rise of Modern Paganism vii, 31 (reissued ed. 1995).

Our political thinking finds increasingly mysterious or indefensible the nationalism and constitutionalism that not only hold surprisingly steady over the modern period, but introduce past-oriented and future-oriented commitments into the heart of modernity itself. More and more, modern thought is obliged to regard these institutions as mere residual expressions, although in new form, of pre-modern attachments to the past. For example, constitutionalism, precisely because it "dispose[s] us to cherish historical continuity," has to be seen as a kind of "ancestor worship," a modern version of the pre-modern "veneration" of the past.[71] From this perspective, the possibility that constitutionalism embodies an entirely new political relation to the past and future—which does not translate into mere pre-modern Burkeanism, "veneration," or "ancestor worship"—is lost to view.

The idea that the earth belongs to the living would have us govern ourselves by our own present will. The issue, then, is the coherence of a conception of self-government that participates in modernity's obsession with currency (or rather *founds* modernity's obsession with currency). Can self-government be conceived as yet another desideratum, like discounted present value, like sexual consummation, like faster computing power, to be had here and now?

The answer is no. But we have no theory of self-government that responds or corresponds to this fact. We have nationalist, constitutionalist institutions that plainly embody the rejection of Jeffersonian presentism, but no theory of self-government appropriate to them.

The written constitutionalism introduced by America in the late eighteenth century, ushering democracy into the modern world, flatly rejects the ideal of democracy as governance by the will of the living. Jefferson lost the battle over the basic contours of American constitutionalism. But Burke lost this battle just as decisively. American written constitutionalism rejected both Jefferson's presentism and Burke's anti-democratic conservatism. It stood for something radically new: a democratic effort by a people to write down and live up to its own foundational commitments over time.

And yet to an extraordinary extent, the Jeffersonian thesis remains the dominant starting point for modern democratic and constitutional theory. Modern political thought may have broadly embraced constitutionalism, but it has never overcome the present-tense conception of self-government in the name of which Jefferson, Rousseau and so many others began to speak two hundred years ago. As the next chapter will show, the ideal of self-government has remained for us an ideal of governance according to the will

71. *See* Yack, *supra* note 55, at 88–89, 100–01.

of the governed, and as a result the concept of constitutional self-government seems almost a contradiction in terms.

Within the Jeffersonian perspective, modernity gives us, at most, a "generation" in which to work. A "generation" is all the future we have, and a generation is never enough. This is why, from Jefferson's declaration of the present's independence, it was but a stone's throw, strangely enough, to our own millennial coding fiasco, the so-called Year 2000 problem.

Why should our early programmers have bothered thinking ahead to the next generation, when members of the next generation were not going to be the buyers of their products? Money belongs to the living. Why should these programmers have adopted an inconvenient three- or four-digit code for identifying years, when the simpler two-digit code would handle all the requirements of their own time, their own generation?

Not that these early codifiers were lazy, greedy, or unpatriotic. They may simply and quite reasonably have supposed that their work would be obsolete by the next generation of software, and here the "generation" naturally gets increasingly compressed, so that it is no longer eighteen years away but only eighteen months away. They may, in other words, have succumbed to modernity's most distinctive and corrosive reason for forgetting the future: belief in one's own imminent obsolescence. We are all passing out of date, into dust, into the ashes that will have to be stirred to nourish the living. Our very genetic composition will no doubt be laughably obsolete within a generation or two. Live in the present, then, since living in the present is—all you can do.

Three

CONSTITUTIONAL SELF-GOVERNMENT ON THE MODEL OF SPEECH

No metaphor is more common in contemporary political theory than the one that figures democracy or self-government in the language of speech, voice, conversation, dialogue, discussion, or some other speech-cognate. "The will of the community, in a democracy, is always created through a running discussion between majority and minority. . . ."[1] "Democracy is government by public discussion. . . ."[2] Self-government is that "state of grace in which . . . the voice of authority is nothing other than the voice of the self."[3] "[M]odern democracy invites us to replace the notion . . . of a legitimate power, by the notion of a regime founded upon the legitimacy of a debate as to what is legitimate and what is illegitimate."[4] More examples could be produced, but this rhetoric is probably at its strongest in the so-called dialogic, discursive, or deliberative models of democracy, which conjure up national "conversations" and now come complete with an entire code of "speech-act ethics."[5]

1. Hans Kelsen, General Theory of Law and State 287 (Anders Wedberg trans., 1961).
2. Holmes, *supra* Chapter 2, note 29, at 233.
3. Paul W. Kahn, Legitimacy and History 8 (1992).
4. Claude Lefort, Democracy and Political Theory 39 (David Macey trans., 1988).
5. Although Habermas is the great figure here, *see, e.g.*, Jürgen Habermas, Between Facts and Norms: Contributions to a Discourse Theory of Democracy (W. Rehg trans., 1996) (especially pages 287–329), excellent discussions may also be found in Amy Guttman & Dennis Thompson, Democracy and Disagreement (1996); Selya Ben-Habib, *Deliberative Rationality and Models of Democratic Legitimacy,* 1 Constellations, Apr. 1994, at 26; and David M. Estlund, *Who's Afraid of Deliberative Democracy? On the Strategic/Deliberative Dichotomy in Recent Constitutional Jurisprudence,* 71 Texas L. Rev. 1437 (1993). For the associated speech-act ethical theory, see, for example, William Rehg, Insight and Solidarity: A Study in the Discourse Ethics of Jürgen Habermas (1994). Democracy and Difference (S. Ben-Habib ed., 1997) contains several other fine essays on the subject.

Why speech?

The answer is that modern political theory has embraced the present-tense temporality proclaimed by Rousseau, Jefferson, and others in the mid- to late 1700s. Speech speaks in modern political theory, as it does in modern psychology, with the promise of eliminating the grip of the past. For this reason, modern political thought had been pursuing a talking cure long before Freud and Breuer proposed theirs. And because a talking cure is supposed to talk away the texts that hold the subject in thrall—because the promise of democracy's talking cure is, like that of psychology's talking cure, to allow its subjects to live in the present—modern political thought always confronts written constitutionalism as a thing antithetical to democracy itself.

The demand for speech in the literature of self-government—for literal acts of speech, said to be essential to liberty—is not a recent development, and it is not limited to one or another ideological camp. It has made itself heard for at least two hundred and fifty years, cutting across the conventional ideological divides, appearing alike in republican, liberal, and even fascist accounts of self-government. Thus Rousseau, who affirmed that the "voice of the people is in fact the voice of God," insisted on a vigorous spoken tongue as a condition of freedom. "[A]ny tongue with which one cannot make oneself understood to the people assembled is a slavish tongue. It is impossible for a people to remain free and speak [such a] tongue."[6] Thus Mill, who wrote that popular assemblies must represent everyone "at all entitled to a voice" in government, insisted that the role of these representatives was not a matter of legislating but of talking. "[I]f [popular] assemblies knew and acknowledged that talking and discussion are their proper business," they would not "attempt to do what they cannot do well—to govern and legislate."[7] And thus Carl Schmitt: "The natural way in which a People expresses its immediate will is through a shout of Yes or No by an assembled multitude, the Acclamation."[8]

The language of voice in these formulations is neither fortuitous nor merely metaphoric. It appears precisely when we are told the necessary,

6. Jean-Jacques Rousseau, *Essay on the Origin of Languages Which Treats of Melody and Musical Imitation,* in On the Origin of Language 73 (John H. Moran trans., 1966).

7. John Stuart Mill, Considerations on Representative Government (1861), in On Liberty and Considerations on Representative Government 173 (R.B. McCallum ed., 1946).

8. Carl Schmitt, *Verfassungslahre* 83 (1928). ("Die natürliche Form der unmittelbaren Willensäußerung eines Volkes ist der zustimmende oder ablehnende Zuruf der versammelten Menge, die Akklamation.")

proper, or natural way for a people or a popular assembly to engage in self-government. Modern political thought obliges us to recognize what I will call a *speech-modeled* conception of self-government.

Among philosophers, only Jacques Derrida seems to have given sustained attention to the distinctive role of the language of voice and speech in political thought. And a basic Derridean insight is inescapable here. The rhetoric of speech and voice marks the operation of a desire for *presence*. But this desire for presence is not the same as that with which deconstruction conjures (I will return to and depart from Derrida's metaphysics later). Speech and voice dominate political thought because political thought has embraced the present-tense demand that the living seize the day and seek governance by their own will here and now.

Speech, not writing, is the linguistic medium of choice for a self that would live by its own present will. So long as the present will of the governed is the ultimate source of political legitimacy, what authority can past will or its defunct legal expressions possibly have? Only as much authority as the *present* will or consent of the governed permit. A self determined to live according to its own present will cannot be governed by a writing, not even by a writing of its own authorship. To such a self, self-government can only be that "state of grace in which the voice of authority is nothing other than the voice of the self."

Thus, having posited that "the general will that should direct the State is not that of a past time but of the present moment,"[9] Rousseau is obliged to idealize the popular voice and the public tongue that would express this will (the general will of the present moment could not be expressed in a writing). Similarly, Schmitt's "acclamation" contemplates not merely a popular will *unmediated* by representatives but a popular will expressing itself in its own *immediate moment.* The same presentism drives Mill's interest in parliament's talk, for in liberal renditions of democracy just as in fascist or republican renditions, the "true consent" of the governed "would have to be continuous—of the living now subject to the laws, not of the dead who enacted them."[10] And today's "dialogic" democrats valorize ongoing dialogue precisely because they too "insist" on a process of "democratic will-formation" that "does not draw its legitimating force from . . . *prior*" expressions of democratic will.[11]

Indeed the very idea of the "will" of the governed is a by-product of this

9. Rousseau, *Geneva Manuscript, supra* Chapter 2, note 1, at 168.

10. Robert Dahl, Democracy and Its Critics 50 (1989).

11. Habermas, *supra* note 5, at 278 (emphasis added).

present-tense temporality. When legitimate political authority is located in the present agency of the governed, what the governed must be thought of as doing, if the polity is to be legitimate, will have to be something that somehow puts popular authority all at once, in a single moment, behind the existing political-legal order. The citizens will have to do something that takes no time to do, something that does nothing—but authorize. Something, in short, like *willing* (or *consenting to*) the present state of political affairs. The concept of the will of the governed takes its place at the forefront of modern political thought as a precipitate of the injunction to locate political legitimacy in a relation between governance and a *present* action on the part of the governed. From the moment that the present moment becomes the exclusive site of legitimate democratic authority, the task of the people can no longer lie in the realm of "doing" at all. It must lie in the realm of *speaking*. This was Mill's point in the passage cited a moment ago:

> Representative assemblies are often taunted by their enemies [as] places of mere talk and *bavardage*. There has seldom been more misplaced derision. I know not how a representative assembly can more usefully employ itself than in talk, when the subject of talk is the great public interests of the country. . . . Such "talking" would never be looked upon with disparagement if it were not allowed to stop "doing"; which it never would, if assemblies knew and acknowledged that talking and discussion are their proper business. . . . It is for want of this judicious reserve that popular assemblies attempt to do what they cannot do well—to govern and to legislate. . . .[12]

If the will of the living is what counts, the political task of the people and the people's representatives will be simply to speak, to give voice to the popular will. (And the freedom of speech will seem the central freedom of a free people.) To conceive self-government on the model of speech, then, is to conceive it as government by the present will of the governed.

But not absolutely, or unreservedly, as government by the present will of the governed. With few exceptions, those who have adopted the speech-modeled

12. Mill, *supra* note 7, at 173. Mill went on to describe representative bodies as follows: "[T]hey are not a selection of the greatest political minds in the country," but rather, when "properly constituted, a fair sample of every grade of intellect among the people which is at all entitled to a voice in public affairs." *Id.* at 173, 174. Thus the members of Mill's "popular assembly" resemble the respondents in a "properly constituted" public opinion survey or focus group: their legitimate role in government derives from their capacity to *speak* representatively.

conception of self-government have never embraced popular will without limitation. There has always been property to protect, or individual liberty, or equality. Hence arises the need for fundamental rights guaranteeing the protection of person or property. And hence the problem of constitutional law.

Within the speech-modeled conception of self-government, a written constitution is a necessity but also a scandal. Old statutes at least remain repealable by recourse to the majoritarian democratic process and are thus, in principle, subject to majority revision at any given moment. But a constitutional text, enacted in some ghostly or backward past, daring to claim superiority over the raised voice of living citizens, is an insult, a perversion, an offense against reason and even against nature. So wrote Jefferson, as we have seen, for whom the continued governance of an old constitution contravened "the law of nature." And so wrote Rousseau, for whom the attempt by a people to lay down constitutional restraints on its own will was "absurd" and "contradictory."[13] Such a constitution would violate the very principle on which it would claim legitimate authority: the principle of the supremacy of present popular voice.

But at the same time, speech-modeled self-government demands constitutional restraints on popular will. Without such restraints, there would be no stability, no security of person or property. A written constitution is necessarily an object of both sacralization and derision in a speech-modeled democracy. Government by present popular voice cannot abide by a written constitution, and cannot abide without it.

As a result, when self-government is conceived in speech-modeled, present-tense terms, constitutionalism and democracy face one another in deep tension, in a seeming antithesis that never ceases to inflame democracy's pride but that can never quite be overcome. That there is such an antithesis between democracy and constitutional restraints is textbook wisdom:

> [T]here must necessarily be some formula or mechanism for the making of decisions or the selection of policies. In a democracy this formula is majority rule.
>
> . . . But democracy has to recognize that a majority can become a tyranny. . . . Thus there must be a balancing of majority power and minority rights. This is the most difficult issue facing any democratic society. . . . For one thing, there is a certain logical dilemma to overcome here.

13. Jean-Jacques Rousseau, *Sur le Gouvernement de Pologne,* in 3 Oeuvres Complètes 981 (B. Gagnebin & M. Raymond eds., 1964) (1782).

> No political philosopher and no constitution-makers have ever quite succeeded in explaining away this dilemma.[14]

But what makes this "dilemma" a "logical dilemma"? The incompatibility of constitutional restraints and democratic self-government need not be figured as a logical dilemma. It could instead be presented, for example, as a failure of democratic courage. Under American written constitutionalism, certain fundamental political matters, the most elemental matters of liberty and justice, are resolved by reference to a document—a piece of crumbling parchment written by persons long dead, ratified in a world very different from our own (indeed a world in which a majority of the governed were denied the most basic rights of citizenship), and interpreted now by unelected, unrepresentative, life-tenured judges. We bow down before our sacred relics and our robed hierophants just like any pre-Columbian people. And we have the temerity to call ourselves self-governing!

Alternatively, the problem of constitutional restraints on democratic will could be thought of as a problem of achieving certain good things—stability, individual rights, the rule of law, the protection of property, and so on—that unchecked democracy cannot be expected to promote. Here too there would be no logical dilemma. There would be only: (1) the theoretical difficulty of identifying which goods are worth preserving at the price of democracy; and (2) the practical problem of devising institutions that can deliver these goods in the face of contrary popular will, without provoking revolt. As in the failure-of-nerve account, there would remain in this picture a basic antithesis between constitutionalism and democracy, but no "logical dilemma."

The antithesis thesis is seen as a "logical dilemma" for democracy because democracy wants—and has always wanted—to claim fundamental guarantees of liberty and justice *as its own.* Democracy does not want to regard individual liberty and justice as foreign, external desiderata that impinge upon its having its way. With few exceptions, partisans of democracy, while balking perhaps at particular instances of judicial review, want to embrace fundamental, constitutional rights as part and parcel of democracy itself. In other words, democracy wants fundamental rights legitimized within the fold of, or under the mantle of, democratic self-government.

But within the speech-modeled conception of self-government, it is very hard to fit such fundamental rights into a democratic system. Fundamental rights would have to stand against the "tyranny of the majority." In order, therefore, to secure such rights within the legal system, wouldn't there have

14. R. Carr, M. Bernstein, D. Morrison, R. Snyder, & J. McLean, American Democracy in Theory and Practice 29–30 (rev. ed. 1956).

to be some kind of dictatorship—even if this dictatorship called itself a judiciary? And isn't dictatorship of any kind antithetical to democracy? This is the "logical dilemma" of constitutional rights in a democracy, the dilemma that has never been "explained away."

In the American constitutional literature, this dilemma, together with the antithesis thesis on which it stands, goes by the name of the "counter-majoritarian difficulty," which has dominated constitutional thought in this country since its inception. Alexander Bickel's 1963 account of this difficulty (mentioned earlier) was seminal, and it reveals in the clearest possible terms how the "counter-majoritarian difficulty" rests entirely on the speech-modeled conception of democracy. According to Bickel, "democracy does not mean constant reconsideration of decisions once made," but it "does mean that a representative majority has the power to accomplish a reversal."[15] This power is "of the essence" to democracy.[16] On the other hand, the "essence" of constitutional law is its counter-majoritarian function. To repeat a passage quoted earlier:

> [W]hen the Supreme Court declares unconstitutional a legislative act or the action of the executive, it thwarts the will of representatives of the actual people of the here and now; it exercises control, not in behalf of the prevailing majority, but against it. That, without mystic overtones, is what actually happens.[17]

None of the "further complexities and perplexities" of American politics, none of the "ingenious" rationalizations of "modern political science," "can alter the essential reality that judicial review is a deviant institution in the American democracy."[18]

In other words, democracy is thwarted when the "actual people of the here and now" cannot get their way. But this diagnosis of constitutional law's deviance from democracy is not the conclusion of *The Least Dangerous Branch.* It is the book's starting point. Bickel goes on to prescribe a physic for constitutionalism's seeming antithesis with democracy, a remedy turning on the possibility of popular will somehow finding a voice in or through the process of constitutional adjudication itself. Bickel's interpretive prescription combines an interesting mixture of prudence and prediction, but the point for present purposes is as follows. "[I]f the process is properly carried out," Bickel

15. Bickel, *supra* Chapter 1, note 16, at 17.
16. *Id.*
17. *Id.* at 16–17.
18. *Id.* at 17–18.

believed, "an aspect of the current . . . popular will finds expression in constitutional adjudication. The result may be a tolerable accommodation with the theory and practice of democracy."[19]

A "tolerable accommodation," not a complete one. "It will not be possible fully to meet all that is said against judicial review."[20] Constitutionalism and democracy inevitably pull "in two opposed directions." What may be hoped for is "some measure of consonance," some "degree of concord between the diverging elements," to keep these nuclear forces from reaching a "critical mass."[21]

Later we will consider Bickel's proposal for achieving "concord between the diverging elements" of this system. For now, the point is only to observe the predominance of the speech-modeled conception of self-government in American constitutional thought and the opposition it creates between constitutionalism and democracy. One more example will suffice: Robert Bork's *The Tempting of America,* published in 1990. In temper, Bork's dogmatic insistence on original intent could not differ more starkly from Bickel's prudentialism and his call for the expression in constitutional law of "some measure" of current popular will. But compare their initial presuppositions.

The "first principle" of the American "system," Bork writes, "is self-government," which "means that . . . majorities are entitled to rule, if they wish, simply because they are majorities." But there is a "second" principle too: "that there are nonetheless some things majorities must not do to minorities, some areas of life in which the individual must be free of majority rule." These are the two principles on which the "United States was founded," and they are "opposing principles," "forever in tension." To protect minority rights from majority "tyranny," courts are entrusted with the constitutional task of "defining these two otherwise irreconcilable principles."[22]

It turns out that courts can discharge this task, according to Bork, by (and only by) adhering to original intent.[23] Hence Bork's interpretive prescriptions differ starkly from Bickel's. But the point once again is that the entire argument derives from a supposed antithesis between self-government and constitutionalism. Constitutional protection of minority or individual rights is

19. *Id.* at 24.

20. *Id.*

21. *Id.* at 27.

22. Robert Bork, The Tempting of America: The Political Seduction of the Law 139–41 (1990).

23. "Only the approach of original understanding meets the criteria that any theory of constitutional adjudication must meet in order to possess democratic legitimacy." *Id.* at 143.

contrary to the principle of self-government. It has to be viewed as a counter-principle, an independent force "forever in tension" with the demand for democratic self-government.

Bork's presentation of this antithesis differs in one important respect from Bickel's. On Bickel's account, only one ultimate norm grounds or defines the American political-legal system: democracy, understood in majoritarian terms. Hence constitutional law is systemically "deviant" and must ultimately accommodate, if only tolerably, present "popular will." On Bork's account, there are two ultimate norms. The principle of self-government (once more understood in majoritarian terms) is offset by a principle of individual rights, a principle demanding protection *against* majority rule, which is set up as a second and co-equal principle of the American founding. Here constitutional rights and restraints are not deviant to, but (at least by half) constitutive of, the American system.

On this point—and perhaps, in a comparison of their respective three hundred pages, on this point alone—*The Tempting of America* reflects a better grasp of the Constitution's place in American democracy than does *The Least Dangerous Branch.* But if Bork, by making constitutionalism constitutive in the way he does, captures something that Bickel missed, still Bork misses what Bickel resolutely kept in view. Within the two-opposing-principles view, what can possibly make the Constitution the legitimate law of the land today? Once an antithesis between constitutionalism and self-government is accepted, the pressing difficulty is to say why it is legitimate to force upon today's majorities a legal text enacted by majorities long dead (a difficulty only exacerbated if that text is interpreted strictly by reference to original intent). Bickel struggled manfully with this problem. It is what drives the entire analysis of *The Least Dangerous Branch.* Bork never confronts it.[24] All is supposed to be taken care of by proclamations to the effect that the two opposing principles were both embraced when the nation "was founded."

This notion of a loyalty-demanding "founding," referred to without explanation or analysis, alone allows Bork to proceed as if the Constitution's legitimacy remains secure despite the antithesis between constitutional restraints and self-government. But he never confronts the fact that the

24. Bork briefly addresses the objection that the living should not be governed by the dead. *See id.* at 170–71. His only response is that the "objection to rule by the dead," whatever its merits, would not justify "activist" constitutional interpretation. But the issue is not whether the "objection to rule by the dead" justifies "activist" constitutional law. The question is whether this objection undermines *all* constitutional law, including an originalist constitutional law. This is the question that Bork never confronts.

"founding" had and has authority—if it ever did and if it still does—not as an act of nature or divine intervention, but only as an act of self-government. As a result, he never worries that one of the two opposing principles supposedly being founded (the principle of self-government) would already have to lie behind the authority of the Constitution, and hence behind its particular anti-majoritarian rights and guarantees, which implies that if self-government should in future come into conflict with these rights and guarantees—if popular will should come to reject these rights and guarantees—then the logically prior principle of self-government ought to supersede that which has been founded upon it.

But we will return below to this difficulty within originalism. For now, three observations. First, despite all the ideological and temperamental differences between them, despite their very different end points, Bork and Bickel share the same basic starting point: the thesis that democracy exists in deep tension with constitutionalism. Second, this same antithesis thesis is invariably in play whenever constitutional scholars grapple with the "counter-majoritarian difficulty." And third, this antithesis thesis arises because democratic self-government has been conceived in speech-modeled fashion, as governance by the present will of the democratic majority.

Constitutional scholars do not invent this conception of self-government. They inherit it—from political scientists, from Jefferson, Rousseau, and all who followed them, from the entire network of cultural forces that render beyond argument the proposition that the world belongs to the living. But would any serious political scientist today equate democracy with simple majority rule? Here is one of the most serious: "Democracy I shall understand as simple majority rule, based on the principle 'One person one vote.' "[25] In this definition, the antithesis thesis is already implicit, even if constitutionalism itself has not yet been mentioned.

Political science need not define democracy as simple majority rule in order to generate the antithesis thesis. So long as democracy is understood in terms that focus on the current agency of the governed, the same result will follow. Thus the disjunction of democracy and constitutionalism is an equally central component of the Schumpeterian school, in which not majority will but electoral competition "is the essence" of democracy—a school carried on for example by Samuel Huntington and to a large degree by social choice thinking.[26]

25. Jon Elster, *Introduction,* Constitutionalism and Democracy 1 (Jon Elster & Rune Slagstad eds., 1993).

26. *See* Samuel P. Huntington, The Third Wave: Democratization in the Late Twen-

In Schumpeterian political thought, the antithesis thesis follows from the need for "analytic precision."[27] To be a useful concept, democracy must be defined without reference to such constitutional values as individual liberty or equality. "[P]opular election of top decisionmakers is the essence of democracy. . . . To some people democracy has or should have much more sweeping and idealistic connotations. To them, 'true democracy' means *liberté, égalité, fraternité*."[28] But such "rationalistic, utopian, idealistic definitions of democracy" cannot "make the concept a useful one." "Fuzzy norms do not yield useful analysis. . . . Democracy is one public virtue, not the only one, and the relation of democracy to other public virtues and vices can only be understood if democracy is clearly distinguished from other characteristics of political systems."[29] In other words, as a matter of analytic clarity, democracy is to be understood as a system of governance accountable to present voter preferences.

A speech-modeled account of democracy can be based on electoral competition or electronic town meetings, on public choice or public dialogue, on majority rule or deliberative communitarian self-definition. But in every case it generates a presumptive skepticism or opposition to constitutional texts. The point is not that the speech-modeled conception of self-government has no means of justifying constitutional restraints. Of course it does. A vast amount of modern political and constitutional thought is devoted to the task of explaining how restraints on popular will can be squared with the principle of government by the present will or consent of the governed. These speech-modeled solutions to the antithesis thesis will be catalogued below. But the destination of these solutions should already be clear.

Speech-modeled efforts at constitutional legitimation remain wholly structured by the conception of self-government with which they begin. They seek to justify constitutional law in the light of an ideal of self-government that has no conceptual resources with which to embrace historical, temporally extended constitutional commitments. The result, as we shall see, is that these speech-modeled solutions to the antithesis thesis can never quite comprehend written constitutionalism.

Modern political thought, having discovered that the earth belongs to the

---

tieth Century 6–9 (1991). For Schumpeter's account, see Joseph Schumpeter, Capitalism, Socialism and Democracy (2d ed. 1947) (especially chapter 21). For an excellent treatment of democracy from the social choice perspective, see William H. Riker, Liberalism Against Populism (1982).

27. Huntington, *supra* note 26, at 7.

28. *Id.* at 6–7.

29. *Id.* at 6–7, 9–10.

living, has a fundamental problem with fundamental rights. Its constant ambition: to reconcile, but without recourse to divine law, the existence of such rights with speech-modeled self-government.

There are in fact four basic speech-modeled solutions to the antithesis thesis, and the elaboration of these four solutions, like ever more sophisticated variations on a theme, has dominated modern political and constitutional thought for two centuries. These four solutions differ from one another chiefly in their temporal orientation. Identifying them will show both the prevalence of the speech-modeled problematic in modern democratic thought and the incompleteness of speech-modeled efforts to rationalize constitutional rights.

The Voice of the People Present

Say that you believe in speech-modeled self-government. You believe that democracy consists, at least ideally, at least in principle, of government by the present will or consent of the governed. But you also believe that governmental actors must be checked by fundamental, constitutional guarantees. How can you justify these constitutional guarantees? Are they not profoundly anti-democratic?

The simplest answer would run as follows. Governmental actors may properly be subject to constitutional checks because and precisely to the extent that those checks have the backing of present popular will. This was Jefferson's solution: the Constitution was to be remade at regular intervals in accordance with the will of the "present generation." So long as constitutional law remained updated to reflect the voice of the "present generation," the conflict between constitutional rights and democracy would disappear.

Observe the slight sleight-of-hand in the concept of "the generation" here. Without it, Jefferson would have provided for no constitutional stability at all. By subtly, covertly changing his central thesis, so that the earth belongs not to the living but rather to the "present generation," Jefferson sought to buy a little time for a stable constitutional order—"18. years 8. months," to be precise, "or say 19. years as the nearest integral number."[30]

But cormorant time is not so easily satisfied. Citizens come and go every day; majority will can in principle change from one minute to the next. Jefferson's generational constitutionalism pictures each generation as a kind of collective subject with a nineteen-year life span, able to bind itself for the duration of its own existence through an authoritative declaration of its will. But if so—if, despite the changing of the constituent individuals, a generation

30. Letter to Madison, *supra* Chapter 2, note 7, at 394.

can be said to have an enduring collective will, binding for the duration of its existence—why can't the same be said of a nation, so that *its* constitutional will might remain binding for the duration of *its* existence? When the earth belongs to the living, the "will of the generation" is no more admissible than the will of the nation. As we have seen, only Rousseau's position—that the law ought to reflect the popular will of the present moment—states the true endpoint of government of, by, and for the living.

Is it possible to construct a constitutionalism responsive to the present will of the living citizens? The embers of Rousseau's pure presentism remain alive today in the work of those now-rare democratic theorists who spurn judicial review altogether. A constitutionalism of present popular will is also the aspiration of those who call for a majoritarian or congressional constitutional amendment process. But most important, through a certain transubstantiation, all-but-obsolete views about how or whether constitutions ought to be *made* can resurface with new vigor in the form of views about how the Constitution ought to be *interpreted*. So it has been with Jefferson's and Rousseau's vision of continual constitutional revision, which began to reappear in a new, interpretive form about a hundred years ago.

After the Civil War, notwithstanding the great burst of constitutional transformation of the 1860s, there followed a period of constitutional disenchantment. The seeming failure of Reconstruction, together perhaps with a feeling that the original Constitution had proved an encumbrance on the nation's ability to deal resolutely with slavery, gave rise toward the end of the nineteenth century to a new body of constitutional thought deeply concerned with the rights and abilities of the living to be their own masters. The proponents of this school of thought were not anti-constitutionalist, but they did not like to see unelected judges setting themselves against the deliberate will of the living majority. One prominent advocate of this line of thinking was Christopher Tiedeman, who reintroduced the living voice of the people into constitutional law, not as a vehicle for Jeffersonian constitutional revision but as an imperative of constitutional interpretation.

The "binding authority of law," Tiedeman wrote, "does not rest upon any edict of the people in the past."[31]

> [I]n countries in which popular governments are established the real lawgiver is not the man or body of men which first enacted the law ages ago; it is the people *of the present day* who possess the political power,

31. Christopher G. Tiedeman, The Unwritten Constitution of the United States: A Philosophical Inquiry into the Fundamentals of American Constitutional Law 122 (1890).

> and whose commands give life to what otherwise is a *dead letter.* Hence, since under a popular government governmental authority rests upon *the voice of the people,* . . . that interpretation, in strict conformity with the fundamental rule of interpretation, must prevail which best reflects the prevalent sense of right.[32]

The "judge . . . who would interpret the law rightly . . . need not concern himself so much with the intentions of the framers of the Constitution."[33] On the contrary: "as soon as we recognize the *present will of the people* as the living source of law, we are obliged, in construing the law, to follow, and give effect to, the *present intentions and meaning* of the people."[34]

Tiedeman's counsel will seem naive to contemporary readers, both in his assumption that there exists a "prevalent sense of right" shared by the people as a whole, and in his conviction that the judiciary can discern it. But he was merely seeking to operationalize what seemed the only legitimate basis for law in a democracy: the present will of the governed. Naive or not, Tiedeman's counsel is rehearsed by all those contemporary scholars and judges who assert that constitutional interpretation should speak for the "contemporary" community,[35] should express "contemporary norms"[36] and "commonly held attitudes,"[37] or should respond to the "fundamental ethos of the contemporary community."[38] Every one of these contemporary-consensus formulations sounds the echo of Tiedeman's voice of the people. In every case, the implicit premise is that constitutional law can achieve democratic legitimacy only if interpreted responsively to popular will.

This school of interpretation is not inherently tied to either an "activist"

32. *Id.* (emphasis added).

33. *Id.* at 151.

34. *Id.* at 154 (emphasis added).

35. Justice William Brennan gave an important address before he retired entitled (with emphasis added), *The Constitution of the United States:* Contemporary *Ratification,* reprinted in Interpreting the Constitution: The Debate over Original Intent 23 (Jack N. Rakove ed., 1990). Justice Brennan argued there that in every "act of [constitutional] interpretation," "it is, in a very real sense, the community's interpretation that is sought." *Id.* at 25.

36. Terrence Sandalow, *Judicial Protection of Minorities,* 75 Mich. L. Rev. 1162, 1193 (1977) ("constitutional law must now be understood as expressing contemporary norms").

37. Harry Wellington, *Common Law Rules and Constitutional Standards: Some Notes on Adjudication,* 83 Yale L.J. 221, 311 (1973).

38. Robert Post, *Theories of Constitutional Representation,* 30 Representations 13, 30 (1990).

or a "restrained" judicial philosophy. The primacy of present majority will, when insisted upon by a Holmes or a Thayer, was supposed to point toward "judicial restraint," with judges invalidating laws only when such laws unambiguously violated the constitutional text or "reason" itself.[39] But virtually all of today's judges and scholars who call for a constitutionalism reflecting contemporary values do so in defense of robust judicial review, unconstrained by narrower historical understandings.

There is a well-known problem with this present-consensus constitutionalism. It presumes that the judiciary can better speak for present majority will than can the people's elected representatives. In response to this objection, some advocates of present-consensus constitutionalism abandon the view that a judge should try to give voice to current popular will. Instead, they say, constitutionalism is reconcilable with democracy because and so long as a majority of Americans continue to consent to the basic institutions of constitutional law (the basic set of individual rights, judicial review, and so on), whether or not a majority agrees with any particular result reached by the Supreme Court. But a still deeper problem confronts even this much more modest present-consensus approach to constitutionalism. The idea of fundamental rights—rights that stand against a deliberate, majority will—is left with no defense. For whenever current majority consent is said to be what really counts, it follows that if a majority genuinely wanted, say, to enslave a minority and genuinely did not consent to a constitutionalism that blocked this result, then the Constitution ought not to stand in their way.

A much more sophisticated variant of present-voice constitutionalism solves these problems. On this view, constitutional rights and institutions are to be understood as a set of basic conditions necessary to establish and maintain the democratic process—where "democratic process" is understood, in classically speech-modeled terms, as governance by present will of the governed. The term "proceduralism" or "process-based" constitutionalism refers to this school of thought.

To illustrate proceduralism, consider the freedom of speech. Free speech,

39. For a general discussion, see Wallace Mendelson, *The Influence of James B. Thayer upon the Work of Holmes, Brandeis, and Frankfurter,* 31 Vand. L. Rev. 71 (1978). For Thayer's classic statement of the doctrine of restraint, see James B. Thayer, *The Origin and Scope of the American Doctrine of Constitutional Law,* 7 Harv. L. Rev. 129 (1893). For one of Holmes's, see *Truax v. Corrigan,* 257 U.S. 312, 344 (1921) (Holmes, J., dissenting) ("There is nothing that I more deprecate than the use of the Fourteenth Amendment beyond the absolute compulsion of its words to prevent the making of social experiments that an important part of the community desires, in the insulated chambers afforded by the several states.").

the proceduralist says, is properly protected by constitutional guarantees in order to ensure the flow of information and the robust debate indispensable to a self-governing citizenry.[40] A judge who enforces the freedom of political dissent, even against majoritarian efforts to suppress it, is not behaving antidemocratically. He does not frustrate present-tense majoritarian self-government at all. Rather, he safeguards the process that is a necessary condition of such self-government.

When this view is systematized from a theory of the freedom of speech to a general theory of judicial review, as John Hart Ely did in his justly famous *Democracy and Distrust,* it yields a thoroughgoing solution to the antithesis thesis. Constitutional law can legitimately constrain the will of the people's elected representatives when, but only when, the constraints are necessary to safeguard the mechanisms whereby the citizens make their voices heard and heeded in the political process. From criminal procedure to equal protection to voting rights, constitutional law could, Ely argued, "overwhelmingly" be viewed as concerned with process. Judges should, therefore, endeavor to read the Constitution's sweeping guarantees as safeguarding the democratic process, rather than imposing any independent "substantive values" on the nation.[41]

Proceduralism is thoroughly speech-modeled. Self-government here means effectuating the present will of the governed. "Self-government is nonsense unless the 'self' which governs is able . . . to make its will effective."[42] Process-based constitutionalism begins with—indeed Ely quotes—the Jeffersonian premise that "the earth belongs to the living."[43] The ingeniousness of the proceduralist solution is that it legitimizes counter-majoritarian fundamental rights on the basis of present popular will without ever claiming that the judiciary is able to speak for the present will of the people.

Because of its ingenious solution to the antithesis thesis, proceduralism has become the dominant account of constitutionalism for contemporary democratic theorists, from Robert Dahl to Jürgen Habermas.[44] When Habermas says that "human rights do not compete with popular sovereignty," but

40. *See, e.g.,* Alexander Meiklejohn, Free Speech and Its Relation to Self-Government 15–16, 24–27, 39 (1948).

41. John Hart Ely, Democracy and Distrust: A Theory of Judicial Review 72–73, 92 (1980).

42. Alexander Meiklejohn, Political Freedom: The Constitutional Powers of the People 14 (1948).

43. *See* Ely, *supra* note 41, at 11.

44. *See, e.g.,* Habermas, *supra* note 5, at 264–66, 274–79; Dahl, *supra* note 10, at 163–75.

"are identical with the constitutive conditions of a self-limiting practice of publicly discursive will-formation,"[45] he indicates both his speech-modeled conception of self-government and his proceduralist solution to the problem of fundamental rights within such a conception. Constitutional rights, for Habermas, are "the constitutive conditions" of the process whereby today's citizens form their will through public dialogue ("publicly discursive will-formation") and transform their will into governance.

The Voice of the People Past

The second basic strategy for justifying fundamental rights within the model of speech is to appeal to the *past* will of the governed. Early social contract thinking provides an example of this strategy and its difficulties. The contractarians sought to derive fundamental rights from a past act of consent: an "original" act of will through which individuals agreed to "enter" into society. The rhetoric of contract suggested a basis both for continuing to recognize the validity of this past act of will and for condemning any present act of state that did not adhere to it.

One small problem: the contracting parties were all dead. At first this problem did not loom as large as it should have, because the contractarians' principal mission, pace Hobbes, was to lay a ground for popular rights against a monarchic government, and as against the monarch, the rhetoric of an original agreement seemed to secure the desired results. The original contractors may be dead, but the government they created can never claim more power than was originally given, just as a corporation remains limited by its original charter even when the original incorporators have passed away.

But when the problem of binding the monarch gives way to that of binding the people, the underlying instability of contractarian logic became increasingly manifest. Hume saw this difficulty early on: the contractarians "suppose[d] the consent of the fathers to bind the children, even to the most remote generations," which "republican writers" would "never allow."[46] In other words, the republican principle of legitimate authority underlying contractarianism—the principle that government derived its legitimate authority solely from the consent of the governed—confuted the effort to bind a disagreeing majority today to the will of individuals long dead.

The usual contractarian reply to this objection was to claim present, tacit consent to the original contract. We who live today were not parties to the

45. *Id.*

46. David Hume, *Of the Original Contract,* in Essays: Moral, Political, and Literary 452, 457 (Oxford Univ. Press 1963) (1741).

original compact, but we tacitly consent to its terms, either by remaining in the polity or by availing ourselves of such benefits as property ownership. Such, for example, was Locke's argument.[47] In this way the present-tense logic of the model of speech proved irresistible. The claims of the social contract, seemingly directed toward a will of the past, turned out to rest on *present* popular will after all.

The colossal embarrassments of this reasoning—the fictitiousness of the original act of will, the factitiousness of the present "tacit" consent of the governed, and the logical weakness of every argument in which a citizen's "tacit" consent somehow manages to trump his *explicit* expression of non-consent—are such that classical social contract thinking no longer plays much of a role in political theory. But as noted above, defunct political theories can reappear with renewed vigor in the forum of constitutional interpretation. In this forum, classical contractarianism has enjoyed a considerable revival—under the name of "originalism" (or sometimes, "textualism").

Like contractarianism, originalism comes in more than one variety. Emphasis may be placed on "the intent of the Framers" or instead on "the intent of the ratifying public." (The latter form of originalism is sometimes called "textualism"; it finds more authority in eighteenth-century dictionaries, which tell us what the "ratifying public" would have understood by certain words, than in the debates of the Philadelphia Convention.) There is a *strict* originalism that insists on limiting constitutional law to what the original parties said or would have said about the meaning of constitutional provisions, and there is a *soft* originalism that allows judges to update the meaning of constitutional provisions so long as they do so in order to be faithful to the founders' original purposes. But all originalism claims to honor the democratic will of the "founding" social compact, so that when the justices enforce the Constitution today, they can always say that they are merely enforcing what the people agreed to.

Certain formidable obstacles to correct originalist interpretation are well known: the difficulty of imputing a single intention to a large number of individuals, the paucity of the historical materials, the emergence of circumstances unforeseeable two hundred years ago, and so on. These are not the difficulties to which I want to draw attention. Consider instead the problem

47. *See* Locke, *supra* Chapter 2, note 29, at 358. *See also* Sheldon Wolin, Politics and Vision 311 (1960) (observing that Locke used "the institution of property inheritance to undercut the favorite notion of radicalism that each generation was free to reconstitute political society"). For a discussion of the latent tensions in Locke's views on this point see Lynd, *supra* note 12, at 69–81.

that arises for originalism as a result of its attempting to combine speech-modeled principles of self-government with a past-oriented constitutionalism.

In what sense is originalism speech-modeled? Originalism reveals its speech-modeling in its insistence on the authority of what the framers "said," "meant to say," or "would have said"—or sometimes on the authority of what the Constitution "says." This "saying" is a reference to the democratic will of the founding "moment." All originalism is an effort to make constitutional law the vehicle for a democratic voice, whether that voice is directly expressed by the utterances of the framers or by eighteenth-century dictionaries, which supposedly reveal what the public "would have said" about the meaning of the Constitution's terms. Originalism, in other words, rests its case on the proposition that the only legitimate constitutional law is law that adheres to the enacted will of the people.[48]

But how can originalism be called speech-modeled if its focus is on the *past* will of the people?

The truth is that originalists, despite their *idées fixes* concerning the "founding" will, do not really believe in the supremacy of the past. True in their hearts to the Jeffersonian ideal, they see themselves as champions of the right of *present* citizens to be governed by their own will. This is why originalists invariably portray themselves as a school of judicial restraint (even though a true originalism would be anything but restrained), vilifying "activist" judges who prevent today's majorities from having their way. *Non*-originalists, the originalist says, are the ones "attempt[ing] to *block self-government by the representatives of living men and women.*"[49] As a result, a massive contradiction organizes most originalism, which simultaneously demands fidelity to the will of the dead and yet condemns non-originalist judges for standing in the way of *"rule by living majorities."*[50]

Doesn't it occur to originalists that they too seek to impede "rule by living

48. *See, e.g.,* Bork, *supra* note 22, at 143. To be sure, originalists also defend their approach in terms of the "fixity" that it will yield and in terms of the need to maintain the Constitution's status as "law." But these arguments are manifestly insufficient. Originalism is no longer on the side of fixity; contemporary constitutional doctrine is non-originalist in so many profound respects that recurring to original intentions would call for an extremely activist jurisprudence. More fundamentally, legal fixity can be had in any number of ways. Interpreting the Constitution in accordance with the views of King George III could in principle provide a fixed body of constitutional law.

49. *Id.* at 171 (emphasis added).

50. *Id.* (emphasis added).

majorities"? Of course it does. But they have an answer to this difficulty—the same appeal to present, tacit consent made by the social contractarians long ago. "We remain entirely free," argues the originalist Robert Bork, to amend the Constitution whenever "we want."[51] If we today have changed our minds about the Constitution, all we have to do is express our new will in the appropriate fashion. The function of constitutional law, therefore, is to enforce the constitutional will of the people until the people changes its mind. Originalism does not exalt past over present will. It is Jeffersonian; it believes that government belongs to the living.

But the argument from tacit consent holds no better for the "constitutional contract" than it does for the "social contract." We, the citizens alive today, do not "remain entirely free" to amend the Constitution whenever we wish. On the contrary, the amendment procedures set forth in Article V of the Constitution famously raise onerous obstacles in the way of constitutional change, including supermajority requirements. Accordingly, as Akhil Amar has skillfully shown, if tacit majority consent to the Constitution were the true touchstone of constitutional legitimacy, the logical result must be a greatly facilitated majoritarian amendment process—perhaps amendment by majority-vote petition and referendum.[52] Only if the amendment process were genuinely open to revision by present majority will could there be a plausible inference of present majority consent from failure to amend.

In other words, the premises of originalism, taken to their conclusion, point back to the Jeffersonian vision of continual constitutional revision. Which means that the logical endpoint of originalism is the abrogation of written constitutionalism itself. Originalism's true principle—its dedication to "rule by living majorities," on the basis of which it claims to demand adherence to enacted majority will until a newly enacted majority will supersedes it, and on the basis of which all of its anti-activist rhetoric rests—calls for the end of written constitutionalism as America has known it.

Readers will think I exaggerate. But this covert and surprising anti-constitutionalism, implicit in originalism, is dramatically confirmed in Bork's recent work. Ex-judge Bork now advocates legislative overrides—by majority vote of the House and Senate—of the Supreme Court's constitutional decisions.[53] How could this champion of original meaning, this constitutional conservative, have come to favor a proposal essentially abrogating American

51. *Id.*

52. *See* Akhil Reed Amar, *Philadelphia Revisited: Amending the Constitution Outside Article V,* 55 U. Chi. L. Rev. 1043, 1064–66 (1988).

53. *See* Robert Bork, Slouching Toward Gomorrah: Modern Liberalism and American Decline 117 (1996).

written constitutionalism? Cynics will say that Bork is merely jealous ("if I don't get to be Supreme in all the land, no one does"). But quite to the contrary, Bork is finally taking seriously his original premises.

Like most originalists, Bork never had any account explaining why the will of the dead should supersede deliberate majority will today. Originalism rests on a picture of the Constitution as America's "social compact," but it is constrained, as classical contractarianism was constrained, to legitimize this compact ultimately by reference to present tacit consent. This means that the "living majorities" of the present *should* "remain entirely free" to overthrow every decision of the Supreme Court, even those that adhere perfectly to the founding will.[54] A popular or congressional constitutional override is, therefore, originalism's natural and proper endpoint.

This is only to say: originalism founders on the same rock that scuttles primitive contractarianism. Because the ultimate principle is government by the consent of the governed, the effort to privilege a single moment of foundational, original popular will ultimately collapses back into a claim of present tacit popular consent, at which point (1) the original will loses both relevance and authority; and (2) the defense of fundamental rights (rights that stand against majority will) can no longer hold. Originalism is trapped in the speech-modeled vise. It seeks to locate authority in a past moment's will, but it can do so only on the basis of a claim to be freeing present majority will from the "usurpations" of activist judges. Its logical conclusion is either a facilitated majoritarian amendment process or, at the least, a legislative override of constitutional decisions.

The Voice of the People Predicted

If you were devoted to government by the will of the governed, but had despaired of treating constitutional law as a vehicle for present or past democratic will, you might yet be tempted by an appeal to a *predicted* popular will.

The appeal to predicted will is a hallmark of utopian thought. (Marx, for example, seemed to believe that communism, when it finally restored each person to himself, would in fact command the free and full consent of all.) In much altered form, an appeal to predicted popular will has also played a role in constitutional interpretation. One illustration appears in an important essay by former justice William Brennan, which characterizes the judge's role in constitutional cases as speaking for the "contemporary community."[55] But

54. *Id.* at 171.

55. *See* Brennan, *supra* note 35, at 23.

Justice Brennan went on to confront the awkward fact that his own position on certain constitutional issues—such as his view that the death penalty was categorically unconstitutional—was not "subscribed to by a majority of my fellow countrymen."[56] To justify this, Brennan appealed to America's future promise: its promise to be a "shining city on a hill." Of the death penalty, Brennan wrote, "I hope . . . to embody a community striving for human dignity for all, *although perhaps not yet arrived.*"[57]

Another illustration is provided in Alexander Bickel's *The Least Dangerous Branch,* which perhaps influenced Brennan. Bickel's eventual solution to the "counter-majoritarian difficulty" lay in an appeal to the future. The hinge of Bickel's argument was the claim that the Supreme Court can shape popular opinion even as it seeks to be guided by traditional values: "The Court is a leader of opinion, not a mere register of it." If the Court leads effectively, today's counter-majoritarian decisions may yet receive tomorrow's stamp of popular approval. Although ostensibly the voice of tradition, the Court is to "declare as law *only such principles as will—in time, but in a rather immediate foreseeable future—gain general assent.*" The Court must be "at once shaper and prophet of the opinion that will prevail."[58]

Others besides Justice Brennan followed Bickel in this justificatory turn to the future.[59] Bickel himself, however, later disavowed it.[60] Predictions of future popular will, Bickel came to think, were not merely unreliable. They failed to address a pivotal question. If democracy essentially meant, as Bickel always believed (in prototypical speech-modeled fashion), that a majority of the present citizens have a right to see their will made law "here and now," then defending constitutional law on the basis of a putative future popular will is no better than defending it on the basis of a putative past popular will. Why

56. *Id.* at 33.

57. *Id.* (emphasis added).

58. Bickel, *supra* Chapter 1, note 16, at 17, 239 (emphasis added).

59. For example, Professor Robert Post first paints a picture of constitutional interpretation whose mission is to "uncover present values" and to "speak for" the "contemporary" "national ethos." This is pure present-oriented speech-modeling of the Tiedemanian variety. But Post goes on to claim that the "national ethos" "may in significant ways be affected" by judicial decisions, and that "a court can, through the eloquent articulation of public ideals, actually help to solidify a national ethos," which will retroactively confirm the propriety of what the court has done. Post, *supra* note 38, at 23, 28, 29.

60. *See, e.g.,* Alexander Bickel, The Supreme Court and the Idea of Progress 173–81 (1970).

should we be governed by the will of tomorrow's majorities any more than we should be governed by the will of yesterday's?

A very different kind of appeal to predicted will escapes this difficulty. Far more sophisticated, it has also been far more influential in contemporary political thought. Here the predicted popular will is not located in the real future at all, so there is never any question of why present majority will should defer to a future majority will. Instead, the predicted act of will is purely hypothetical. What is predicted here is not what the people *will* say at some future moment, but what the people *would* say under ideal deliberative conditions, of which those specified by Rawls in his *Theory of Justice* are the most famous.

In Rawls, the familiar constellation of speech-modeled politics—an assembly of citizens, deliberation, production of a popular will—appears again, but now in hypothetical form. The genius of Rawls's solution is that it justifies fundamental principles of justice on the basis of the unanimous consent of the governed, without being the least bit troubled by any contrary views in fact held by real people. One difficulty in hypothetical-consent theory is relevant to the present discussion.

Operationalizing hypothetical-consent theory—translating it into the arena of constitutional law—would require judges either to be or to consult philosopher-kings. Democratic constitution-writing would be largely out of this picture, because constitutional law would become a subset of moral philosophy. This is a consummation devoutly to be wished according to a number of philosophically minded legal academics. In this scenario, the rights that ought to be enforced *might* be expressed in the constitutional text, but if they were, this result would be purely fortuitous. The right rights would be accessible only through recourse to the hypothetical conversation taking place under ideal deliberative conditions. At this point, the appeal to predicted will would have crossed over into the fourth and final speech-modeled strategy for resolving the problem of constitutional rights—the appeal to timeless truths transcending temporal power—and further remarks must therefore be put off until that strategy has been more fully described.

The Flight from Temporality

Most of those who framed and ratified the United States Constitution were probably believers in some version of "natural law." Natural law, understood as an emanation from a divine will, supplies another simplistic answer to the antithesis thesis. Of course constitutional rights conflict with democracy, but that is because constitutional rights express God's will, which properly supersedes all temporal power.

But an appeal to timeless rights can be in play even without explicit invocation of divinity. Reason, science, moral truth, or even hypothetical-consent theory can equally serve as the source of fundamental, timeless rights. In these forms, the a-temporal solution to the problem of fundamental rights continues to be a powerful component of political thought today, visible not only in the moral-political literature but also in the practices of international law, where a vigorous discourse of national self-determination co-exists in perfect contradiction with an equally vigorous discourse of universal, a priori human rights.

The appeal to timeless rights stands in a complex relationship to the speech-modeled ideal of self-government. In principle, an appeal to timeless truth can displace the claims of democratic self-government altogether. Believers in timeless law might believe, depending on how extensive or comprehensive they imagine this law to be, that there is little role for democracy at all. Perhaps on some "policy" issues the voice of the people could have its little say, but on all issues of "principle," truth should prevail. In fact, however, the defenders of timeless rights have frequently cast themselves as champions of democratic freedom. How?

The answer to this riddle lies in a special reconciliation that has emerged between natural-law thinking and the speech-modeled conception of self-government. There was a price to be paid for this reconciliation on both sides. Natural law would have to be de-theified, while self-government would have to be de-politicized. This transformation took place when natural law and speech-modeled self-government converged on the supremacy of the voice of the *individual:* on individual autonomy, on each individual's right to act according to his own free will, provided only that he respect the right of other individuals also to act on theirs. The ultimate timeless solution to the problem of fundamental rights within the framework of speech-modeled self-government is—liberalism.

When Mill, for example, famously pronounced his skepticism about such terms as "popular will" and popular "self-government" (in a passage from *On Liberty* that we will consider in more detail later), he did not break from speech-modeled self-government. On the contrary, what changed was the locus of inviolable voice. The voice to which political authority had to answer shifted from that of the body politic to that of the individual. As a result, Mill ends with two basic political prescriptions for a free society: (1) a speech-modeled democratic politics in which representative assemblies voice the current opinion of the people; and (2) a principle of individual autonomy, organized around the freedom of speech and of will, within the individual's own proper domain.

Liberalism remained, in this way, dedicated to an ideal of self-government, but the self that was to govern itself was the individual, not the people. (The only "true" self-government, Mill wrote, is "the government of each by himself.") This transposition of self-government from the domain of a people to that of the individual made possible a reconception of democracy wholly stripped of the ideal of collective self-government. A democratic politics, from the liberal perspective, becomes definable in terms of electoral competition, then in terms of interest-group competition for goods, and finally in terms of an immense network of individual-wealth-maximizing rational-choice operations. Here, following Mill's lead, the notion of a collective will or popular voice is wholly exploded, and democracy ends as an essentially economic enterprise, whose principle is or ought to be efficiency.

In a sense, individual self-government is the predestined home of the present-tense temporality on behalf of which Rousseau and Jefferson spoke. Collective understandings of self-government require a sense that those who live today are members of a temporally extended polity—at a minimum, Jefferson's "generation." But if today is ours, tomorrow is not. It belongs to those who will be alive then. Hence the very premises of speech-modeled self-government inaugurate a transition away from political self-government toward individual self-government. The nation gives way to the generation, and the generation gives way to those alive at the present moment. At this point politics can be only an exercise in counting and reconciling individual wills, and self-government can be understood only as "the government of each by himself."

This individualist ideal of self-government in turn produces a solution to the problem of fundamental constitutional rights in a speech-modeled democracy. Through such precepts as one-person-one-vote, and through far more elaborated conceptions of individual autonomy or equal regard under law, liberalism sustains a present-tense, majoritarian democratic politics, while yet justifying anti-majoritarian, fundamental rights. The tie that binds liberalism to the older natural-law tradition is its naturalistic dedication to pre-political rights. On the liberal view, individual equality or autonomy exists as a fundamental principle prior to the formation of the state and definitive of the proper sphere of government. The individual's fundamental right to be governed by his own voice is not dependent on some past political act, nor on present majority consent, nor even on predicted popular will. It is rather the given that underlies the legitimate authority of the political-legal order itself. The freedom of each to act on his own will, here and now, "consistent with a like liberty for each" (or on the basis of "reasons justifiable to all rational actors," or in accordance with laws reflecting "equal regard for all") is to be understood not as a particular, substantive, egalitarian commitment of a given nation. It does not derive from the domain of temporal political power at all. It stands prior to that domain. It is derivable only by recourse to a priori, timeless moral philosophy.

There can be no doubt about the influence of liberalism on American constitutional law and particularly on Americans' understandings of the fundamental rights their Constitution guarantees. This influence was perhaps most dominant from the end of the nineteenth century to the 1930s, when something very much resembling Mill's principle of self-regarding acts—the principle that society had no business regulating acts merely private or self-regarding in nature—was engrafted into constitutional law under the name of the liberty of contract. (Relying on this liberty of contract, together with other related doctrines of the period, the Supreme Court struck down minimum-wage laws, maximum-hour laws, union-protection legislation, and a host of other state and federal commercial regulations, characteristically on the ground that the government had no authority to interfere with any individual's actions unless those actions had a material effect on the public.) Today, the inclination to read constitutional law as a working out of liberal axioms of free and equal individuality remains an important thread in the constitutional literature.

I am not interested here in trying to refute any of the speech-modeled solutions to the problem of fundamental rights. But observe how thin, how hollow a picture of written constitutionalism they leave us with. None of these solutions can comprehend written constitutionalism as America has known and practiced it.

As noted above, the more simplistic of these solutions—for example, present-consensus constitutionalism and originalism—ultimately make the legitimacy of constitutional law depend on its conformity with present popular will. As a result, they demand in principle a constant process of updating constitutional law to ensure that present popular will remains behind it, either by way of an interpretation that looks to present consensus or by way of legislative or plebiscitary overrides of constitutional decisions. But whenever constitutional law's legitimacy is made to depend on conformity with present democratic will, the result is that the Constitution, to be fully legitimate, could no longer be a constitution at all.

A legitimate constitution, where legitimacy has been defined by reference to present national majority will, could rein in wayward state actors, or stand against a president that sought to exercise dictatorial power, but it could no longer stand against an oppressive majority will. Thus is lost a central idea of American written constitutionalism: the idea that the fundamental principles laid down in the Constitution may *rightfully, legitimately* supersede democratically enacted law, no matter how accurately this law reflects majority will, and no matter how deliberative the lawmaking processes may have been. If today's citizens deliberately, genuinely decided by majority vote to establish a church, or to enslave a minority, the Constitution could not rightfully, legitimately stand in their way. Here constitutional law becomes a hollow shell of what America has understood it to be.

The more sophisticated speech-modeled solutions discussed above—proceduralism, for example, or liberalism—overcome this problem. Each provides a basis for counter-majoritarian constitutional rights. But to do so, each is obliged to cast aside another central feature of American written constitutionalism: the constitutional text in its propositional and historical particularity. To the extent that any rendition of liberal fundamental rights is pressed as the basis of constitutional law, judges and other interpreters are directed away from the actual constitutional text. They are asked to shift their inquiry instead to determining the true postulates of free and equal individuality.

No doubt efforts can be made to show that these postulates are safely nestled in the Constitution's actual provisions, but such efforts are inevitably anachronistic and deeply artificial. Thus when Ronald Dworkin finds a "textual home" for *Roe v. Wade* in the Constitution's *religion* clauses, there is no escaping a certain felt artificiality.[61] The desired liberal outcome finds a textual peg to hang on, but the post-hoc nature of this hanging is all too visible.

Neglect of the written Constitution characterized the Supreme Court's most obviously liberal period, in which it elaborated the notorious liberty-of-contract jurisprudence mentioned above. To be sure, in the contemporary ideological vocabulary, "conservatives" favor property rights and the freedom of contract, while "liberals" prefer to focus on reproductive rights and more generally on a vision of moral autonomy and equality. But all philosophically liberal constitutionalism, whether politically "conservative" or "liberal" in today's terminology, wants its judges to be mouthpieces of philosopher-gods. The only difference lies in the choice of deity: Mill or Locke, Kant or Coase, John Rawls or—Ayn Rand.

In its ingenious double devotion—to the will of living majorities through one-person, one-vote processes and to a-temporal, unabridgeable individual rights—the liberal conception of self-government leaves little room for a prac-

61. *See* Ronald Dworkin, Life's Dominion 160–68 (1993).

tice in which judges interpret a written constitution. There is plenty of room here for judges to recur to the original position, or to the best moral theory of a political community, or to equations of Kaldor-Hicks efficiency. But there is precious little room for them to participate in the discipline of interpreting a legal text democratically enacted a hundred or two hundred years ago, with its own history, its own particular context and substance, handed down over time and elaborated upon by ever-growing incrustations of precedent.

The same is true of proceduralism. If constitutional rights are legitimate only to the extent that they set forth "the constitutive conditions" of the democratic process, there is little or no place for the "substantive" commitments that the actual Constitution embodies. The prohibition of slavery is an example of a substantive constitutional commitment. Even John Ely concedes that this prohibition cannot candidly be regarded as a process guarantee. He ought to concede as well that the entire equal protection guarantee, which is perhaps the most important provision in contemporary constitutional law, similarly escapes process-based thinking. For no amount of proceduralism can answer the question of which persons are to be treated as full members of the polity, entitled to the full panoply of citizens' rights.

Ely's argument for equal protection as a proceduralist guarantee runs as follows. Legislators who enact laws reflecting prejudice against certain groups characteristically fail to take into account all the costs and benefits of the laws they pass. Either they mistakenly believe in false generalizations about the group in question ("stereotyping"), leading them to undercount the harms suffered by members of the subject group, or they mistakenly count the harms suffered by members of this group as benefits ("valuing their welfare negatively," for example because of animus against them). According to Ely, these are "malfunctions" in the legislative *"process,"* in the sense that the proper inputs are not getting factored into the legislative process.[62]

But this "process-based" account of equal protection means that a law banning blacks from, say, institutions of higher learning would not violate the equal protection clause and would do no cognizable constitutional wrong, provided that the legislators enacted this law after a full, open, accurate consideration of all the expected harms and benefits of the law. For so long as all the relevant information came into the legislative process, and so long as the legislators performed their cost-benefit calculus correctly, then there can be no allegation of a "process error" in the resulting law, and there can be denial of equal protection.

Proceduralist equal protection cuts the heart out of the substantive, his-

62. Ely, *supra* note 41, at 103, 157.

torical commitment memorialized by the Fourteenth Amendment, leaving in its place a process-based shell. I will say more about this substantive commitment in a later chapter. The point for now is this. Constitutional law is a set of substantive, foundational commitments—commitments to principles of justice and liberty and power—laid down by the nation to govern itself. These temporally extended commitments cannot be captured in proceduralist terms, nor indeed in any speech-modeled logic.

If legitimate political authority derives from the will of the governed, then fundamental rights can be legitimized only by deriving them either (1) from the will of the governed at some particular moment—whether past, present, or predicted—or else (2) from truths lying outside the domain of temporal authority altogether. Contractarianism, originalism, proceduralism, hypothetical-consent theory, liberalism—these and other great movements within political and constitutional thought have all responded, in highly determinate, predictable fashion, to the basic difficulty of justifying constitutional rights in light of a conception of self-government as government by the self's own will.

Written constitutionalism, however, as America has understood and practiced it, cannot be comprehended within the speech-modeled conception of self-government. Constitutional law is irreducibly temporal, and yet also irreducible to the political will of any given moment. Are we obliged then to admit a fundamental contradiction in constitutional democracy, a "logical dilemma" that no philosophy will ever succeed in "explaining away"? Are we obliged to choose between self-government and constitutionalism?

This choice would be inevitable if the speech-modeled conception of self-government were the only possible conception. But it is not. It is not even an adequate conception, whether the self-government at issue is that of an individual or that of a nation. Or so I will argue in the chapters that follow.

Four

THE ANTINOMIES OF SPEECH-MODELED SELF-GOVERNMENT

I have tried to show: (1) the existence of a predominant conception of self-government, which I call speech-modeled, of which the organizing term is government by the present will or voice of the governed; (2) the distinctively modern temporality for which this conception of self-government speaks; (3) the fundamental problem it confronts when faced with a constitutional text laying down fundamental rights; (4) the limited matrix of solutions it makes available to address that problem; and (5) the considerable extent to which modern political and constitutional thought has played itself out within this matrix.

I have not claimed that every speech-modeled solution to the problem of fundamental rights is doomed ultimately to conceptual incoherence. Little would be gained by proving an ultimate irreconcilability between speech-modeled self-government and constitutional rights. Proving this irreconcilability would simply reconfirm the antithesis thesis, with which speech-modeled constitutional thought begins. The real question is not whether the speech-modeled conception of self-government offers a satisfactory account of fundamental rights, but whether it offers a satisfactory account *of self-government.*

Put the problem as follows. Imagine a people governing itself in ideal speech-modeled fashion. Imagine nationwide electronic town meetings. Make them as participatory, enlightened, rational, open, and thorough as you like. Put aside Condorcet paradoxes (but only for now; we will return to them later). Perhaps we should even stipulate, to top it off, that deliberation continues until the citizens reach unanimous decisions, which, on every matter large and small, are instantaneously effectuated. Imagine, in other words, government by the pure but deliberate voice of the people. Have we imagined self-government?

This is not to ask: have we imagined an utterly infeasible form of democratic politics? Undoubtedly so, but remember that this impractical picture remains the regulative ideal organizing most theories of democracy, including theories of representative democracy. Nor is the question: might this perfect democratic politics fail to protect against majority tyranny? The question now is different. We are asking whether the speech-modeled conception of self-government, even when taken in ideal form, offers a coherent picture of what it means for a people to be self-governing.

The point of this chapter will be to demonstrate an ineradicable antinomy in the regulative ideal of governance by pure present popular voice. This antinomy, built into the very logic of the speech-modeled ideal of self-government, makes that ideal presuppose what it cannot accept: the presence of texts, enacted in the past, governing the polity on fundamental matters of justice today and in the future.

Jacques Derrida has made this point repeatedly, for example in his long analysis of Rousseau in the *Grammatology.* There are substantial differences between Derrida's deconstruction of what he calls "logocentrism" and the critique to be pursued here of speech-modeled thought. Nevertheless, Derrida—especially Derrida on Rousseau—is pertinent here.

According to Derrida, Rousseau is so adamantly committed to a "logocentric" (or, roughly, speech-centered) politics, in which citizens must express their will "in their own voice, without proxy," that he is forced into a kind of contradiction. Here is the passage with which Derrida concludes his analysis of *The Social Contract:*

> The instance of writing must [in Rousseau] be effaced to the point where a sovereign people *must not even write to itself,* its assemblies must meet spontaneously, without "any formal summons." Which implies—and this is a writing that Rousseau does not wish to read—that there were "fixed and periodic" assemblies that "cannot be abrogated or prorogued," and therefore a "marked day [*jour marqué*]." That mark had to be made orally since the moment the possibility of writing were introduced into the operation, it would insinuate usurpation into the body of society. But is not a mark, wherever it is produced, the possibility of writing?[1]

Why should we think, as Derrida wants us to, that this marking of a day for popular assemblies poses a problem for Rousseau? The significance of this *jour marqué* requires some elucidation and emendation, but it is in fact, as Derrida suggests, the mark of a deep problem that cannot be solved within the terms of speech-modeled self-government.

1. Jacques Derrida, Of Grammatology 302 (G.C. Spivak trans., 1976).

Rousseau did indeed maintain that in the ideal polity popular assemblies would meet without "formal summons" on a "marked day." Now, this requirement did *not* mean, as Derrida might be read to indicate, that the assemblies were to meet "spontaneously," as if the call to assemble had to go out solely by word of mouth ("orally"). Then Rousseau would have contradicted himself in a very obvious way, simultaneously demanding that the popular assemblies be spontaneous (springing up "orally") and planned in advance ("marked" down in some kind of writing).

Rousseau did not fall into this contradiction. He condemned "spontaneously" gathered assemblies as illegitimate. *Only* an assembly convened on the marked day could make law. "[E]xcept for these assemblies, lawful by their date alone, every assembly of the people that has not been called by the magistrates . . . ought to be considered as illegitimate and everything done at it as null." If one of these illegitimate, spontaneous assemblies purports to enact a law, such a law "is null; it is not a law."[2] So Rousseau rejected spontaneous assemblies; how then can he also have rejected a "formal summons" to assemble?

Rousseau's requirement was that the marked-day assemblies would need no formal summons *from the currently governing officials.* Rousseau imposed this condition not to ensure "spontaneity" or "orality," but rather to ensure that the "fixed and periodic" popular assemblies would need no blessing from the current rulers, who "will never spare efforts, nor objections, nor obstacles, nor promises to discourage the people from holding them."[3] The day had to be marked in advance in order to establish the right of the people to assemble without regard to the will of the current governors. How was it to be marked? The day had to be marked, without possibility of prorogation, *in the form of law.* There needed to be no "formal summons," not because the call to assemble was to erupt spontaneously, but because the call to assemble was to *"emanate from the law."*[4]

Thus despite Derrida's statement that Rousseau's "sovereign people must not even write to itself," Rousseau's very point (but at bottom this is Derrida's point as well) was that the people *must* write to itself in order to preserve its sovereignty. The people must pass a law addressed to itself, expressly calling on itself to assemble on particular dates, and this self-addressed writing must further provide that the convocation of the assemblies will not require any formal summons by the current governors.

2. Rousseau, The Social Contract, *supra* Chapter 2, note 1, at 100, 102.
3. *Id.* at 101.
4. *Id.* at 100.

But in a society that aspires to governance by the present voice of the people, this self-addressed, self-written law, the one that marks the day of every legitimate popular assembly, is foundationally problematic.

The law that marks the day is a law that the voice of the people here and now cannot propound or ratify, because this law precedes any authoritative pronouncement of that voice. If the people can speak with legitimate, sovereign authority only when assembling on a marked day, that date must be marked *before* the people can authoritatively speak. Popular voice cannot, therefore, govern alone. A writing is essential to its governance, a foundational text enacted in the past that precedes and helps constitute the authority of the democratic voice today.

Which implies a broader point: in order for the voice of the people to govern, there must be a set of constitutional rules in place identifying the process whereby the voice of the people authoritatively speaks and makes law. There must be rules of recognition. There must always already be a preestablished constitutional process of some sort, which, because it is a necessary condition for the authoritative speaking of the democratic voice, cannot be installed by that voice.

All this is or should be familiar ground. But it is important to distinguish the point just made from an equally familiar one with which it is often bundled up: the supposed problem of infinite regress. Obviously, the legitimate authority of any law or lawmaking body cannot be founded on its own sayso. Thus the authority of every lawmaking institution and of every law seems to require a reaching back into the past, to prior authoritative norms or laws that establish the authority of the legislature or law in question. But of course the same problem would attach to these prior norms or laws, which would seem to require a further reaching back, and so on. Much is sometimes made of this foundationalist problem of infinite regress, but it is *not* the problem just described.

The regress problem is meant to highlight the impossibility of providing "ultimate" foundations for any legal order. The regress problem is said to show that no political-legal order can be founded without some kind of lawless act, some instituting act of force that cannot be justified without circularity or without assuming the existence of normative foundations that cannot themselves be ultimately grounded. This difficulty is not addressed with any particularity to speech-modeled systems of legitimate political authority; it applies to all systems of legitimate authority. Because it is in no way particular to the speech-modeled conception of self-government, the strategies for responding to this infinite regress problem in no way address the problem

I mean to raise concerning the *jour marqué,* which *is* a problem specific to speech-modeled self-government.

Consider how an infinite regress argument could be framed and answered in the case of the *jour marqué.* The regress argument would claim that within Rousseau's logic, *no* legitimate law could ever be made. Doesn't Rousseau expressly require a day-marking law as a condition necessary to the enactment of all legitimate law? But if so, then obviously there can *never* be any legitimate law. For the law that marked the day, in order to be a law, would have to have been ratified at an assembly convened on a previously marked day, which would require a prior law marking *that* day, which would in turn have to have been ratified at an assembly meeting on a previously marked day, and so on.

This regress problem, however, is not very serious. The Rousseauian answer would be to grant the propriety of an initial, revolutionary assembly, gathering despite the repressive efforts of the existing illegitimate government. Let this revolutionary assembly mark a day, and let it provide a further set of constitutional processes (voting rules and so on) to govern subsequent assemblies. Unless these rules are complied with, no assembly that gathers afterward is legitimate. In this way, the infinite regress is brought to a kind of halt by the introduction of a revolutionary, founding act.

To be sure, this act of revolutionary violence will not terminate the infinite regress in the sense of providing an ultimate normative ground. To begin with, a revolutionary act will not be legally justified at its own foundational moment. Moreover, if a principle of popular sovereignty is said to legitimize this revolutionary act, this principle obviously cannot itself be established by reference to popular will. This legitimizing principle, or some other principle, or some reference to convention, will ultimately have to stand as it were on its own bottom. In this sense there can be no end to the infinite regress; every normative system suffers from an Ultimate Lack of Foundations. But the force of this kind of infinite-regress objection is far from obvious, because any point supposedly derived from the Ultimate Lack of Foundations will itself be equally lacking in ultimate foundations. For example, it is logically impossible to say, on the basis of an Ultimate-Lack-of-Foundations argument, that the principle of popular sovereignty is *unjustified,* without presupposing some normative ground (even if only a normative demand for justification) that would itself be equally unjustified. A normative system cannot be *criticized* for its Ultimate Lack of Foundations without presupposing a norm to which the infinite regress problem would equally apply.

This problem is by no means confined to normative systems. Consider the critique of scientific truth associated with Thomas Kuhn, according to which the science of any particular era and field is governed by prevailing "paradigms" that change over time and that are themselves foundationally unjustifiable and unverifiable (because they set the terms of what count as facts). Now, this critical history of science cannot be taken, as it often is, as a critique of "objective" truth—nor as a "disruption" of it, a "dislocation" of it, etc. The obvious reason is that to provide any leverage against truth at all, the Kuhnian position would have to proclaim itself as true. But as noted above, this truth would be subject to its own critique, i.e., to a showing that the practices and knowledges that go by the name of "history," or the "history of science" in particular, are just as governed by changing, dominant paradigms as are those that go by the name of science. In other words, the most that can be said, on the basis of the Kuhnian position, is that it is always possible for any currently dominant scientific theory to be replaced by a new one based on new data inconsistent with the old paradigm. But this claim does not disrupt scientific truth; it merely restates what science itself already acknowledges. Needless to add, what I have just said about the Kuhnian history of science applies a fortiori to claims about the Social Constructedness of Reality. Such claims always depend on one assertion of "real" truth—namely the truth of their own claims about the social constructedness of reality.

So let us put away the infinite regress and consider instead a very different foundational problem raised by the *jour marqué,* a problem particular to speech-modeled thought. The invocation of an initial, legitimate, revolutionary assembly, even if it brings the infinite regress more or less to a halt, concedes that the *present* voice of the governed cannot exclusively govern. In other words, the writing that marks the day and sets up the other constitutional processes, even if it could be traced to a legitimate historical source, still cannot be regarded as an expression of *present* popular voice. This writing must always remain prior to, and constitutive of, any authoritative pronouncement of that voice.

Hence the voice of the governed—the will of the governed, here and now—*cannot* be supreme. It must itself be governed by a text, whether written or unwritten, established in the past, providing rules for its own speaking.

This logic might not overly discountenance a partisan of speech-modeled self-government. He might willingly grant the necessity of a pre-established constitutional process. Whoever supposed that a town meeting could conduct itself without rules of parliamentary procedure? And who cares what day the assembly meets? So long, he will say, as the constitutional rules do no more than allow the present popular will to govern on all matters of *substance,* the ideal of government by present popular will has not been substantially damaged by the fact that it depends on a *process* established in the past.

I will not pause here to observe that matters of process may sometimes be more substantial than matters of substance. The constitutional intrusion of the past into the present is by no means limited to marked days or even, more generally, to matters of process. It extends to the most fundamental matters of justice, equality, citizenship, and political identity.

Who are we—we the living, we who are to govern ourselves? This *we* cannot announce itself, not in its own present voice. It must always presuppose a prior determination of its boundaries, its lines of inclusion and exclusion, without which the ideal of government by present popular will is unintelligible. If there were no prior determination of this *we* inscribed already into a nation's institutions, *we* would be unable to speak now at all. For the will of the governed to govern today, we must have more than constitutionally marked days. We must also have—we must also be—marked men.

In any particular nation, this *we* will have been the product of a history, a constitutional struggle, usually waged at the cost of considerable blood and fortune. (This point does not depend in any way on the concept of the nation-state; it would apply equally at a more localized level or at the level of world government.) To be who we are, our being must be governed by the past. To quote Derrida again, whose words echo Heidegger and in a strange way Burke: "the being of what we are *is* first of all inheritance, whether we like it or know it or not."[5]

The inherited nature of political identity does not refer merely to the fact that certain geographical limits and border lines must have been marked out in advance. Within a polity—of whatever size or location—the problem of border lines repeats itself in the form of the struggle over equality and membership. These internal border lines will govern matters of race, sex, age, religion, and so on. Here too, the *we* whose will is to govern *here and now* cannot by reference to its own present will proclaim the operative principles of equality, for the simple reason that a particular set of equality (or inequality) principles must already be in place in order to identify the present will of this *we*.

We may be tempted today to think of our current equality principles as a priori truths or as derivable from the very concept of democracy itself. They are neither. They are a legacy: contingent, historical, substantive, written in blood, sustained imperfectly in the form of constitutional commitments, and elaborated through a democratic politics. Speech-modeled thought cannot grasp this point. It is obliged to conceive the *we* either as a product of undemocratic force or else as a product of a-prioristic reason.

5. Derrida, *supra* Chapter 1, note 15, at 54.

Robert Dahl, whose recognition of this difficulty is more sophisticated than most, provides an example. As noted earlier, Dahl's basic picture of democratic self-government is speech-modeled. To be genuinely authoritative, he says, the "consent of the governed" "would have to be continuous—of the living now subject to the laws, not of the dead who enacted them."[6] As a result, there is for Dahl a serious foundational difficulty when it comes to saying "what constitutes 'a people' for democratic purposes." The present consent of the people cannot, as a logical matter, tell us what group of persons is the group of persons whose consent counts, because we would have to have identified this group in advance in order to consult its present will. Democratic theorists, says Dahl, have for the most part "either ignored" or "provided facile answers" to this problem.[7]

One conventional response, he notes, is to shrug off the problem with the thought that "every people defines itself," which, as Dahl observes, seems to take the position that the definition of the people should, like all other matters, be left to popular "consent." But Dahl points out that this answer cannot do, for the reason just discussed: popular consent cannot be measured until a political unit has already been determined. If the determination of the units of self-government were genuinely left to present consent, the only logical result would be that each individual would be called on to decide for himself which unit (if any) he belongs to, a result tantamount to "anarchism." Dahl's conclusion: "we cannot solve the problem of the proper scope and domain of democratic units from within democratic theory."[8]

How then is the problem to be solved? There are, Dahl finds, only two possible sources for determining the *we* of a democratic people: "reason" and "violence." If nations heeded reason, he argues, they would embrace a universal equality principle (essentially universal adult citizenship, with exceptions in the case of the mentally defective), together with general criteria for selecting good geographical boundaries. But in reality, he acknowledges, the "answers to the question, what constitutes 'a people' for democratic purposes," will "far more likely come" from "violence and coercion" than "from reasoned inferences."[9]

This logic is unassailable given its starting point. If self-government is understood as governance by present consent, then the *we* must be established in some fashion external to the process of self-government itself. "Like the

6. Robert Dahl, Democracy and Its Critics 50 (1989).

7. *Id.* at 193.

8. *Id.* at 196, 207.

9. *Id.*

majority [rule] principle, the democratic process *presupposes* a proper unit."[10] Because democracy cannot determine its own unit, "reason" and "violence" (where "violence" includes both coercion and accident) would therefore seem the only sources through which a people's border lines—its lines of exclusion, internal and external—can be established.

Which is to say: speech-modeled self-government produces an antinomy at the heart of self-government. It produces the necessity of quitting the domain of democratic self-government in order to answer a democracy's most fundamental questions of justice, equality, and citizenship. This antinomy is driven entirely by the present-tense temporality of speech-modeled thought. These fundamental questions cannot be answered democratically when democracy has been compressed into the punctuated temporality of governance by present will. But they can be and have been answered democratically, when democracy is permitted temporal extension.

Consider a United States court holding that a particular state voting law violates the Fourteenth or Fifteenth Amendment's citizenship and equality guarantees. Does this decision represent a leap into the domain of reason or violence? To be sure, the court's decision will presumably employ both reason and coercion, as does every judicial decision. But in enforcing the Fourteenth or Fifteenth Amendment, a United States court ultimately enforces century-old constitutional commitments enacted and maintained through repeated, intense democratic struggles.

A people cannot *in the present* determine its own operative principles of inclusion and exclusion, because any expression of present popular will must already presuppose the operation of certain principles of inclusion and exclusion. But a people can *have determined* its operative principles of inclusion and exclusion *over time.* The embarrassment of speech-modeled theory is that, as Dahl illustrates, it has no conceptual resources through which to recognize the degree to which a country like America has *democratically* forged its own foundational principles of equality and citizenship over time. In speech-modeled thought, America's constitutional equality principles dissolve into either a continuing act of violence or a vehicle for a priori reasoning.

Dahl is by no means alone on this point. At the heart of the work of such important legal academics as John Hart Ely and Ronald Dworkin is the effort to understand the equality principles of the Fourteenth Amendment through a-prioristic reasoning about the nature of democracy. But there is no single set of equality postulates that can be said to underlie democracy. There is any number of such postulates, so that the most that can be said is that democracy

10. *Id.* at 207 (emphasis added).

requires that the selection of a particular set of equality principles ought to be made—democratically. And the only way a democracy can give itself such principles democratically is by doing so *over time.*

It will be replied, however, that this "over time"—this recourse to history—merely defers, but cannot solve, the impossibility of democratically establishing principles of equality and justice. After all, it might be said, America's constitutional achievements of the 1860s were ultimately the spoils of war, a war in which one set of claims of nationhood and self-determination triumphed over another set by force. Sooner or later, any attempt to trace this nation's equality and citizenship principles to its constitutional history will necessarily run up against acts of undemocratic force. In any nation there must be, whether just yesterday or long ago, an initial drawing of lines, which may have provided the starting point for a democratic process but which, in its own time and place, cannot have been democratically accomplished.

Here the claim has become once again a version of the infinite regress, and this regress proves nothing. It can show at most that a people must *initially* be brought into being by force or by accident. Such a people, however, even if brought into being by powers outside its control, may yet be the author of its own foundational commitments, including its own equality principles, *over time.* A person too is violently brought into the world, through little or no agency of his own, but this person may still, much later, be the author of his commitments.

A constitutional enactment like the Fourteenth Amendment can always be traced to a war or to the imposition of governance by one group (say, the white men of one region) upon another. Nevertheless, the trichotomy of reason, force, and present will is simply too impoverished a grid on which to try to map what happens when a nation like the United States constitutionally remakes its own principles of equality and citizenship. The inheritance of the Fourteenth Amendment cannot be reduced to the language of a-temporal reason on the one hand or undemocratic violence on the other. It is a violent but democratic inheritance. American constitution-writing processes have been lamentable in a wide variety of ways, but they were in their own time more democratic than almost any such processes the world had ever known. The point is that the speech-modeled conception of self-government cannot embrace or work within—it has no conceptual resources through which to embrace or work within—this democratic inheritance.

The struggle for law that every democracy must wage is a struggle in which force, reason, and present popular will all figure, but in which there may also unfold an effort that exceeds every one of these terms. This is the effort by which a people would remake the state, over time, in the light of its own self-given political commitments. (But is there such a thing as a people, capable of acting as the "author" of constitutional commitments? Is it possible to speak meaningfully or even intelligibly of "peoples" as inter-generational political subjects? Permit me to continue to postpone this objection. It is the subject of Chapter Eight.) A people today must be governed by rules of equality and inequality, of inclusion and exclusion, that it will necessarily have inherited from its constitutional past. As a result, self-government cannot be had on the model of speech. When self-government is conceived as governance by the present will of the governed, self-government is impossible with respect to the polity's most fundamental questions of equality and membership.

Grant, then, that on some of the matters most fundamental to any polity, present popular will cannot govern. Self-government must always be, on these matters, even in the most idealized system of electronic town meetings, government of the present by the past. But perhaps a partisan of speech-modeled self-government will concede this too. Perhaps he will agree that governance by the will of the governed requires the existence not only of a set of inherited constitutional processes (voting rules and the like), but also of a set of inherited citizenship and equality principles. On all other matters, he may say, the will of the people can and should be supreme. Of course self-government requires the prior establishment of a democratic process and a democratic "unit"—a people—but once such a process and such a unit have been put in place, what can self-government mean other than governance by the present will of the people?

Even this deeply compromised version of speech-modeled self-government cannot survive. The reason is that democratic self-government is not only bound up with the past. It is also entrained in the future. Self-government is never a matter of governing what is; it is always a matter of governing what will be. Political decisions made today, no matter how perfectly expressive of present popular will, can be realized only tomorrow. Self-government is always government of the future.

Imagine a perfectly consummated, original "constitutional moment" at which a free people brought itself into being and defined every inch of the nation's legal landscape. This sublime moment would not constitute the achievement of self-government—not then, not *at that moment*. Indeed, as Derrida says, at a genuinely foundational moment of this sort, when a people declares its own independence and its own constitution, the "people does not exist."[11] At this originary moment, if there ever were such a moment, the people's independent existence could be rendered only in the "will have been" of a "future perfect."[12]

The people *will have* existed, it *will have* achieved independence, if the law laid down at that original moment *holds*. At a truly foundational constitutional moment, an expression of popular voice would have to be like a performative speech act that must itself bring about the very conventions within which alone it can felicitously perform. It could only gesture toward a future perfect, the "more perfect union" that it promises and that alone can secure, retroactively, its legitimate authority. "There are cases in which it is not known for generations if the performative of the violent founding of a state is 'felicitous' or not."[13]

But this temporal extension—this projection toward a future perfect—is not only a necessary part of a revolutionary founding; it is part of the internal structure of every act of lawmaking. Say that a law is enacted at time t_1 in accordance with the democratic will at t_1. Is this enactment what it claims to be—law? It *will have been law* only if at some later time t_2, this act that calls itself law *holds*. A putative act of law that never holds anyone under any circumstances, whether by force, threat, moral suasion, or otherwise, never was law. It might have been an attempt to make law, but it would have failed. Even if an act of putative law were applied at the very moment of its announcement but never again (as if, for example, a court announced a new rule in a given case but this "rule" never applied to and never governed anyone in any way ever again), the act would not be one of law. It would merely be an act of force—perhaps just, but not law.

For there to be law, there must be a *holding*. Two moments at least are required for law: one at which a rule is established, and one at which it holds. Law, therefore, cannot be made, and never exists, in a present. It exceeds the here and now; it exceeds the present-tense temporality in the name of which speech-modeled self-government proclaims its prerogatives. Law is something that exists only *over time*.

This was Holmes's insight when he famously defined law as a "prophecy."

11. Jacques Derrida, *Declarations of Independence,* New Political Science 7, 10 (Summer 1986).

12. *Id.*

13. Jacques Derrida, *Force of Law: The "Mystical Foundation of Authority,"* 11 Cardozo L. Rev. 919, 965, 993 (Mary Quaintance trans., 1990).

What the law is now is always a matter of what is to come. Law is a prefiguring today, of something that is to be tomorrow, according to rules established yesterday.

For this reason the voice of the people here and now can never give itself law. The speech-modeled ideal of self-government is *antinomic* in the strictest sense: it is opposed to law. The self that would live by its own voice hates law. It cannot abide by law, and it cannot make law. Law is always, from its point of view, a lapse from authenticity, a compromise with freedom, a fall from grace.

Government by present voice is incompatible with law, because law can never be merely spoken. It requires a writing; it requires language preserved over time. Law is always written. (Even in a society whose law is preserved solely by oral tradition.) And government requires law. Which is to say: a people can govern itself only by both *being governed by its past* and *governing its future.*

This double intrusion of past and future into present voice explodes the entire constellation of concepts behind the speech-modeled ideal. It explodes the picture of self-government as an ideal type of "being in the present." A people never governs itself in its own here and now. It will have governed itself in its own there and then if it successfully maintains its constitutional past and projects itself and its law into the future. A constitution can never be founded in a sublime moment from a revolutionary past. It can find its foundations only—in its own future.

Thus a people can never be *autonomous,* self-law-giving, in the present. Should it really be surprising to say so? Nothing a people can do can be done in a moment—nothing, at least, of any moment. The important things a free people can do may take generations to accomplish. The equal protection of the laws is not made real the moment (if there ever is such a moment) it is declared by the Voice of the People. It becomes a reality only over time—perhaps over centuries. If, therefore, self-government is to be of any moment, if it is to concern real achievements under law rather than mere declaratory proclamations, self-government cannot be of or for the moment. Self-government cannot be an exercise merely of the *freedom of speech* and all that the freedom of speech entails (political dialogue, formation of the "public will," responsiveness of the representatives to the "voice of the people"). Self-government requires an inscriptive politics, a politics that exercises the *freedom to write,* a politics oriented around the production and enforcement of a democratic text laying down enduring principles and institutions for generations to come.

To achieve self-government, a people must do more than seize the moment. A people must attempt the reins of time.

Although speech-modeled self-government is opposed to law, it is not the case that speech-modeled thinking has no devices for accommodating law or the values of legality. The problem for speech-modeled thought is that it can reach this accommodation with legality only by compromising its ideal of self-government.

For example, when originalism locates the authoritative democratic voice in a past moment, the values of legality are preserved. The two moments minimally necessary for the existence of law are now in place: one at which law is established (the "original" or founding moment) and another at which it is to be enforced (the present moment). This is the true appeal of originalism and the other past-oriented schools of speech-modeled self-government: they stand for the virtues of legality, such as stability, predictability, the importance of settled expectations, and constraints on governmental action. (Which is why purveyors of the past-oriented schools of interpretation always hold themselves out as the champions of the rule of law and of the Constitution's status as law.) But the present moment secures the virtues of legality only by giving up what should have been its god-given speech-modeled right: the right to rule itself by its own living voice.

A similar disjunction occurs with respect to justice and self-government. Within the model of speech, justice too is a desideratum in tension with the ideal of self-rule in the here and now. Once again, this is not to say that speech-modeled thought can find no way to accommodate justice. Speech-modeled thought makes this accommodation whenever it locates foundational law neither in the past, nor in the present, but in the domain of predicted will or timeless rights. Which is why the predicted-voice and timeless-voice schools of speech-modeled thought, such as Rawlsianism or other forms of liberal constitutionalism, make their case ultimately in the name of justice. But as soon as democracy is rendered in the language of hypothetical consent or timeless truths, the actual truth is that the living have lost their speech-modeled right to be their own masters in the here and now. In other words, the model of speech can claim the mantle of justice, but only, once more, at the cost of seriously compromising its ideal of self-government in the here and now. Only the present-oriented speech-modeled schools—the contemporary-consensus constitutionalists, the discursive democrats, the believers in strong participatory democracy, the process-based constitutionalists—attempt to preserve this ideal, and as a result they make their case in the name of freedom (conceived as present-tense self-rule).

Thus the model of speech ends by disintegrating the three deepest aspirations of democratic self-government—legality, freedom, and justice. Punctuating time, the ideal of governance by the will of the governed carves up the domain of political legitimacy by associating these three aspirations with, respectively, the claims of the past, the claims of the present, and the claims of a time to come. The result is a strange three-fronted battle visible throughout modern political and constitutional thought, in which the rhetorics of law, freedom, and justice unceasingly contend one against the other.

Originalists and other conservatives demand respect for the past, appealing to the need for order, stability, and the rule of law. More thoroughgoing democrats insist on the freedom of the living to define for themselves their own conception of constitutional liberty. Against both these parties, moral philosophers like Rawls, through an appeal to the will of an ideal community, try to theorize the entire legal system and particularly the entrenched principles of constitutional law through the lens of justice. And all will *defend their positions by reference to the will of the governed*—past, present, or predicted.

So long as its conception of self-government is dominated by the model of speech, political thought can proclaim itself in the name of the law, of freedom, or of justice—but it can do so only *one at a time*. It can never do justice to self-government under law. Freedom, conceived as a desideratum of the here and now, becomes a thing at war with the rule of law and the reign of justice. Worse still, freedom itself becomes impossible—a thing unintelligible in itself. Freedom cannot exist here and now; it is always, itself, a thing of the past and future.

To begin to do justice to self-government under law, we would need to elaborate a conception of human freedom that incorporated temporal extension into the very structure of the self and its government. We would need to replace the speech-modeled conception of self-government with a conception of self-government on the model of writing, in which self-government was understood in terms of living under self-authored, temporally extended commitments. Why the "model of writing"? Not because there is a necessity for a literal writing, but because temporally extended self-government is available only to beings who have what I will call the freedom to write—who can communicate with themselves over time, who can give themselves texts, including legal texts, to govern their futures.

What needs to be explored, then, is the kind of freedom that is at stake when self-government is reconceived to incorporate temporal extension—when it is reconceived, in other words, on the model of writing.

Part II

BEING OVER TIME

Five

COMMITMENT

If we think candidly about how we live, how we modern Western men and women exercise the tremendous degree of autonomy so many of us undeservedly possess, we will find that we do not "live in the present" at all. Much of our time we spend working out the possibilities and requirements of projects and attachments—to persons, places, purposes—to which we engaged ourselves some time in the past. We decide what to do *given* these temporally extended projects and attachments. In other words, we constantly act now on the basis of decisions, relations, and intentions formed in the past. And if we ask why this is so, we may find that—we cannot quite say.

The cult of the present inclines us toward two different, contradictory views about this. The first is one of embarrassment and longing; here we abashedly confess to inertia, moral laziness, or failure of nerve. From this standpoint, we see ourselves caged, on treadmills, failing to hear or to follow our true voice, which would evidently call on us, in its purity, to live without regard to yesterday or tomorrow, to live a life of "flight," in and for the moment.

The second view is self-satisfied. From this second perspective, we carry on with past-commenced projects and past-formed attachments because (and to the extent that) carrying on is at each moment the rational thing to do. Change is uncertain; transaction costs may be high. Even deliberation has its costs. Indeed, action could hardly occur at all if we had to re-decide at every moment what to do. Hence it is eminently rational for us to treat many matters in our lives as more or less settled.

The significant gains to be achieved if a person coordinates his conduct at different times in a purposive, systematic, path-dependent way are well understood by those who have tried to parse out, within prevailing conceptions of instrumental rationality, the phenomenon of acting now on previously formed intentions.[1] But these consequentialist explanations, while doubtless

1. For an introduction, see Michael E. Bratman, Faces of Intention (1999); Edward

sound as far as they go, leave something out. As David Velleman has remarked of "consequentialist or instrumental" theories of why persons form intentions for the future and later act on those intentions: "There is something more to being a self-governing person, something more than being systematic about pursuing goals, and a theory of intention ought to help us understand what it is."[2] This "something more" is what I hope to explain in what follows.

I do so, however, through a theory not of intention, but of *commitment.* The man who longs for a state of grace disentangled from all temporally extended attachments, and the man who rationalizes those attachments as present-preference-maximizing, both overlook something basic about the significance of past and future in our present lives. They overlook the relation of self-government to time and, as a result, the possibility that passionate engagement with the world and with the future is a central element of human freedom. This possibility is the defining thesis of self-government on the model of writing: *the self that governs itself over time is governed by commitments of its own making, apart from or even contrary to its will at any given moment.*

The core question, then, is simple to state. A commitment is an enduring normative determination made in the past to govern the future. The committed self permits this past determination to push aside consultation of what it would do if it were to act on its own present preferences, or on its own present all-things-considered judgment. The question is why. What reason is there (apart from instrumental or consequentialist considerations) to adhere to past normative determinations when present preferences have changed or when present all-things-considered judgment is now to the contrary?

The answer to this question will take three chapters to explain. Let me say a few words, therefore, about how the argument will proceed, what it will confront, and what will make it so long.

To begin with, I will be offering a kind of phenomenology of commitment: its style of being lived under, its passion, its normative force, its rationality. This is more difficult than might be supposed. For example, as we will see, the "standard . . . model of rational action does not seem to have clear room

F. McClennen, Rationality and Dynamic Choice: Foundational Explorations (1990); David Gauthier, *Commitment and Choice: An Essay on the Rationality of Plans,* in Ethics, Rationality, and Economic Behavior 217 (F. Farina, F. Hahn, & S. Vannucci eds., 1996).

2. J. David Velleman, *Book Review,* Philosophical Rev. 100 (1991), at 277, 284 (reviewing Michael E. Bratman, Intentions, Plans, and Practical Reason [1987]).

for . . . a commitment to future action."[3] Commitments give agents reason to act, but to make this commitmentarian reason intelligible requires a break with standard modern accounts of rationality, which are oriented to an agent's *present* aims or preferences. Specifying how commitments create obligation presents comparable difficulties. When a person makes a commitment to himself, he does what modern philosophy has told us for hundreds of years that he cannot do: "because he that can bind, can release; and therefore, he that is bound to himself onely, is not bound."[4]

Explaining the reason-giving and obligation-creating force of commitments is complicated by the fact that I will be rejecting the one prominent strand of contemporary moral philosophy that credits commitments with a decisive normative force different from that of more familiar will-based obligations. According to this line of thought, the communal memberships most central to our identity make claims on us antecedent to any act of will on our part. These memberships are "commitments" whose force a person is bound to recognize because they in part define him as the person he is. This communitarian account of the moral obligations of membership omits a feature critical to commitments as I will define them: their self-givenness. If commitments are not self-given, they do not bind. They create no obligations and provide no reason to act.

But *individuals'* commitments are not the endpoint of the discussion. Ultimately I will be arguing that democratic self-government is also commitmentarian (meaning that it too consists of living under self-given commitments) and that written constitutionalism is properly understood as a nation's struggle to lay down and live out its own fundamental political commitments over time. As a result, I will be obliged to confront the great difficulties involved in supposing that a *people* might be regarded as a collective agent, persisting over time, able to make and to live under its own commitments. One objection to this way of thinking is ontological: there is no such thing as "a people" existing across generations. Persons exist; "peoples" do not. A second, related objection is normative. It holds that talk of "peoples" masks or even invites oppressions, exclusions, and violence of the most obvious kinds. The third objection concerns rationality. According to this objection, which leans on Kenneth Arrow's work, talk of "popular will" is meaningless and irrational because, in conditions of sufficient heterogeneity, the will produced by any democratically acceptable voting rules will be self-contradictory. All these difficulties will have to be answered.

3. Bratman, *supra* note 1, at 41.

4. Hobbes, *supra* Chapter 2, note 29, pt. 2, ch. 26.

Finally, to complicate matters still further, in working out this commitmentarian account of constitutionalism, I will also have to reject the one strand in constitutional philosophy that has taken most seriously the analogy between popular and individual self-given commitments. According to this line of thought, constitutional constraints can be usefully analogized to the figure of Ulysses tying himself to the mast, *pre-committing* himself against the irrational passions he expects to encounter in future. This "pre-commitment" account of constitutionalism not only operates wholly within the standard models of rationality mentioned above; it also relies on a reason/passion trope very poorly suited to constitutional reality. The Constitution does not speak with the pure voice of Timeless Dispassionate Reason; nor is it credible to dismiss what the Constitution blocks as Ephemeral Irrational Passion. On the contrary, what the Constitution blocks may be the seductive voice of rationality. What is necessary is just the opposite of Ulyssean pre-commitment: an account of commitment that captures the sometimes superior claim of feeling over reason—of an enduring normative passion over day-to-day rationality.

A phenomenology of commitment begins by differentiating what might be called distinct "modes of deliberative agency." Consider three.

The first involves full-blown, all-things-considered reflection. Here we would demand of ourselves that we act on the basis of all the reasons that apply to us. At every given moment, we would ideally take the measure of all relevant considerations, weigh them, and decide accordingly. Through this process, we might happen to find that we do best by carrying on with our existing attachments or projects, but in an important sense all our present engagements would be bracketed. They would figure in our reasoning as contingent and relinquishable, with no special weight attached to them merely in virtue of the fact that they are engagements to which we committed ourselves (if we did) at some time in the past. Part of the question that we would put to ourselves in this mode of deliberative agency is whether our present attachments are, all things considered, for the best. If we choose to carry on with these attachments, it ought to be because we have decided to re-found, as it were, or to re-embrace these attachments anew at each successive moment in an exercise of present affirmational will.

A second mode of agency involves maximal fulfillment of present desire. Here once again we would bracket or put aside every temporally extended commitment in which we might be engaged. Instead we would try simply to act on whatever it is we most desire to do here and now. On such occasions, we might or might not contemplate "returning" to our "real" lives afterward. This mode of agency should not be thought of as unreflective or automatic.

On the contrary, we might need reflection both to see what it is we most desire and to see how best to go about satisfying this desire.

These two modes of agency are very different, but both are versions of living in the present. Both pursue a certain deliberative, motivational "emancipation" from the temporal trajectory and enduring attachments of one's life. Both seek to achieve, in very different ways, conformity here and now between what we do and our present will. Both see governance by the self's full or authentic will here and now as the touchstone of self-governing agency.

Now consider someone who lives within the terms of commitments already embarked upon. This agent tries to understand what he ought to do *given* certain important lines—relations, attachments, purposes, and so on—with which he has already inscribed his life. He does not in his deliberation try to bracket or to step outside his ongoing attachments, either in the name of present desire or in the name of a present demand to consider all the reasons that apply to him. He is, rather, entrained in the task of working out the implications and possibilities of certain engagements he already has with the world.

We live, most of the time, in something like this third, commitmentarian fashion. We do not generally do, or even try to do, what we would most prefer to do at every moment. (Is there really nothing else that you, the reader, at this moment, the moment you are reading this sentence, would prefer to be doing?) Nor, ordinarily, do we engage in genuine all-things-considered reasoning, re-deciding at every moment that this course of conduct, this life—the one we are engaged in, with all the commitments and temporally extended activities, large and small, that describe it—maximizes whatever it is we want to maximize. Ordinarily the question we put to ourselves concerns what we ought to do *given* certain commitments in which we are engaged.

But what are commitments? The potential objects of commitment—that which one can be committed to—are innumerable. A course of action, a person, an institution, a principle, most anything that persists over time can be the object of a commitment. No ideological or moral credentials are required; commitments can be purely self-interested. Nor is any traditionalism or conservatism implied. There can be commitments to context-smashing as well as to the status quo, commitments to revolution as well as to maintenance, to a constitution or to a constitutional. There could even be a commitment to—living in the present.

Living in a committed style is not a matter of defining and adhering to rigidly defined duties. On the contrary, it is a matter rather of the degree to which the self permits itself to be *thrown* into its own engagements. The uncommitted self may want to experience the present moment to its "fullest," or to follow his best all-things-considered judgment of the present moment, but in either case he *reserves* or *withdraws* himself from that moment. He cannot fully engage himself with his own relationships or projects; doing so would entail investments and attachments that he is loath, deliberatively and motivationally, to undertake. By contrast, the more a self is committed, the more he throws himself into his engagements.

This does not mean that he throws his *whole* self, so to speak, into every one of his engagements. It means that he participates in them without the reserve, the withdrawal, that characterizes the uncommitted self. It does not mean he loves his life. But it does mean this: he does not constantly complain, to others or himself, that he hates his life even as he lives it.

Three points of emphasis. First, like any other mode of deliberative agency, commitmentarian agency can of course be conducted shallowly, rigidly, or unreflectively. But if done well, elaborating and honoring commitments requires the opposite of these qualities. Living out a commitment demands, first of all, an ongoing and sometimes profoundly reflective activity of interpretation (of the commitment's requirements). It may well call on us to change, to shake up, to destabilize. Indeed, the idea of being against *all* commitments in the name of "fluidity" is self-contradictory. Such a stance, if taken seriously, would itself *be* a commitment. This is the mistake postmodernism makes, conjuring up a "life strategy" of living in a "continuous present" as if the very concept of a "life strategy" did not already exceed and explode such a present.

Second, taking one's commitments as given, for purposes of a good deal of day-to-day life, is not to be disparaged as mere moral or deliberative laziness. It may be that. But the force of will necessary to recognize and honor a commitment, in the face of contrary present preferences, can be far more considerable than anything required in present-desire or all-things-considered agency. The committed self does not necessarily consult his present preferences when he acts, but he may know what they are, and he may well be called on, without promise of return, to accept considerable sacrifices.

Third, commitments are breakable. There is always the freedom to repudiate, to walk away. Indeed this freedom—which does not, however, demand continuous reappraisal, at each successive moment, of the life or project in which we are engaged—is more than a *possibility* within commitmentarian self-government. It is a *necessity.* The reason is that commitments exert their normative force on us only if they are and remain ours. We must have given them to ourselves, and they must remain recognizable as self-given, if they are to be normatively forceful at all.

Commitmentarian freedom is an exercise of the freedom to write. The committed self wants to be governed not by his present will or voice, but, in important part, by texts of his own authorship, whether or not these texts are literally written down. Every commitment is a kind of text that the self gives itself to govern itself over time. And we cannot live without such texts. They may be self-authored or not, but we will live, one way or another, within lines laid down for us in the past to govern our future. This means: freedom is always a struggle over the authorship of our commitments. Man must commit himself to be free.

To see the importance of self-givenness in commitmentarian freedom, turn to the lucid work of Michael Sandel. In his communitarian philosophy, Sandel also has been concerned to articulate a place for "commitments" in individuals' lives irreducible to and independent of any acts of will on their part. It will be helpful to distinguish Sandel's commitments from the kind of commitment I am describing.

Sandel develops his thinking about unwilled commitments as part of his critique of liberalism. According to Sandel, liberalism at least in the Kantian tradition rests ultimately on a picture of an abstract, "unencumbered" self choosing its own ends, a self figured with particular vividness, for example, in Rawls's "original position." The task of liberal political philosophy is to theorize the conditions of state power that rational, "unencumbered" individuals would choose for themselves.

But the unencumbered self, Sandel says, supplies a deeply inadequate picture of our identity and our relations to others. Specifically, it leaves out of account the moral claims upon us arising from our membership in various communities, as for example our religious or political affiliations. Owing to these memberships, we have "moral ties antecedent to choice." These "involuntary" "obligations of membership" exercise "moral force" on us not because we willed them but because they make us who we are. Such "commitments" are deep personal engagements constitutive of identity. They are binding on us because we cannot unbind ourselves from them: our "identity is bound" up with them already. Their "moral force consists partly in the fact that living by them is inseparable from understanding ourselves as the particular persons we are."[5]

5. Michael J. Sandel, Democracy's Discontent 13–17 (1996).

On this view, we do not make our commitments; they make us. They make us "the particular persons we are." We do not lay claim to them; we are "claimed" *by* them. We feel their claim, we feel their "moral force," as a matter of knowing ourselves. Self-knowledge demands that we "think of ourselves as encumbered selves, already claimed by certain projects and commitments." When we see that some of the "projects and commitments" that define our identity are "antecedent to choice," we will let go of liberalism's conception of the self as a being that exists "prior to its ends."[6]

The choice opened up by Sandel's critique of Rawls reprises the two forms of subjectivity described by Merleau-Ponty, touched on in the first chapter. On the Rawlsian picture, we are to imagine ourselves as bearers of an "empty subjectivity," an I that remains what it is even when stripped of all its attachments to the world, an I whose only obligations to others are those it has freely willed (or would freely will in an original position). On Sandel's picture, we are to imagine ourselves as bearing a much fuller subjectivity, defined by our attachments to the world, and hence "claimed in advance" by those obligations of membership that "are inseparable from understanding ourselves as the particular persons we are."

In other words, we are to choose between autonomy and self-knowledge. Rawls's subjects are free (to choose their own commitments), but know nothing of themselves. Sandel's subjects know themselves well, but they are not free (to choose their own commitments). The autonomous being recognizes no obligations binding upon it except those embraced by its own will; the self-knowing subject is obliged to recognize unwilled commitments that are *not self-given at all,* but are binding nonetheless because they are self-constitutive.

Neither of these pictures is adequate to the phenomenon of commitment that I am trying to describe, nor to the distinctive kind of freedom that commitment makes possible. Commitment entails obligations that are *neither* willed by the self *nor* imposed on it "in advance" as a constitutive condition of its identity. Commitmentarian obligation is *irreducible to will,* but nonetheless it is binding only insofar as it is *self-given.* Between the poles of pure voluntarism and pure involuntarism, there must be space for the self-made commitments that character our lives.

This space is not difficult to describe. To live out a self-given commitment, contrary to or apart from one's will at any given moment, is a quotidian phenomenon. We do it in large and small ways every day. It is the dominant

6. *Id.* at 12–14. Rawls describes the self as "prior to the ends which are affirmed by it" in *A Theory of Justice* 560 (1971).

mode of work, of learning, and of relationship. Living within the engagements that inscribe and describe your life cannot profitably be understood in terms of effectuating a "founding" will, or in terms of effectuating each successive moment's will, or in terms of effectuating a hypothetical reasonable will. But this does not mean that commitments should be treated as *"involuntary"* obligations, obligations *"antecedent to choice,"* obligations not self-given at all. We deal rather with self-given projects whose possibilities and requirements we ourselves have brought into being.

Hence the committed self is not the "empty" or "unencumbered" subject against which Sandel warns. The commitmentarian subject is not stripped of entanglements with the world—neither in the sense of having freed itself to follow the call of its own voice, nor in the sense of having stepped back from all its engagements in order to pursue an all-things-considered form of reflection. But at the same time, this I is not "sucked down into the world." The self who aspires to commitmentarian freedom is not claimed in advance, or defined, by the "involuntary commitments" that his world may purport to impose on him. His future is infinite within the bounds of the actual temporal trajectory that he inhabits.

Commitment offers a third term beyond the dichotomy of willed and unwilled obligation, beyond that of present desire and all-things-considered reflection. Commitments are neither willed nor unwilled. Sandel is correct: the willing subject is too thin an impersonation of ourselves to make sense of our moral and political engagements. But the thinness of this subject does not consist in the fact that its being is conceived as standing prior to its ends. Its thinness consists in its temporal compression: the compression of its agency and its being into a single moment of unfettered will, whether present or original. We do not *will* our commitments. It does not follow, however, that we do not *make* them, over time.

Indeed if we have *not* made them, if they are *not* self-given, then commitments cannot exercise normative force. This is an unsolved problem for Sandel. Communitarianism asks us to accept obligations we incur as a result of involuntary memberships in particular communities. We are to see these communities as making claims upon us that ought to be respected, that are morally forceful, because they are central to defining us as "the particular persons we are." But if these "obligations of membership" are both *self-defining* and *genuinely unauthored,* their moral force is lost.

Imagine a person defined as the particular person he is by virtue of having been born and raised as a member of the sewage-shoveling caste. Perhaps his family has belonged to this caste for generations. This membership is central to his identity. Everyone sees him as a sewage-shoveler; even he, despite himself, thinks of himself as a sewage-shoveler. Is he obliged to give moral weight—any moral weight at all—to this self-defining "commitment"? Must he too learn to think of himself as an "encumbered self," "already claimed by" the "moral ties" of sewage-shoveling as one of the "projects and commitments" that are "inseparable from understanding [himself] as the particular person[]" he is?

The *more* fully a commitment satisfies Sandel's two criteria—the more fully it is both involuntary and definitive of "the particular persons we are"—the *less* normative force it exercises. Such a commitment is the opposite of freedom. An individual involuntarily committed in this way lives in a state of confinement. Worse: he lives under dictation. His life is dictated; it is written for him by others. When we live in such conditions, we are no longer the makers, not even the co-authors, of the scripts that we live out. On the contrary, our lives have been *con-scripted*—impressed into service, forced into scripts of others' drafting.

Commitmentarian freedom insists on authorship of one's commitments. It retains the priority of the self in relation to its ends. This is why commitmentarian self-government not only allows but requires reexamination of the commitments by which we live. The demand that we live out commitments of our own authorship demands the ongoing freedom to tear down and rewrite our commitments over time. A commitment that was once one's own, but is no longer, is no longer self-given.

But to repeat: this is not a demand for continual re-decision or reappraisal. At each moment, the self does not ask himself whether he is acting on his present preferences or whether he wants here and now to rededicate himself to his commitments, all things considered. Reexamination is a requirement of commitmentarian agency, but it is a requirement to be discharged over time. Repudiation is always possible, but it need not be always on the table.

Nor does the continuing possibility of rewriting one's commitments slip in at the last moment the picture of an empty, unfettered, undetermined I engaging in "self-determination." Commitmentarian freedom is not a freedom of self-definition or self-narration. It recognizes that our subjectivity is always already far too deeply formed to indulge in fantasies of self-creation. The self that reexamines, repudiates, and rewrites its commitments is not an empty subject; it is, inescapably, a thing made by the histories in which it lives and, in part, by the very commitments it is called on to reexamine.

Commitmentarian freedom holds only that within the forces, the histories, and the limits that inscribe our positions on earth, we nevertheless have the freedom, if we are fortunate, to give and re-give purposes to our lives over time. It holds, in other words, that we have the freedom to write, and that we must be exercising this freedom if our commitments are to exercise normative force. But if we do exercise this freedom, we necessarily try to understand and to honor what we have made or are struggling to make of our lives. In this way, commitment overcomes the false dichotomy between self-knowledge and freedom.

Even as we live in and through channels we have cut for ourselves, we may yet protest that we are not *committed* to anything. We may say: if I choose to carry on with projects or relationships formed in the past, it is because I think it best, here and now, to do so. And if I have any *obligation* to carry on with a particular relationship or course of action, it is because I have duties to *others,* not to *myself.* In other words, apart from obligations we owe to others, we might protest that we are never obliged to do anything just because we committed ourselves to doing it some time in the past. How could we be? What reason could we possibly have to adhere to a commitment if our preferences have now changed or if in fact our best all-things-considered judgment is now to the contrary?

It is difficult to isolate a situation in which the "pure" normative force of commitment, independent of any other arguable sources of normative or instrumental reasoning, can become visible. To construct such a situation is necessarily artificial, given the multiple and competing explanations readily available for almost all of our conduct. But with these caveats, imagine the following, overdramatic picture.

You are visiting a friend in a hospital. He is dying. He says he wishes that a particular thing would be done after he is gone. Then he falls into unconsciousness. You cannot now promise him to do the thing he wishes; or at any rate, you do not make such a promise to him, perhaps believing that promises cannot be made to unconscious people. Nevertheless, you try to commit yourself to doing this thing. You do not merely decide to do it, forming an intention. You try, rather, to impose on yourself an obligation that will persist past this moment. You may say nothing aloud, but you give yourself, as it were, your word. Your friend dies, and of course, when the time comes, you no longer want to do the thing you tried to commit yourself to doing.

Say that you have no independent reason to do this thing. It does not inure to your benefit in any way. It will not clearly make anyone else better off. Stipulate, for completeness, that doing it will not increase your utility (the benefits of feeling better about yourself are exceeded by the costs of doing it). The claim is that, if you have successfully committed yourself, your commitment gives you a weighty reason, in the nature of an obligation, to do the thing notwithstanding. The claim, in other words, is that persons can—give themselves law.

Grant, if only for the sake of argument, the *possibility* and the *intelligibility* of this self-law-giving. The question remains: what reason would a person have for giving weight to past normative determinations he has made? Why wouldn't he want to depart from these determinations whenever his preferences or his best all-things-considered judgment changed?

It is not usually sensible to try to answer one set of difficult questions by bringing up another. But I am going to do that here. Recall the objections stated earlier to the idea of *popular* commitments. Two of those objections are: the Arrovian argument against the rationality of collective decisionmaking; and the ontological argument against the very existence of a generation-spanning "people." I bring up these objections now because answering them is necessary to complete the phenomenology of commitment, to complete the account of the self that commitmentarianism entails, and to explain the importance of commitment in an adequate account of human freedom.

The argument that does all this is complex. In brief: taking up the rationality and ontology objections in turn in the next two chapters, I will argue that the problems these objections identify are, contrary to what is usually supposed, as applicable to persons as they are to peoples. More than this, I will try to show that the way we solve these problems of rationality and ontology in the case of individuals not only indicates how they are to be solved in the case of peoples but also reaffirms the central role of time and commitment in human freedom, human rationality—in human being itself.

Six

REASON OVER TIME

The first time Arrow's name appeared in this book, the subject was the reappearance, within contemporary economic thought, of Jefferson's proposition that the earth belongs to the living. (Rational economic policy, Arrow suggests, would take into account the interests of future citizens only to the extent that there is a present preference among living individuals to do so.)[1] A similar observation applies to Arrow's famous Impossibility Theorem. It relies on an understanding of rationality that, while characteristic of modern economic thought and much analytic philosophy, is untenably compressed in its temporality—compressed into the present.

This conclusion, which may seem opaque on first impression, and which will require considerable argument to explain, should ultimately be unsurprising. Everyone knows that there is a direct line back from Arrow to Jefferson's contemporary, the Marquis de Condorcet. Arrow's theorem depends in important part on certain voting "paradoxes" discovered by the extraordinary Condorcet, and these paradoxes in turn reflect—the very fact that they are viewed as paradoxes reflects—the present-tense conception of democracy to which Condorcet (as we have seen), no less than Jefferson, was devoted.[2]

The Impossibility Theorem[3] holds that, for any social choice among three or more alternatives, no "method of voting," neither majority rule, nor plurality voting, "nor any scheme of proportional representation, no matter how com-

1. *See supra* at 27.

2. *See supra* at 16. Condorcet famously showed that majority rule could be justified, in certain conditions, by its greater likelihood of producing right answers, but ultimately he held, with Jefferson, that each "generation" was categorically entitled to make its own law. *See supra* Chapter 2, note 6.

3. For Arrow's own brilliant statement and explication of the theorem, which he called the "General Possibility Theorem," see Kenneth Arrow, Social Choice and Individual Values (2d ed., 1963).

plicated,"[4] can guarantee compliance with five simple conditions—conditions that seem uncontroversial in or even indispensable to an acceptable democratic process. For example, condition five is: not giving dictatorial power to any single voter.[5] The first condition: yielding rational results.

What does rationality mean here? A virtue of Arrow's rationality condition is that it requires so little. Essentially, its only requirement is that preferences be transitive.

Transitivity of preferences means this: if someone prefers steak to chicken and chicken to tofu, he also prefers steak to tofu. Suppose this person told us that, on the contrary, tofu is even better than steak. This statement would be hard to understand; it would not seem consistent. One way to see this irrationality is to observe that an individual who genuinely held these intransitive preferences would seem prone to "cycling" crazily among the three choices. Say he is served a plate of nice soft tofu. His preference for chicken over tofu is worth a dollar to him. So he will pay a dollar to get the chicken instead. But his preference for steak over chicken is also worth a dollar to him, so he will pay a dollar to get the steak. But now he says that tofu is a dollar better than steak, so he pays a dollar to get the tofu back, and on and on he will go until he is so poor that the trade up to his preferred meal is no longer worth the marginal value of the next dollar.

Thus rationality, it is said, requires that preferences be transitive. An intransitive preference set would be "bizarre."[6] It would indicate that a person "does not understand what it means to prefer something or that he is just mixed up and confused."[7] Accordingly, the standard "concept of rationality," which Arrow employs in deriving his theorem, and which, as he observes, lies "at the heart of modern economic analysis,"[8] posits transitivity of preference and presumes as a general matter that the preferences of ordinary, rational individuals are transitive.[9]

But this requirement of transitive preferences, minimal and unproblematic as it is assumed to be for individuals, poses a profound problem for democ-

4. *Id.* at 59.

5. For Arrow's discussion of the relevant conditions and their necessity, see *id.* at 59–60, 96 et seq. For Sen's influential version of the conditions, see Amartya Sen, Collective Choice and Social Welfare 37–38 (1970).

6. William H. Riker, Liberalism Against Populism 17 (1982).

7. Jon Elster, Nuts and Bolts for the Social Sciences 155–56 (1989).

8. Arrow, *supra* note 3, at 19; *see* Amartya Sen, On Ethics and Economics 12 (1987).

9. "The modern economist assumes as working hypotheses that the average individual is able to rank . . . all alternative[s] . . . placed before him and that this ranking is transitive." J. Buchanan & G. Tullock, The Calculus of Consent 33 (1962).

racies. The problem is not that citizens in a democracy are somehow prone to bouts of irrational, intransitive preferences. The problem is that despite the rationality of every individual voter, any acceptably democratic rule for aggregating their votes into a collective decision—say, the rule of majority rule—can yield an intransitive and hence irrational preference set. Even though each individual voter is perfectly rational, "majority will" will in such cases still be irrational.

Why? Because of the operation of so-called Condorcet paradoxes.[10] If, say, candidates A, B, and C are ranked {A, B, C} by a third of the voters, {B, C, A} by another third, and {C, A, B} by the final third, it will be the case that a majority would prefer A over B, B over C, but C over A. In other words, when Condorcet paradoxes exist—and it is supposed that they exist, or may exist, very often—"majority will" is irrational. In such circumstances, so long as the agenda remained open, and so long as popular will governed, the system ought in principle to cycle irrationally from A to B, from B to C, from C back to A, and on and on.

Another way to put the same problem: no matter which of the three candidates is elected by "majority will," it will be the case that this same will *would prefer someone else.* In the acidulous glare of the Impossibility Theorem, the very concept of majority rule begins to dissolve, for majority will comes to be seen as an incoherent construct, its outcomes "self-contradictory"[11] and "meaningless,"[12] its will opposing every choice that the majority is said to make. As Arrow put it, so long as there is "a wide range of individual orderings, *the doctrine of voters' sovereignty is incompatible with that of collective rationality.*"[13]

How frequent are Condorcet paradoxes in reality? No one knows. Grant, however, that they exist with enough regularity to pose the problem just described. What I want to consider is whether transitive preferences are properly regarded as a requirement of rationality. In part, this question turns on the place that Condorcet paradoxes are supposed to hold in the case of individuals.

As noted above, it is supposed that individuals ordinarily do not hold intransitive preferences, and it is said that they could not hold intransitive preferences without being irrational. In other words, it is generally believed that

10. Condorcet's account of the voters' paradox can be found in M. de Condorcet, Essai sur l'Application de l'Analyse à la Probabilité des Décisions Rendues à la Pluralité des Voix (New York photo reprint 1972) (1795).

11. Arrow, *supra* note 3, at 5.

12. Riker, *supra* note 6, at 128, 130.

13. Arrow, *supra* note 3, at 60 (emphasis added).

Condorcet paradoxes are not problems for ordinary individuals, who are presumed rational in economic modeling as well as in the "social choice" analyses powerfully influenced by Arrow's work.

But intransitive preferences can exist in individuals—in rational, ordinary individuals. I do not refer here to the results of certain studies in empirical psychology in which individual intransitive preferences seem to have been found in relatively narrow situations suggestive of cognitive malfunction, endowment effects, non-linear preference functions, and the like.[14] I refer instead to much more ordinary situations in which the precise kind of decisional paradox described by Condorcet and made central by Arrow can also occur in individuals. Condorcet paradoxes are *just* as possible for persons as they are for peoples—where "just as possible" means that such paradoxes can be expected to occur both in persons and in peoples in similarly structured decisional situations. The next several pages will be occupied with this point; let me first say, therefore, what turns on it.

I am *not* trying to pursue the demonstration, familiar in behavioral economics, that real-life individuals are not the perfectly rational actors that economists are said to assume them to be.[15] The subject is rather: (1) the relationship between rationality and intransitive preferences; and (2) the supposition that Arrow's theorem identifies a special problem of irrationality for democratic (but not for individual) decisionmaking, undermining the ideal of collective (but not individual) rationality and thus of collective (but not individual) self-government. I will be arguing *not* that individuals can be just as irrational as groups but that rational agents are able to deal with Condorcet

14. *See, e.g.,* Amos Tversky, *Intransitivity of Preferences,* 76 Psych. Rev. 31 (1969); *see generally, e.g.,* Daniel M. Hausman, The Inexact and Separate Science of Economics 227–44 (1992). It has been said that these studies "undermine[ ] the core commitment of rational choice theory to the transitivity of preferences," Brian Leiter, *Incommensurability: Truth or Consequences,* 146 U. Penn. L. Rev. 1723, 1727 n.17 (1998), but the claim is overstated. A typical finding is that subjects prefer bet A (with a higher chance of success) to bet B (with a higher payoff) when asked to choose one, but then set a higher selling price for B when asked to sell them. *See* Hausman, *supra,* at 228–29. The findings are interesting, but indecisive.

15. *See, e.g.,* Itamar Simonson & Amos Tversky, *Choice in Context: Tradeoff Contrast and Extremeness Aversion,* 29 J. Marketing Res. 281 (1992). *See generally, e.g.,* Christine Jolls, Cass Sunstein & Richard Thaler, *Behavioral Responses to Law and Economics,* 50 Stan. L. Rev. 1471 (1998). As Kelman points out, the differences between "behavioral" and "rational choice economics" may be less important than the basic methodological premises common to both. *See* Mark Kelman, *Behavioral Economics as Part of a Rhetorical Duet: A Response to Jolls, Sunstein, and Thaler,* 50 Stan. L. Rev. 1577 (1998).

paradoxes in a fairly straightforward way, and that this way of solving intransitive preference problems is as available to polities as it is to persons.

The importance of this point is as follows. A characteristic social-choice interpretation of the Impossibility Theorem views the theorem as supplying a reason to abandon efforts to understand democracy in terms of collective self-government. The irreducible possibility of Condorcet paradoxes, it is said, means that "popular will" (whether constructed through majority rule or some other system of voting) may always oppose any choice made in its name, and hence the very enterprise of thinking of democracy in terms of a "collective will" is flawed. Individual will exists; it is rational. Collective will is a fiction—and, in conditions of sufficient heterogeneity to allow for Condorcet paradoxes, a "meaningless," "irrational," "self-contradictory" fiction. Hence we should stop thinking of democracy in terms of collective will and collective self-governance. The Impossibility Theorem, on this view, tells us that the only rational way to understand democratic politics is to analyze the process in terms of individualistic decisions made by voters and politicians maximizing their own (transitive) individual preferences.[16]

This view is mistaken. The Impossibility Theorem identifies no special problem of rationality afflicting democratic decisionmaking that does not pertain as well to individual decisionmaking. Individuals in ordinary circumstances are also prone to intransitive Condorcet preferences, and such preferences are in no way antithetical to rationality. Rational actors can solve problems of intransitive preferences *by displacing will in favor of commitment.*

Arrow's theorem does indeed undermine efforts to see democracy in terms of present-oriented popular will-formation and will-effectuation. The so-called deliberative democrats who want to see democracy this way have had little to say to the challenge that social choice theory poses to their fundamental premises.[17] But the ineradicable possibility of intransitive popular preferences does not argue against the ideal of popular self-government, any more than the possibility of intransitive individual preferences argues against the ideal of individual self-government. Instead it argues for rejecting a *will-based* conception of self-government in favor of a *commitmentarian* conception.

But the hinge of this argument lies in the idea that individuals, and not just groups, are subject to Condorcet paradoxes. To that subject I now turn.

16. This position is, for example, elaborated at length in Riker, *supra* note 6.

17. Richard H. Pildes & Elizabeth S. Anderson, *Slinging Arrows at Democracy: Social Choice Theory, Value Pluralism, and Democratic Politics,* 90 Colum. L. Rev. 2121, 2142 (1990), is an important and welcome exception.

Let me "model" a choice someone has to make. I will call this choice the case of M's marriage. In the way of such things, the description will be crushingly simplistic, but in the way of such things, this simplification may make it useful.

Imagine, then, a man, M, trying to choose one of three women to marry. All three are extremely intelligent. All are willing to marry him. Indeed all are perfectly identical except in three respects. Here is how M describes these differences: "Lotion is sensationally attractive and a good person, but the truth is she doesn't like me. Jane loves me, and she's pretty, but she's evil. Gertrude is morally beautiful and rather fond of me, but I really don't find her pleasing to look at."

Say now that M compares Lotion and Jane "pairwise." He finds that on two of the three dimensions on which they differ, Lotion is superior to Jane. ("Lotion is better-looking and a better person, morally speaking.") Likewise, on two of the three dimensions, Jane is superior to Gertrude. ("Jane is more attractive, and she loves me.") But Gertrude is superior to Lotion along two dimensions as well. ("She is morally beautiful and likes me better than Lotion does.")

Under these conditions, nothing can rule out the possibility that M will prefer Lotion to Jane and Jane to Gertrude, but Gertrude to Lotion. To be sure, this conclusion assumes that M does not have a single metric into which he can precisely quantify the "utility" he derives from each woman's beauty, her morality, and her liking him. If he does have a unifying utility metric of this sort, and if he could rank the women cardinally as well as ordinally, then of course he could tally up the "total value" of each woman. In that case, there could be ties, but no intransitivity.

But there is no sufficient reason to believe that there exists, even in principle, a metric that would make the three qualities and hence the three women commensurable.[18] There is no law of neurophysiology such that every experience of something valued must come to an individual through a single neural or chemical channel, allowing every such experience to be cross-compared and internally ordered along a single gradient. Indeed it would be strange to suppose that there was: what would it mean to think that someone's nobility of character is worth "50 units" of what that person's handsomeness is worth "100" of?

If incommensurability obtains, then for any decision among three or more

18. Raz's discussion of incommensurability, Joseph Raz, The Morality of Freedom ch. 13 (1986), seemed to spark a considerable burst of scholarship on the topic. *See, e.g.,* Incommensurability, Incompatibility, and Practical Reason (R. Chang ed., 1997).

alternatives, differing along three or more dimensions of value, the situation within an individual's mind can have a structure identical to that of a Condorcet voters' paradox. When M tries to compare Lotion and Jane on the three relevant dimensions, he receives not three commensurable inputs into a single calculus but rather three different, independent "votes." And in this situation, M may well prefer by "majority vote." He may, in other words, prefer Lotion to Jane just because, on the three dimensions incommensurably important to him (with everything else being equal), Lotion prevails on two. As between Jane and Gertrude, Jane prevails on two dimensions, so he may well prefer Jane. But as between Gertrude and Lotion, he gets two "votes" for Gertrude, and so he may well prefer Gertrude.

It might be objected, however, that M's "majority vote" preferences are too crude to be taken seriously or that they should be rejected just because they lead to intransitivity. Philosopher Susan Hurley has made arguments of this kind. A person in M's position should not, says Hurley, "just . . . add up the numbers of criteria that favour each alternative and select the one that's favoured by a majority." To do so is "crude and unappealing." On the contrary, if rational, a person in M's position will seek a "coherent" "theory" of his conflicting values, and he "would not have arrived at a satisfactory theory about the values that apply" until he "had found one that would avoid intransitivities."[19]

To see whether Hurley is stating an objection to the argument presented so far, we have to distinguish carefully between claims about M's preferences and claims about what he ought to do. Observing that a person can have Condorcet preferences does not mean that this person is obliged to act on his intransitive preferences—doomed, say, to cycle uselessly from one alternative to another. If Hurley is saying only this much—that a rational agent with Condorcet preferences would avoid wasteful or self-destructive conduct based on those preferences—there is no disagreement. But Hurley appears to be claiming something more: that a rational agent in M's position would not suffer from intransitive preferences at all. " '[W]e cannot make good sense of an attribution of preference except against a background of coherent attitudes,' " and "coherence" implies transitivity.[20]

But isn't it quite "coherent" for a person to choose alternative *a* over *b* just because *a* dominates *b* on two out of the three (incommensurable) dimensions on which they differ? Hurley concedes as much. She even concedes, on this basis, that a person might understandably *choose* intransitively; it's just

19. S.L. Hurley, Natural Reasons 259–62 (1989).

20. *Id.* at 260 (quoting Donald Davidson, Essays on Action and Events 237 [1982]).

that he cannot, "all things considered," *prefer* intransitively. "[W]e can understand how someone, without a change of mind, might choose *a* over *b*, *b* over *c*, and *c* over *a*, by supposing that he acts on discrete, conflicting values, all of which he accepts. . . . What we can't understand is someone thinking it better, all things considered, to do *a* rather than *b*, *b* rather than *c*, and *c* rather than *a*."[21]

It is not clear, however, why or in what sense "we can't understand" this. Certainly we can understand M thinking it better to dine with Lotion rather than Jane, Jane rather than Gertrude, and Gertrude rather than Lotion, on *successive* evenings. Obviously what is intended, then, is a certain unintelligibility in M's thinking it better, "all things considered," to do these things *at the same time*. In that case, however, it seems that we are dealing not with the unintelligible, but with a desire for the impossible—which *is* intelligible. We can understand someone's thinking it better, all things considered, to be in two places at the same time.

Consider the possibility, then, that Hurley has it exactly backward: we *can* understand how M might *think it better* to have *a* rather than *b*, *b* rather than *c*, and *c* rather than *a* (at the same time). What we *can't* understand is his *choosing*, all things considered, *a* over *b*, *b* over *c*, and *c* over *a* (at the same time). M cannot *choose* intransitively. He cannot choose Lotion rather than Jane, Jane rather than Gertrude, and Gertrude rather than Lotion all at once. But that does not mean he cannot *prefer* intransitively. What it means, rather, is that he cannot act at a given moment to satisfy his (intransitive) preferences at that moment.

Hurley essentially wants a person in M's position to bring himself, through "theory," to a transitive set of preferences. All-things-considered deliberation is supposed to deliver transitive, all-things-considered preferences. But this view of preference is overly rationalistic. Even assuming that "a good theory about the relationships among the values that apply to any two alternatives has to take into account the way those values apply to other alternatives as well," and has to supply a transitive adjudication of the conflicting values, perhaps M cannot find such a theory. Or perhaps his preferences are unyielding to this degree of rationalization. He may have no control over the fact that, when he compares his alternatives pairwise, he prefers Lotion over Jane, Jane over Gertrude, and Gertrude over Lotion—just because, in each case, the former is superior to the latter on two out of the three dimensions at issue. A person's rationality needs to be deployed not only in arriving at his preferences, and not only in figuring out how to maximize satisfaction of

21. *Id.*

his preferences, but also, on occasion, in deciding what to do *in the face* of them.

Perhaps, however, it will yet be objected that M's "majority rule" preferences are not even intelligible, given the supposition that the three dimensions are genuinely incommensurable to him. For what unifying metric would permit him to say that Lotion's two superiorities vis-à-vis Jane are better than Jane's one, when by hypothesis there was no common metric in terms of which he could compare these superiorities in the first place?

The addition of incommensurables is not so mysterious. Given a set of incommensurably valued items {A, B, C, . . . N}, surely it is plausible to imagine an agent increasingly preferring a subset of these items (over the remainder) the larger the subset is. The same holds for a choice between items with competing superiorities along several incommensurable dimensions. The claim is not that M must "prefer additively" in this way in the case of his marriage, only that he might very naturally do so.[22] And if he does, he will indeed prefer Lotion to Jane, Jane to Gertrude, and Gertrude to Lotion.

Individual Condorcet paradoxes are therefore possible. More than possible: isn't the phenomenon described here—a choice between alternatives with competing superiorities differing along incommensurable dimensions of value—a deeply familiar one? Every LSAT essay for the past several years has presented students with a problem in which they are asked to choose (and to defend their choice) between two options, each of which is superior to the other on one of two important dimensions that, at least given the information available, are difficult, if not impossible, to render commensurate.[23] There

22. A much stronger claim would transpose Arrow's Impossibility Theorem in toto from collective to individual choice and would argue that, so long as incommensurability obtains, then no matter what decision rule M uses, he cannot avoid intransitivity. *See* Kenneth O. May, *Intransitivity, Utility, and the Aggregation of Preference Patterns,* Econometrica 1 (1954). May concluded that "transitivity holds just when a money price (a utility expressed in money terms) can fully express the preference pattern"; but "where choice depends on conflicting criteria, preference patterns *may* be intransitive." *Id.* at 5, 7. As Hurley points out, May's argument depends on the questionable claim that the conditions Arrow imposed on social welfare functions properly apply to individual preference functions as well. *See* Hurley, *supra* note 19, ch. 12.

23. In the (unscored) writing sample portion of the test, examinees are invariably asked to write an argument in favor of one of two courses of action open to a decisionmaker with two competing goals, as for example a city that wants both to create jobs and "to preserve the integrity" of a wildlife refuge. The two courses of action inevitably have competing superiorities as measured by the two criteria. Thus one alternative open to the city will be a large commercial project near the refuge; the

is a word we use when we have to make this kind of choice. We say we are "torn." And whenever we are "torn" among three or more options, we have a potential Condorcet paradox.

Whether an individual's preferences are occasionally or even frequently intransitive along these lines is a question of, we might say, speculative empirical psychology. I present no evidence of such intransitivities, but my primary goal is a purely formal one, as Arrow's was (the Impossibility Theorem was similarly offered without evidence of any actual Condorcet cycling having ever occurred in any democratic system). The object is to defeat the claim that the ineradicable possibility of intransitive preferences poses a special problem for *collective* self-government and *collective* rationality inapplicable to *individual* self-government and *individual* rationality. Contrary to what is usually thought, the Condorcet problem *does* apply to individuals.

Moreover, we should expect *not* to see the one kind of evidence that would best corroborate the existence of intra-individual Condorcet paradoxes: namely, evidence of persons cycling irrationally through intransitive preference sets. We do not see much evidence of such cycling in democratic decisionmaking either; the reason is that rational agents find ways to avoid such results. To repeat: from the fact that an agent has intransitive preferences, it does not follow that he is therefore irrational. The question is rather: how would rational actors deal with their occasionally intransitive preferences?

In asking this question, I am emphatically not trying to argue about how the word "rational" should be used, an ultimately uninteresting enterprise. The point is to look squarely at those features of intransitive preferences that lead us to regard them as antithetical to rationality (for example, the apparent paralysis that they might "rationally" induce or their apparent propensity to motivate wasteful cycling) and ask how a clear-headed, instrumentally motivated, right-thinking—in short, an otherwise rational—person could deal with them.

Before we turn to this inquiry, however, consider one more way that M's preferences might be intransitive. The argument to this point has depended on the concept of incommensurability,[24] which is much contested and which

---

other will create fewer jobs but impose lesser environmental risks. At least without more information, the incommensurability of the two criteria makes it almost incoherent to argue that one alternative is superior to the other.

24. Actually, Condorcet results would also obtain on the above analysis for choices where the competing superiorities were along *equally* valued dimensions (not merely

I have not seriously defended here. But M's preferences can be intransitive in an important sense even without incommensurability.

Imagine now what I earlier denied: that M has internal access to a universal metric of his own utility, allowing him to quantify all objects of desire on all relevant dimensions of value. He can thereby produce total-value utility scores for every commodity he confronts. Still M's preferences might be intransitive as follows.

Say Lotion "scores highest" when the total numbers for each woman are finally in. As a result, M marries Lotion. But after a week of being married to Lotion, M begins to wish he were married to Jane. The problem is not that he made a mistake in his earlier calculations. Living with Lotion has changed his utility function. Now he is sorry he chose Lotion. He wants to change to Jane, and he does change to Jane. But after a week of Jane, it becomes more pleasurable for M to have Gertrude. So he changes to Gertrude. But after a week with Gertrude, it becomes once again more pleasurable overall to have Lotion. And so on. Here M's preferences might be called *functionally intransitive,* in that they are intransitive over a very short period of time, even though they are not actually intransitive at any one moment.

But perhaps the reply will be that M *did* make a mistake in his initial calculations: "You seem to think that the relevant calculation for M to make at each moment is to measure how much utility he would derive, there and then, from each of his options. But of course M's correct strategy, before marrying, is to calculate his total *future* expected utility from marrying each woman, factoring in how he would feel after he began living with her. He should have married the one who scored highest on this total future utility measure. There is no paradox here. M simply failed to make the right calculation."

But why is M constrained to make a long-term decision of this kind?

"He's not," it might be replied. "M is free to live with Lotion for a week, Jane the next, Gertrude the next, and so on, if that's what makes him happy. Nothing paradoxical there either."

Perhaps it is not paradoxical, but it is functionally irrational on the definition of irrationality presupposed by the Impossibility Theorem. M would pay money to switch from Lotion to Jane, but then pay money to switch to Gertrude, but then pay money to switch to Lotion, and so on. In other words, M will engage in just the sort of irrational cycling that was described earlier.

"No, there's nothing irrational in such cycling, provided that M is maxi-

---

incommensurably valued dimensions), if the agent could rank the items only *ordinally* (not *cardinally*) along those dimensions.

mizing total utility that way. It would be irrational only if M's total (expected) utility is smaller because of this cycling than it would be if he stuck with one of the women for a longer period of time."

But let's say that M's total expected utility *is* smaller, much smaller, this way. The reason is that after a round or two of this cycling, no one will return his calls, and he will live a life of lonely and bitter desperation thereafter.

"Still no paradox and no problem. A rational actor, knowing his short-term preferences to be liable to such cycling, will consider the adverse consequences of continually cycling through his intransitive preferences. If cycling produces misery or waste, then instead of engaging in such cycling, he will find a way to hold himself to a single course of action, at least for some substantial period of time."

Just so.

Which is to say: it is wrong to conceive of transitive preferences as a requirement of rationality. There is no incompatibility between rationality and intransitive preferences. On the contrary, rationality requires an actor faced with a problem of intransitive preferences to *forswear acting on present will* and instead to *commit himself* to a course of action. This will be so both in cases where the actor's preferences are formally intransitive, meaning that they are actually intransitive at a given moment, and in cases where his preferences are functionally intransitive, meaning that his preferences "go" intransitive over short periods of time. In both cases, the actor may be rationally required to find a means through which to choose and to hold himself to one of his options, rather than to cycle wastefully or self-destructively as he would if he acted at each moment on his then-present preferences.

It is also wrong, therefore, to think that the Impossibility Theorem tells us something important about the rationality of democratic decisionmaking in contrast to that of individual decisionmaking. There is no reason to conclude that democratic decisionmaking is irrational or prone to an irrationality that does not afflict individuals. Instead, the lesson to be derived from Arrow's Theorem concerns the present-tense conception of democracy motivating the Marquis de Condorcet's voter "paradoxes."

The Impossibility Theorem reconfirms that governance by the present will of the governed cannot be had, at least under conditions of heterogeneity sufficient to create Condorcet paradoxes. In such conditions, government by the will of the governed cannot supply an adequate or even coherent picture of self-government. The "majority will" of the governed, whenever Condorcet conditions exist, at each moment *opposes* whatever outcome results from the democratic voting rules that purport to establish majority will. But this self-opposition within majority will does not prove that a heterogeneous democracy cannot be rational. It proves only that *democracy cannot rationally pursue governance by present popular will,* meaning that it ought rather to pursue governance by enduring popular commitments. Instead of a powerful argument from rationality against the possibility of collective self-governance, we have a powerful argument from rationality in favor of commitmentarianism.

I imagine economically minded readers resisting the idea that individual Condorcet paradoxes are real possibilities. But individual Condorcet paradoxes pose no threat to economics, to individual rationality, or to the ideal of individual self-government. Neither, however, does Arrow's Theorem pose a threat to politics, to collective rationality, or to the ideal of collective self-government. The point is this: the self that would govern itself, whether personally or politically, must turn from effectuating its present will to living out, over time, its own self-given commitments.

But how is a person, or a citizenry, possessed of an intransitive preference set, supposed to make a commitment to one of the available courses of action? The idea of commitment, it might be objected, cannot alter the problem of intransitive preferences at all. For if the alternatives are intransitively preferred, which alternative is to be committed to? There will simply be another outbreak of the same Condorcet paradox when the question becomes which option is to be committed to.

It is not the case that intransitive preferences make rational choice impossible. To be sure, an agent, aware that he has intransitive preferences of the sort described above, has no reason to make *any particular* commitment to any of the courses of action available to him. So far as rationality is concerned, a commitment to any of the options will be equally well-motivated. Such a person is not paralyzed, however, like the too-rational ass who, caught between identical troughs of feed, starved to death. He can, at a minimum, throw dice. Or he might have someone else make the choice for him. Indeed, he might be maximizing his own happiness in the latter case, avoiding the "psychic costs" of having to make the decision himself.[25]

But here rationality begins to run out in its capacity to explain the phenomenon of commitment. Commitmentarian freedom, as I have suggested, is not satisfied with merely arbitrary choices, nor by a commitment that was not self-given. Commitments are rational, but they cannot be fully explained by reference to rationality. In other words, a pure rationality-based account of commitment is missing something essential. What is it missing?

25. *See, e.g.,* Jennifer Gerarda Brown, *The "Sophie's Choice" Paradox and the Discontinuous Self: Two Comments on Wertheimer,* 74 Denver U. L. Rev. 1255 (1997).

To answer this question, generalize from the argument so far. The problem of intransitive preferences, I have suggested, turns out to involve an instance of a broader and familiar state of affairs, in which an actor has reason today to try to prevent himself tomorrow from indulging in foolish or self-destructive preference-satisfaction. Examples of this kind of problem are legion. The figure perennially invoked is Ulysses tying himself to the mast of his ship in order to hear the music of the Sirens. A well-plumbed line of constitutional thought has sought to justify constitutional constraints by analogy to this kind of self-binding, in which reason prepares itself in advance against a wave of excessive or self-destructive passion.[26]

But the venerable Ulyssean analogy is inapt and misleading for our purposes. This kind of self-binding is often called "pre-commitment," and I will use this term too, because pre-commitment differs in important respects from commitment.

Ulysses has literally bound himself. The justification for this forcible privileging of his time-1 preferences over his time-2 preferences depends on his superior claim to reason at time 1. At time 2, we are to understand, the Sirens will have deprived Ulysses of his capacity either to reason or to hold himself to reason's counsel. We might say that at time 1, Ulysses knows what he will "really" want at time 2 better than he will know it then himself. In any event, the normative structure of the transaction is: rational self at time 1 acts to prevent himself from falling prey to irrational desire at time 2.

The limits of this rhetoric, as it is extrapolated into other settings and particularly into political affairs, are well known. It is often unclear why the censored time-2 preferences are not equal in their rationality, their reason-giving status, or their "authenticity," to those of time 1. Moreover, the ideal of Ulyssean self-denial can always be recharacterized, as Horkheimer and Adorno sought to do, as the triumph of a modern, dehumanizing rationality, "a denial of nature in man."[27] But the point on which I want to focus is this:

26. *See, e.g.*, Jon Elster, Ulysses and the Sirens (1979). Stephen Holmes summarizes this line of thought: "A constitution is Peter sober while the electorate is Peter drunk. Citizens need a constitution, just as Ulysses needed to be bound to his mast." Stephen Holmes, Passions and Constraint: On the Theory of Liberal Democracy 135 (1995). The reason/passion trope is a strong theme in the Federalist Papers. *See, e.g.*, The Federalist No. 1 (Alexander Hamilton) at 1 (Clinton Rossiter ed., 1999); *id.* No. 42 at 236 (James Madison) ("the mild voice of reason, pleading the cause of an enlarged and permanent interest, is but too often drowned, before public bodies as well as individuals, by the clamors of an impatient avidity"). For an excellent general discussion, see Kahn, *supra* Chapter 3, note 3.

27. Max Horkheimer & Theodor W. Adorno, The Dialectic of Enlightenment 54

nowhere in this story of reason and passion does Ulysses's action of self-binding provide him with a *reason* to act.

The ropes that hold Ulysses when he hears the Sirens explain why he stays on board his ship in a causal sense; they do not supply a reason in a normative sense. What is the difference between the causal and normative sense of reason? Thomas Scanlon describes it this way: "I might ask, 'Why is the volcano going to erupt?' But what I would be understood to be asking for is an explanation, a reason why the eruption is going to occur, and this would not . . . take the form of giving the volcano's reason for erupting."[28] When struggling to follow the call of the Sirens, Ulysses is like the volcano; the ropes explain why he stays on board, but they are not his reason for staying. At time 1, Ulysses *causes* himself to be unable to act on his future preferences; he does not give himself an *obligation* or a *reason* to resist the Sirens. Precommitments generally take this form.

A commitment, however, does provide a reason to act. A person committed to a purpose, principle, relationship, etc., has a special reason to adhere to this purpose, principle, or relationship that someone else would not have: namely, that he has committed himself to it. What is the nature of this commitmentarian reason? The answer is complicated. Rationality as it is set up in the Ulyssean analogy makes it difficult to see the nature of commitmentarian reason, which exceeds the simple terms of the reason/passion distinction on which the intelligibility of Ulysses's self-binding rests. Indeed commitmentarian reason exceeds the entire present-tense conception of rationality that underlies modern accounts of rational action.

The standard modern account of rationality, which is traceable at least to Hume and which dominates contemporary decision theory, economics, and much analytic philosophy, holds action to be rational if it maximizes satisfaction of the agent's *present* aims or preferences.[29] This does not mean that a rational agent is supposed to be unconcerned about his future. On the contrary, it is expected that his present preferences will include preferences about

---

(1972); see Elster, *supra* note 26, at 108 et seq.; Claus Offe, Modernity and the State, East, West 37–45 (1996).

28. Thomas M. Scanlon, What We Owe to Each Other 18 (1998).

29. For a discussion of, and an attempt to depart from, the standard account, see Thomas Nagel, The Possibility of Altruism 61–74 (1970). For a typical affirmation of the standard view, together with some variations on the theme, see Philip Petit and Michael Smith, *Parfit's P,* in Reading Parfit 78–81 (J. Dancy ed., 1997) [hereinafter Dancy].

how his life should go in future. Nonetheless, at each moment rationality is supposed to consist of acting in a fashion instrumentally responsive to the agent's present preferences.

(To be sure, conventional economic analysis typically assumes that rational agents seek to maximize discounted *future* utility, but it is a source of persistent confusion in economic thought whether this means: [a] that a rational agent is obliged to be impartial between present and future preferences, only allowing future utility to be discounted because of its uncertainty; or [b] that agents are simply assumed as a general empirical matter to be concerned today, at discount rates varying from individual to individual, with how things will go for them later. Economic analysts sometimes suggest [a], but ultimately are obliged to embrace [b].

(Richard Posner provides a good example. "What is true," says Posner in a discussion of future-utility discounting, "is that any personal discount rate higher than necessary to adjust for the risk of death is suspect from the narrowest rational-choice standpoint, as it implies an arbitrary preference for present over future consumption."[30] Here Posner seems to suggest position [a]; "preferring" present preferences over future preferences is said to be "arbitrary" and hence presumptively inconsistent with rational action "narrowly" construed. But economics cannot opt for [a] without giving up too much. Nearly everyone, Posner concedes, is a "hyperbolic discounter," changing "time preferences" markedly as expected harms or goods become more imminent, and doing so at a rate far "higher than necessary to adjust for the risk of death." More fundamentally, a major thrust of the entire concept of instrumental rationality is to eliminate the inquiry into whether an agent's particular preferences are "arbitrary." For these reasons, Posner ultimately opts for [b], reclaiming the presentism that is the hallmark of modern accounts of rationality, and allowing the "rational actor" to act on his particular "time preference" just as he is allowed to act on "altruism" if he is so motivated.[31] Indeed, Posner opts for the most radical, extreme presentism possible, and his solution simultaneously reflects the considerable anxiety in conventional economic thought concerning this problem as well as the ultimate loss of grip on personhood produced by the present-oriented conception of rationality. Posner concludes by suggesting that "hyperbolic discounting" can be

30. Richard Posner, *Rational Choice, Behavioral Economics and the Law,* 50 Stan. L. Rev. 1551, 1568 (1998).

31. *Id.* at 1567 (describing the "success of modern economics in enriching the simplest rational-choice models, not only with risk aversion and risk preference but also with altruism [and] time preference").

squared with "rational choice" by positing "multiple selves" in each person: a "present self" acting to maximize his own present welfare, and numerous "future selves" whose welfare the "present self" "disvalues.")[32]

A present-oriented account of rationality has no difficulty accounting for *pre-commitment,* because the self that engages in pre-commitment is never imagined as voluntarily acting against present preferences. Ulysses, for example, acts on his present preferences when he ties himself to the mast, and he tries to act—but is prevented from acting—on his present preferences when he hears the Sirens. Present-oriented rationality meets pronounced difficulties, however, when it confronts the phenomenon of commitment. For the phenomenon of honoring a commitment precisely requires counter-preferential action.

Philosophers are well aware of this difficulty. To repeat a formulation quoted earlier: "The standard . . . model of rational action does not seem to have clear room for . . . a commitment to future action."[33] This is because the idea of commitment starts with the "phenomenological given" that "people often act in ways that are contrary to their present preferences,"[34] but the "standard account of rational action," tying rationality to the agent's preferences *"at the time of action,"* has "no resources" through which to understand the idea of a rational agent at time 2 following a commitment "counter-preferentially."[35] At time 2, the agent's then-present preferences either do or do not point in favor of the conduct called for by the commitment. If they do, then performing this conduct is rational, but the agent is not actually following the commitment in any meaningful sense. He is simply acting, as always, on his present preferences. If, however, his time-2 preferences do *not* point in favor of the conduct called for by the commitment, then the agent acts irrationally if he follows the commitment. In either case, the commitment fails to provide a reason for action.[36]

The difficulties produced by rationality's presentism are a source of constant puzzlement, consternation, and increasingly bizarre hypotheticals in

32. *Id.* at 1568. He elaborates on this thought in *Are We One Self or Multiple Selves? Implications for Law and Public Policy,* 3 Legal Theory 23 (1997). *See also infra* note 42 (discussing George Ainslie's similar multiple-self reasoning). I return to the question of time's place in personhood in Chapter 7.

33. Bratman, *supra* Chapter 5, note 1, at 41.

34. *Id.*

35. Edward F. McClennen & Scott Shapiro, *Rule-Guided Behaviour,* in 3 The New Palgrave Dictionary of Economics and the Law 363, 366 (1998) (emphasis added).

36. The same difficulty is generalizable to all instances of rule-guided behavior. *See id.*

contemporary analytic philosophy. Individual A, stranded in the desert, can induce motorist B to rescue him only by sincerely assuring B that he (A) will pay B tomorrow, when they arrive in town. A's problem is that he is perfectly rational (and a very bad liar): he knows that when they arrive in town he will have no reason to pay B. (It is always stipulated in such cases that A will have no further dealings with B, will not "feel so much better" if he pays B that his utility will increase in any event, will suffer no reputational damages if he fails to pay, and can make no binding moral or legal engagements with B, as by entering into a contract, waiving claims, etc.) So A cannot assure B of his help, and his rationality condemns him to death.[37]

Then there is the "toxin problem," in which the rational agent will be paid a million dollars tonight if he intends (tonight) to drink a really foul but harmless toxin next Wednesday. To get the money, the agent doesn't have to drink the toxin; he just has to intend to. But a rational agent cannot intend tonight to drink the toxin Wednesday, knowing that Wednesday the money will be in the bank and there will be no reason then to drink.[38]

Or consider the "rational self-torturer," who gets ten thousand dollars for permitting himself to be implanted with a device that can subject him to increments of pain from 1 to 1000. The difference between any particular unit of pain and the next is too slight to be detected by human sensibility; but at 1000, the individual is wracked with unthinkable agony. The device cannot be removed and can be ratcheted only up, not down, a fact that becomes significant when the rational self-torturer is offered another $10,000 for ratcheting up to 1 and for each unit thereafter. Soon enough, he rationalizes himself into $10,000,000, but he cannot enjoy his good fortune because he is too busy begging for death.[39]

37. On a rational agent's inability to assure future reciprocation of benefits, see, for example, Joe Mintoff, *Rational Cooperation, Intention, and Reconsideration,* 107 Ethics 612 (1997).

38. *See* Gregory S. Kavka, *The Toxin Puzzle,* 43 Analysis 33 (1983). For comments on Kavka's toxin puzzle, see Daniel Farrell, *Intention, Reason, and Action,* 26 Am. Phil. Q. 283 (1989), and several of the essays in Rational Commitment and Social Justice (Jules L. Coleman & Christopher W. Morris eds., 1998) [hereinafter Rational Commitment].

39. For the self-torturer, see Warren Quinn, Morality and Action 198–209 (1993). The rational self-torturer suffers from a kind of intransitivity; he prefers 1 to 0, 2 to 1, and so on, but he also prefers 0 (with no money) to 1000 (with $10,000,000). *See id.* at 199. This is an instance of a phenomenon described by Amos Tversky in 1969: intransitive preferences can be produced in any two-dimensional choice where the agent cannot distinguish incremental differences along one dimension. *See* Tversky, *supra* note 14.

In all such cases, pre-commitment would be an obviously desirable strategy,[40] but the philosophers who treat these issues stipulate to the unavailability of pre-commitment mechanisms because they are concerned, as they should be, with the riddle posed by a conception of rationality that seems, at least when unaided by "external mechanisms," to obstruct the agent's capacity for welfare-maximizing planning or, to put it in another way, that seems so unreasonable. Several of these philosophers claim that the utility-maximizing plan can be reached within the standard account of rationality, but their solutions are unsatisfactory, because in every case a temporally extended commitment is the needed "internal" normative operation, and the present-tense conception of rationality cannot deliver commitment.[41]

Stranded in the desert, rational agent A would survive if only he could effectively *commit* himself to paying motorist B when they arrive in town. Having thereby given himself an obligation and a reason to pay, he could sincerely assure B that he intends to pay. Similarly, the rational recipient of the toxin offer would make his million if only he could tonight commit himself to drinking the toxin on Wednesday (having committed himself, he would have a reason to drink and could then rationally intend to drink). And the rational self-torturer would not have ended in wretched agony if only he had successfully committed himself to stopping somewhere along the way. But none of these commitments is possible, because within these agents' stipulated present-tense rationality, a decision made today never provides them with a reason to act counter-preferentially tomorrow. This problem has no satisfying solution within present-tense accounts of rationality.[42]

40. *See, e.g.,* Thomas Schelling, The Strategy of Conflict (1980); Thomas Schelling, Choice and Consequence 58, 83–112 (1984).

41. One suggestion is that the agent at time 2 may simply prefer sticking to his time-1 choice. *See, e.g.,* Wlodek Rabinowicz, *To Have One's Cake and Eat It Too: Sequential Choice and Expected-Utility Violations,* 92 J. Phil. 586, 611 (1995). To avoid bootstrapping, the claim here needs to be that a "resolute" choice at time 1 can causally alter the agent's time-2 preferences, or causally induce the agent at time 2 to regard the disallowed conduct as "infeasible." *See* McClennen & Shapiro, *supra* note 35, at 365–66. These claims essentially treat commitment as a species of pre-commitment; they assume away counter-preferential action by stipulating that a time-1 commitment not to x causes x to be something the agent at time 2 either does not *want* to do or *cannot* do. But the precise problem of commitment is that, phenomenologically and normatively, a commitment not to x must exert its force just when x *is both preferred and feasible.* An adequate account of commitment would explain counter-preferential action, not explain it away.

42. Some rational actor models claim to solve these problems by viewing them as multi-person, sequential-move games, with the agent at various times occupying the

The difficulty here—or rather the way out of the difficulty—lies in finding a way to grasp how we address ourselves to, how we engage ourselves with, temporally extended courses of action as such. David Gauthier suggests this line of thought when he says that a rational agent should at time 1 "embrace" and afterward follow through with the "best course of action" *"as a whole"*—the course of action "maximally conducive to [his] life going as well as possible."[43] The problem is that Gauthier's decision criterion here—the concern with "one's life *going* as well as possible"—does not quite break with, indeed seems to imply, the from-now-on perspective that makes these problems so intractable. As a result, it is not clear why the agent at time 2 should not decide what course of action "as a whole" is *then* "maximally conducive to [his] life *going* as well as possible."

We move still closer to the heart of the problem with the proposal that we should take seriously, in making decisions today, our own *anticipated future regret* about what we might or might not do. Rawls, who makes this proposal in his *Theory of Justice,* connects it with the idea of the self's regarding itself as "one continuing being over time."[44] More incisively still, Michael Bratman locates the relevance of a person's anticipated future regret in the very project or structure of temporally extended agency: "In being engaged in planning agency, one seems to be committed to taking seriously how one will see matters in the relevant future. One seems, in particular, to be committed to taking seriously how one will see matters at the conclusion of one's plan."[45] The claim here is that if at time 2 an agent expects to be regretful later if he succumbs now to his preference for x, this anticipated future regret gives him a reason to hold to his intention, formed at time 1, not to x.

Observe, however, that this appeal to future regret can solve only some of

---

roles of different persons in the game. The claim is that the time-1 person can "bargain" with his later selves to achieve the optimal result. *See, e.g.,* George Ainslie, Picoeconomics: The Strategic Interaction of Successive Motivational States Within the Person (1992). The problem is that: (1) a self genuinely temporally individuated in this way would have no reason to engage in future-expected utility maximization; and (2) optimization in multi-person sequential-move games depends on the continuing existence of the players over the relevant sequence, a condition that does not obtain if a time-1 person is regarded as "bargaining" with future persons. *See, e.g.,* Bratman, *supra* Chapter 5, note 2, at 48; Frank Döring, *Le "Choix résolu" selon McClennen,* in 1 Les Limites de la Rationalité (J.-P. Dupuy & P. Livet eds. 1997).

43. David Gauthier, *Rethinking the Toxin Puzzle,* in Rational Commitment, *supra* note 38, at 47, 48, 57.

44. Rawls, *supra* Chapter 5, note 6, at 421–23.

45. Bratman, *supra* Chapter 5, note 2, at 86.

the cases described above. It can help the "rational self-torturer," for example, who will live to regret it if he does not adhere to his decision to stop, say, at 15. But as Bratman acknowledges, it cannot help A, stranded in the desert, who needs to assure B of being paid tomorrow; for under the terms of the hypothetical, at the moment of truth (which is tomorrow, when A must choose whether or not to pay), if A *fails* to pay, he will *not* regret it later.[46] And neither will anticipated regret help you hold to the commitment you made when visiting your dying friend in the hospital. By hypothesis, you will be unhappier if you honor this commitment, and hence you will actually be regretful if you *do* honor it.

If only you could at time 2 take seriously your *earlier* perspective, the one you held at the *beginning* of your plan, rather than merely your future perspective, at the *conclusion* thereof. Then you *would* have a reason at time 2 for adhering to your commitment. But such backward-looking reasoning is said to be excluded by the standard premise of rational action, according to which, as Bernard Williams puts it, the "correct perspective on one's life is *from now.*"[47] The rational agent may *not look back*. Our "agency is located temporally and causally": the temporal location is *now,* and the causal location gives us some control over how things will go for us in the future, but none over how things went for us in the past.[48] Therefore, at time 2, when we no longer want to do what we earlier decided to do, while we may and should "take seriously" how we "*will* see matters" "at plan's end," we may *not* take seriously how we *did* see matters at plan's inception.[49]

There is a profound instability in this reasoning. In considering future regret, we are *already looking back*. We are looking ahead *to* our looking back, and we are taking this future looking-back seriously. Regret is of course backward-looking, and its backward-lookingness is central to the argument for its relevance. The appeal to anticipated regret, in this picture, is "*not* grounded simply" in "a concern with one's future desires."[50] (If rationality called on us to act now directly to satisfy future desires, there could never be

46. *Id.* at 82 ("I would later favor not following through, for then I would have thereby gotten the benefit without the burden"; the "no-regret condition, then, seems . . . not to be satisfied by follow through in . . . cases . . . of reciprocation."). Similarly, regret would not help the would-be toxin drinker, who would *not* feel regret later if he chose at time 2, with the money already in the bank, to refrain from drinking. *Id.*

47. Bernard Williams, Moral Luck 13 (1981).

48. Bratman, *supra* Chapter 5, note 1, at 80.

49. *Id.* at 86.

50. *Id.* at 87.

a conflict between rationality and future utility, but it is just this conflict that creates the problems we have been discussing. The rational self-torturer, for example, has present preferences inconsistent with maximizing his long-term utility. So does Ulysses when he hears the Sirens; so, in a different way, does A when, after receiving B's help out of the desert, he no longer wants to pay. The precise difficulty philosophers try to answer here is to say how or whether rationality, understood to call on agents to act in conformity with their present preferences, can be squared with achieving the optimal result.) On the contrary, anticipated regret is here said to be relevant because it will be the self's own later view of the course of conduct in which the self is already engaged. To repeat: the appeal to regret is "grounded" in "one's actual engagement in planning agency," by virtue of which one is already "committed to taking seriously" "how one will see matters specifically at plan's end."[51]

But once future regret is taken seriously *in this way*—once it is acknowledged that an agent's (future) *looking back* on his course of conduct can supply a reason for action now—then we are entitled to ask why the agent *now* may not look back, and specifically why he may not find a reason for action in his (earlier) *looking ahead.* If, in other words, we may *look ahead to our future looking back* (at "plan's end"), why may we not also *look back to our earlier looking forward* (at plan's beginning)? The reply that agency is "temporally and causally located," and that the agent must ultimately decide what to do *"from now,"* begs the question. For the very question to be decided is whether it is appropriate for an agent, in deciding what to do *from now,* to take seriously his earlier determinations. And if this agent, who despite this *from now* turns out to be licensed both to look ahead and to look back by virtue of being engaged in "planning agency," if he is thereby intrinsically interested in how he *will* see his course of conduct at plan's end, then surely he may also take an interest in how he *did* see it, at plan's beginning.

The idea that "the correct perspective on one's life is *from now"* is acceptable so long as it is recalled that this "now" is intelligible only within the temporal trajectory, extending into both past and future, that makes it what it is. We are always *in medias res.* The very term "one's life" is not understandable *now* or even *from now.* We are obliged to ask, at any particular now, not only how one's life *is* going, or how it *will* go, but also how it *will have gone,* where this will-have-gone necessarily involves us in a constant engagement with the broader temporal trajectory of our lives, extending both into the past and future just as the courses of action in which we are engaged extend

51. *Id.* at 86–87.

into the past and future. It is this engagement that obliges us to take seriously our prior determinations of what was right or wrong for us to do.

To be sure, the weight we should place on our past determinations can depend on a number of factors: whether we were well informed at the time, whether circumstances have changed, whether our preferences have changed (expectedly or unexpectedly), and so on. But most of all, the weight will depend on a further specification of the kind of "planning agency" we are engaged in. If we merely formed an *intention* at time 1, we will presumably have only efficiency reasons for adhering to or departing from this past decision. But if we are engaging in *commitmentarian* activity—if we *committed* ourselves to something or to some course of conduct, if we gave ourselves an *obligation*—we will have to take this earlier determination much more seriously.

The task, then, is to say what it means for a person to give himself, without literally tying his hands (pre-committing himself), a rule, an obligation—a commitment—that he recognizes as binding or at least as exerting strong normative force on him over time. We might say that we do this whenever we enter into a contract. But the analogy to contracting is as potentially misleading as is the analogy to pre-commitment. A contract *is* a pre-commitment. Through a contract, one creates an expectancy in another agent, who may enforce this expectancy in court. The threat of a lawsuit or of reputational damage ties a monetary rope around you, causally constraining your future preferences and options. By contrast, through a commitment, the self imposes on itself a normative obligation that provides a reason for, not merely a cause of, its own future action.

But can't a contract be thought of as a promise, and can't we imagine an agent performing a contract not to avoid damages but rather to keep his word? Yes, and this point of view begins to shift contract into the domain of commitment. From this perspective, every contract and every promise can be viewed as creating a commitment. Nevertheless, the normative structure of contract, even of contract-as-promise, remains different in important respects from that of commitment.

The person who makes a promise is understood to create a moral obligation to another, flowing from his act of promising. But in the cases we are discussing, the agent has by stipulation no other with whom or for whom he can create such an obligation. He has only himself to deal with. And a person cannot contract with himself. The same is usually said of promises. The reason is explained this way: because a contractual or promissory obligation can be released at any time by the promisee, a person cannot meaningfully bind himself to himself, because he could always release himself whenever he didn't care to perform. On the basis of such reasoning, a position long familiar to political thought holds that a "free," "sovereign" agent (whether individual or collective) cannot be "bound to itself." Thus Hobbes:

> The Soveraign of a Common-wealth, be it an Assembly or one Man, is not Subject to the Civill Lawes. . . . For he is free, that can be free when he will: Nor is it possible, for any person to be bound to himself; because he that can bind, can release; and therefore, he that is bound to himself onely, is not bound.[52]

Hobbes's reasoning is correct within the normative structure he assumes, which is nothing other than that of speech-modeled self-government—self-government understood as government by the self's own will. The model of speech, together with its ever-present presentism, is unmistakable here: the free self is one who "can be free when he will." Within this speech-modeled normative structure, the termination of a promise or contract is almost necessarily dependent on the future present will of the parties (the promisee, to whom the obligation runs, remains free at any moment to release the obligation; the parties remain free together, at any moment, to modify or rescind as they like). Commitment offers a solution to the problem of self-binding precisely because it does not conform to this speech-modeled logic.

Unlike a contract, a commitment does not require two or more agents. It is an act of self-binding that does not conjure up—does not even allow for—a will that is authorized to release the obligation at any moment. The normative structure of commitment is one of *self-re-collection.*

A self that commits itself gives itself its word. This word-giving is like a promise, but it is not a promise, which is an act of will creating a debt to another. A commitment is an exercise of the freedom to write: the freedom of a temporally extended self to engage itself, for and by itself, with special determination, to a course of action—inscribing into its life a text, even if nothing is literally written down, demanding that a certain purpose be honored, or course of action followed through. This engagement and this text, if they hold, *recall* the self to itself. Self-re-collection: a commitment both calls upon the self to *recollect* what it is "about"—recalling the self to that which

52. Hobbes, *supra* Chapter 2, note 29, pt. 2, ch. 26. Bodin, Pufendorf, and Rousseau made similar arguments; the conclusion drawn was usually that a constitution binding the sovereign was logically impossible. *See, e.g.,* Jean Bodin, Six Bookes of a Commonweale bk. I, ch. 8 at 91–9 (1962) (1576); Samuel Pufendorf, De Jure Naturae and Gentium bk 1, ch. 6, § 7 at 94, bk. 7, ch. 6, § 8 at 1064 (C.H. & W.A. Oldfather trans., 1934) (1672); Rousseau, *supra* Chapter 3, note 13. For an excellent discussion, see Holmes, *supra* note 26, at 113–15, 143–58.

it knows to be the right thing to do—and serves to *re-collect* the temporally disparate experiences of the self's life into the self-governed experiences of a temporally extended agent.

A commitment is like a swearing, or a vow, but it is not a vow, because a vow requires a god to whom it can be sworn, and hence recreates in alienated fashion the normative structure of a promise. Vows are mystified commitments: the self that makes a sacred vow believes he needs God as a source of his moral obligations, failing to see that man may be—must be—his own lawgiver. A committed self gives himself his word that he will x, but this word-giving can never be effected or released, as a promise can, in a single moment. One who vows or "promises himself" to x, even if this vow or promise is sincere, may or may not be committed to x. Only time will tell. A commitment must be inscribed in one way or another into the agent's life; it must engage the process of self-re-collection, before the agent can really be said to be committed.

In fact, we have a convention for making non-waivable promises to ourselves (a kind of secular vow): the convention is called the New Year's resolution. Anyone can make such a promise or vow. But this is not a commitment. For the self to give itself its word, the word must be *accepted.* I am not equal to describing this, but the self must in a sense invest or (in Frankfurt's term) identify itself with the word it gives. To be given, the word must *take.* So that out of the *fort* and *da* of our good and bad intentions there occurs a determinate throwing of the self, an irretrievable throwing, from which one may never go back, although one may always repudiate and go forward in a different direction. For the word to *be* given, it must become *a* given: it must become a given in the person's life. Some have a greater capacity to determine themselves, to make things *given* in this way, than others. Some can commit themselves almost as a matter of will. But it is not a matter of will. It is a matter of making investments and accepting bequests.

Commitments, once made, exert normative force on a person not merely because their object is worthwhile but also because they are his. A person who lives by a commitment is committed to living in a certain deliberative mode of agency—the commitmentarian mode described earlier. He must, therefore, retain a belief in the commitment's being his, and hence he must retain a kind of belief in the commitment's rightness, but the latter belief has distinctive features. The rightness of the commitment need not be present to his consciousness at every moment. A man may honor a commitment while damning himself for a fool to have made it. Indeed, the experience of honoring a commitment, as an experience of acting counter-preferentially, characteristically involves a person who cannot, then and there, rank the commitment more highly than he ranks doing the thing that he prefers. Yet a person acting on a commitment must always be moved by a kind of belief, even if only presumptive, that he is doing what is right. He must believe in the rightness of honoring his commitments, and he must at least believe in the possibility that he would see the rightness of his having made *this* commitment were he to see things more deeply, more feelingly, than he is currently able to do.

In other words, a commitment's self-re-collecting function may, at any particular moment, only be potential. A commitment need not operate by bringing into the person's present consciousness at the moment of action a sublime recovery of lost time. But it is in search of his being-over-time that a person determines to live by his commitments. (Of this being-over-time, more in the next chapter.) And if this search should fail, if a commitment's self-recollecting potential should come to nothing, then the commitment does not bind. While a commitmentarian obligation does not depend on the self's will at any given moment, if a person genuinely comes over time no longer to be able to recognize a commitment as his own, he has no commitmentarian reason to follow it.

Hence there is no doom laid upon the committed self to follow through on its own commitments come what may. We can always walk away. The challenge is to understand that we do not attain a true or pure freedom at such moments of rupture. On the contrary, we will be obliged to start again, to find other temporally extended engagements within which to live.

Commitments, then, are precisely the kind of normative embrace of the future necessary to a self that conducts itself, much of the time, within temporally extended engagements that it has given itself. An agent who honors a commitment to x need not say, at each moment of action, that he was ultimately right to have committed himself to x. Rather he lives within the commitment, he takes it as given, thereby giving a shape—a spine—to his life, understanding as he does so that his assessment of the commitment will be informed by this unfolding, this living out, of the commitment itself.

So a commitment expresses and inscribes in a person's life a determination about what is right or wrong for him to do in future (but not necessarily right or wrong in a moral sense). Where do such determinations come from? I take it that no one knows. Perhaps, out of the fog of irresolution that ordinarily envelops our lives, we may occasionally find that we do, after all, have a definite sense of what is genuinely important to us. We may not be sure when we came to this determination. It may seem that we have long felt this way without knowing it. Or perhaps the experience is one of discovery. More familiarly, in living out some previously commenced course of action, we may be made forcibly aware that something we thought was acceptable is not.

Such determinations can happen in a polity as well. At a certain point, a large group of persons may come to feel that a certain course of action long engaged in is in fact intolerable. Perhaps a particular event, no different from a hundred other similar events, will suddenly galvanize a conviction of this sort. A commitment can then become possible, for example a commitment against slavery, cutting through the Condorcet paradoxes that may have obtained in the past or even those that obtain in the present. Individuals who come to believe that slavery is intolerable may yet, in a substantial sense, prefer slavery to the other available options or expect themselves to prefer it in future. They may prefer it, that is, precisely in the sense both that they desire it now and know that it will maximize their expected future utility. And hence they might want to memorialize a commitment against it, anticipating that their sense of what is right is likely to succumb over time to rational preference-satisfaction.[53]

The commitmentarian self knows that just as it is capable of succumbing to passion, so too is it capable of succumbing to rationality. Commitment, in this way, turns Ulysses inside out.

Ulyssean pre-commitment appeals to rationality as against the seduction of transient passion. *Commitment appeals to passion as against the seduction of rationality*—of everyday, cost-benefit, preference-maximizing rationality. Commitments are always made feelingly. The feeling involved need not be love or hate, and it need not be a distinctly moral feeling. But feeling there must be, for in all commitments the self throws itself into an enduring engagement with an object that exists at least in part outside itself, and it is impossible for a self to be so engaged with an object without feeling.

Consider in this light the fact that constitutional provisions tend to be enacted at times *not of sober rationality, but of high political feeling.* The enactment of the Fourteenth Amendment is notorious in this respect. Within a few years, American justices and constitutional scholars were characterizing the revolutionary propositions of the Fourteenth Amendment as a product of the "excited feeling growing out of the war," an expression of a "flushed" and

53. Of course it could also happen that differing segments of the voters could come to different determinations about what courses of action are intolerable. In such a case, it might happen that the earlier Condorcet paradoxes produced by differing preferences might simply be replaced by a new Condorcet paradox produced by differing determinations. The *possibility* of political commitment is no guarantee against voters' paradoxes, just as the *possibility* of individual commitment is no guarantee against intra-individual intransitive preferences.

"inflamed" passion, which "the people in their cooler moments," repossessed of their rational faculties, would not and did not sanction.[54] On the basis of such reasoning, the most important provision of the Fourteenth Amendment was simply erased—interpreted into nothing at all by the Supreme Court of the United States—and this result was perfectly defensible from the viewpoint that sees the Constitution's authority in terms of pre-commitment.[55]

In the long tradition of reason/passion thinking in constitutional philosophy, the passionate nature of constitutional enactments is an unpleasant little truth that needs constantly to be swept under the historical rug. For if the legitimate authority of constitutionalism is conceptualized in the Ulyssean terms of "Peter sober" legislating for "Peter drunk," the world is turned upside down when we seem to find, in actual constitution-making, Peter drunk legislating for Peter sober. The entire logic and normative structure of pre-commitment, as a vehicle for understanding and justifying written constitutionalism, founders on the passionate nature of constitution-writing. But this passion is necessary and proper from the perspective of commitmentarian self-government.

Thus the rationality of commitment and its passion. Yet we still have not arrived at the bottom of commitment's reason-giving force, nor have we confronted the metaphysical-ontological difficulty involved in supposing that a set of voters can meaningfully be regarded as "a people," committing "itself" for the future even after these particular voters are all dead. These two issues are linked. I will try to get to the bottom of the first, and to begin to answer the second, in the next chapter.

Referring earlier to the normative structure of commitment as one of self-re-collection, a matter of the self's trying to put itself into a certain self-governing relation with its own being-over-time, I committed myself to giving an account of this being-over-time. The final piece of commitmentarian reason, and the beginning of an answer to the ontological objection against popular commitments, has to do with the relationship of time to human being as such. I turn, therefore, once again to the most recalcitrant subject—the I itself.

54. *See, e.g.,* The Slaughter-House Cases, 83 U.S. (16 Wall.) 36, 82 (1873); Tiedeman, *supra* Chapter 3, note 31, at 101–02.

55. Tiedeman expressly defended the *Slaughter-House* Court for nullifying the Fourteenth Amendment's privileges or immunities clause on the ground that the Court was merely enforcing the people's "cooler" "will," as opposed to their overly "excited" "whim." Tiedeman, *supra* Chapter 3, note 31, at 101–02, 164.

Seven

BEING OVER TIME

The ontological objection against popular commitments, it will be recalled, maintains that there is no such thing as a "People," understood as a collective subject persisting across generations. This chapter, like the last one, will attempt to show: (1) that contrary to what is usually thought, the objection applies to persons as well as to peoples; and (2) that the way we answer the objection in the case of persons further explains the place of time and of commitments in an adequate account of human self-government. In addition, the answer to the ontological objection in the case of persons furnishes the beginning of the answer to the same objection in the case of peoples, which will be the subject of the next chapter.

In what sense can the ontological argument against peoples be thought to apply to persons? One possible claim would be that we are at each moment not one self but many different selves, whose schizophrenic plurality is hidden by the fiction of unitary personhood. A different claim, and the only one that will interest us here, is that we are composed of many different selves not at a particular moment, but over time.

Against claims that "a people" did this or that a hundred or two hundred years ago, it is often pointed out that the long-dead people who actually did the thing in question are not the same as the ones living today. For this reason, claims implying the existence of a generation-spanning "people," bound today by "its own" past actions, are supposed to be particularly spurious. The claim that the unitary "I" existing over time is a fiction raises similar questions about the existence of persons.

Philosopher Derek Parfit has famously made the strongest case in recent years for the factitiousness of the self, the unitary I, over time.[1] Here is how Parfit's argument works. Consider a person at time 1, whom we will call A, and a

1. *See* Derek Parfit, Reasons and Persons 199–306 (corrected ed. 1987).

person at time 2, whom we will call B. What must be the case about A and B, what relation must they bear to each other, such that they are the same person?

The answer cannot be that A and B must have the same body. If you undergo a kidney transplant, receiving one of Q's kidneys, wouldn't it be you, rather than Q, who wakes up after the operation? And wouldn't the same be true if you received a new leg, a new heart, and so on? "Some people continue to exist," Parfit observes, "even though they lose, or lose the use of, much of their bodies."[2]

If, however, you underwent a *brain* transplant, receiving Q's brain in place of your own, would you survive? Most people think that in such a case, the person who survived the operation—the person who woke up afterward—would be Q with your body, not you with Q's brain. This intuition implies that the brain is somehow the primary carrier or locus of personal identity. But if so, it is not because of anything special in the particular cells that happen to make up your brain, any one of which we could imagine being replaced by an exactly similar cell, one after the other, without thereby causing you to cease to exist. It must instead be that the psychological contents of our minds—the memories, thoughts, dispositions, values, and so on—are what really matter to personal identity.

Hence, Parfit argues, what matters in saying whether a "present person" A is the same as a "future person" B is a relationship not of bodily connectedness, but of "psychological connectedness."[3] What matters is not the continuity of A's particular body parts, not even the continuity of the particular cells that make up A's brain, but rather the continuity, in B, of many or most of A's memories, feelings, beliefs, and so on.[4] On this view, if I have undergone a substantial enough psychological change over the last several years, it would be fair to say that I am no longer the same person "I" used to be. On the

2. *Id.* at 204.

3. *Id.* at 263. Parfit does not argue that "pyschological connectedness" and personal identity are equivalent. Because he understands the concept of identity to require that the relationship of identity must hold "*uniquely* . . . between one present person and *only one* future person," Parfit concedes that personal identity and psychological connectedness are not identical (psychological connectedness could in theory obtain between "one present person" and an infinite number of "future person[s]"). *Id.* at 263. He says, however, that psychological connectedness is the ingredient of identity that "matters." *Id.*

4. I use "psychological connectedness" and "psychological continuity" indiscriminately here, although Parfit distinguishes the two terms in a fashion not relevant to the present discussion. *Id.* at 206.

basis of more sophisticated versions of this kind of argument, Parfit derives very disturbing conclusions.

For example, imagine that a friendly scientist made a perfect replica of you—not a clone, but a replica, with a psyche identical to yours at the moment of replication, complete with all your memories, desires, dispositions, and so on. Imagine further that this scientist advises you that he has to terminate one of the two of you, and the one to be terminated happens to be yourself. On Parfit's account, you should not mind. For the "I" to whose self-preservation you are so devoted inheres not in physical connectedness but rather in psychological connectedness, and the replica will in future be almost exactly as psychologically connected to you as your "own" body and brain would be. You are going to survive in the person of your replica just as well, or just about as well, as you would have survived in your "own" person. To be sure, you will probably feel anxious at "your" upcoming termination; but this, Parfit says, is merely an "irrational fear."[5]

Here is another, simpler argument by which Parfit arrives at the same unsettling point. Picture a stereo. Call this stereo A. Now imagine that the stereo's speakers are replaced. Call the speaker-replaced stereo B. Say that every material fact about the stereo and all its components, including the old and new speakers, is fully known. Is B the same stereo as A?

When we think about this question, Parfit says, we will see that we are not asking about a "further fact," a fact above or beyond all the facts known to us about the stereo's composition before and after its speakers were replaced. There is no further fact that remains to be discovered, no occult truth about the stereo's identity over time that would tell us, if only we knew it, whether A is the "same stereo" as B. We know all the facts. All that remains to be decided is the description to be given to these facts. The question in this sense is empty. To suppose otherwise would be to postulate some kind of mysterious stereophonic soul, which existed behind the stereo's material components, and which may or may not, upon the replacement of speakers, have escaped to audio heaven.

Asking whether I am the same person I was a few years ago, says Parfit, is just like asking whether the stereo is the same stereo it was before its speakers were replaced. The pertinent facts, whatever they are—perhaps I took a new job in the meantime, perhaps I underwent a religious conversion, or perhaps I am merely "a few years older"—would remain whatever they are. If we knew all the pertinent facts about the person calling himself Jed Rubenfeld now and all the pertinent facts about the person calling himself Jed Rubenfeld

5. *Id.* at 279.

then, we would know all that could be known. Asking whether the person calling himself by that name remains the "same person" he was before is not to ask for any further fact.[6] To be sure, Jed Rubenfeld may instinctively feel that there could be no question more interesting than whether *he himself* will still exist next year. But the question of whether a person survives a year's psychological changes, once the relevant facts have been specified, is empty in just the sense that it is empty to ask whether stereo A "survives" its speaker replacement.

Cartesians and believers in certain religious faiths may embrace the idea of an incorporeal soul inhabiting the body, potentially surviving the body's death, or even jumping from one body to another so that a person alive today might also have lived a thousand years ago. But this hypostatic I must be laid to rest. My body may house a number of rather different persons over time. I might even be a different person from one day to the next. If science should learn to replicate me in my entirety, only superstition or irrational instinct would cause me to prefer my own body's survival over that of my replica's.

Parfit's arguments demand that we see the "I" in a fashion similar to the way many people see a nation's "We."[7] The "individual self" is here broken down into a series of time-separated selves—"present persons" and "future persons"—just as some would insist on breaking down a "popular self" into a host of present and future persons. The result is a claim that we suffer from a kind of delusion if we believe in a unitary, temporally extended I persisting over time, just as some say we suffer from a delusion if we believe in a unitary, temporally extended "We" persisting over generations. How do we answer these objections in the case of persons?

One temptation is to answer Parfit with a kind of vulgar Kantian rejoinder: whatever logic may say, individuals are obliged to think and to act *as if* they possessed a unitary, determinate, continuous I. But this rejoinder is hardly sufficient. For we would still want to know, as Simon Blackburn puts it, whether the "reminder that we conduct our judgment 'as if' there were a transcendental unity involved, rather than indicating a reservation about the Humean or Parfitian approach, represents a prejudice that with their help we should overcome."[8]

Another strategy is to say that Parfit has made a mistake about "superve-

6. *Id.* at 242.

7. In fact Parfit expressly invokes the way we think about nations as an analogy for thinking about the identity and existence of persons. *Id.* at 204.

8. Simon Blackburn, *Has Kant Refuted Parfit?* in Dancy, *supra* Chapter 6, note 29, at 180, 191.

nience." A statue is an example of a supervening entity, and it is surely an entity independent of its component parts in at least this sense: the statue might be destroyed, say by melting, even though the metal of which it was made continued to exist. Supervening entities are thus not fully "reducible" to their component parts; and thus the I, it might be said, even if composed wholly of psychic contents, remains independent of those contents. But Parfit's argument does not deny supervenience. What Parfit challenges is not the existence of supervening entities at any particular moment but the substantialness of asking whether a given supervening entity continues to exist over time, as "its" component parts change.

Yet another strategy in resisting Parfit's conclusions is to say that, on reflection, a person's particular body parts (this face, these legs, this torso) are indispensable after all to his or her identity. This view has implausible implications. For example, on this view, you cannot intelligibly imagine yourself waking up with a different body. It would not be you opening your eyes, but someone else opening his or hers.[9] So it would seem that the coming era of surgical replacement and modification of our natural body parts (if this era is not already upon us) will be one in which people pay great sums to their physicians in order to be killed on the operating table.

Let us consider, then, a very different way of differing with Parfit, one that would attempt to open a wedge between the ontology of most objects (such as stereos) and that of persons. The point of departure lies at the beginning of Parfit's argument. As described earlier, Parfit's arguments take the form of trying to say what must be the case in order for a "present person" A, who exists at time 1, to be the same person as a "future person" B, who exists at time 2. To acquiesce in this way of putting the question is to accept the idea that a person's being is fully realized in a present moment. If we add to this premise the ruling out of a wholly incorporeal ego, then the question of a person's identity over time must indeed present itself as an empty one.

Having ruled out a Cartesian ego, we understand that what a person is consists in some way or other, or in some combination or other, of his body, his mind, and/or his relations with the world around him. Add to this thought the concession that a person's being is fully realized in a present moment, and it follows that all we can do, in trying to decide whether "present person" A and "future person" B are the same, is to compare "present person" A's body, mind, and relationships with those of "future person" B, so that, ultimately, we are in the same position, as we struggle to say whether A and B are the same person, as we would be when struggling to say whether

9. *See* Judith Jarvis Thomson, *People and Their Bodies,* in *id.* at 202, 217–18.

stereo A is the same stereo after its speakers are replaced. If it is ultimately an empty question to try to decide whether stereos A and B are the same stereo, so too it must be an empty question to try to decide whether "present person" A and "future person" B are the same person.

Conceding that persons fully exist at a particular moment prevents us from asking the only question that circumvents the entire Parfitian reduction. That question is: how long does it take to be a person?

A sociologist plays us two videotapes, each showing an inning of baseball. He asks, "Are these the same?"

Although the two innings seem to involve the same teams, the events are completely different. We point this out and say, on this basis, that the two innings were not the same.

"That's not what I meant," he says. "I want to know whether it was the same game in both cases."

"Oh, then the answer is yes. It was the same game in both cases: baseball."

"That's still not what I meant," he says. "Do the videotapes show the same *particular* baseball game?"

How would we respond now? Perhaps: "But I don't know if I was even watching a *game* of baseball in that sense. For all I know, it might have been a simulation or an exhibition."

"Trust me," says the sociologist. "In each case, you were watching a major-league baseball game."

"So your question is whether the two innings were from the same game?"

"No," he says, "I am not asking whether they were *from* the same game. I want to know whether these two innings *are* the same game. Examine each closely. You may press this button to see the plays from different angles, and that button for slow motion. Tell me whether the two innings bear the degree of sportological connectedness to one another that entitles us to call them the same game."

Wouldn't we now want to say that this sociologist had misunderstood what a game is? A game is a temporally extended thing, and two innings are innings of a single baseball game not by virtue of the connectedness in the athletic qualities displayed in particular innings but by virtue of their being within a given sort of temporally extended unit, whose unity derives ultimately from what we might call a text or set of texts—texts that prescribe for baseball games their beginnings, middles, and ends.

Of course it will be said that there can be no analogy between a person and a game. Persons are things; games are events. Events happen to or involve things. Events are extended in time; things are not. Things are extended in space, and while they may persist through time, they exist, as it were, all at once. Richard Wollheim expresses this thought: a person is a "thing" that "persists through time," he says, but is not "extended in time."[10]

Why should we say so? A person is distinguishable from all other things precisely by virtue of a certain relation it bears to itself over time. Locke famously put this relation as follows: a person is a being that can "consider itself as itself, the same thinking being, in different times and places."[11] If this thinking-of-itself-as-itself-in-different-times is a definitive characteristic of our consciousness, then there can be, as John McDowell puts it, no "identity-free account of continuous 'consciousness.' "[12] In other words, consciousness cannot be specified, cannot be made intelligible, without being placed within an account of the subject's persistence over time. The point here is not to recreate the Kantian argument mentioned above, in which the phenomenon of consciousness requires us to think "as if" we had temporally extended identities, even if "logically" we cannot make good on the concept. The "as if" argument derives a temporally extended I from the fact of self-consciousness. But the temporally extended I is not to be derived from self-consciousness; self-consciousness is rather a part of having (or being) a temporally extended being. Self-consciousness is necessary to this state of being, but it is only, as McDowell says, the "subjective angle on something that has more to it."[13]

What more? We might put it this way: personhood just *is* being-over-time. To be a person is to live a certain kind of life, the kind of life open only to a self-re-collecting being. Self-consciousness at any one moment does not constitute this being-over-time. It is the apperceptive experience of being-over-time.

If personhood is intrinsically—in its very being—temporally extended, the question becomes: how long does it take to be a person? And if being a person means living a certain kind of life, then one natural answer might be: a lifetime.

10. "[T]here is a thing, and there is a process, and there is a product. The thing, which is a person, is extended in space, and it persists through time. Being spatial, it has spatial parts, but it does not have temporal parts. The product, which is a person's life, is extended in time. . . . The process, which is the leading of a life, occurs in, though not necessarily inside, the person, and it issues in his life." Richard Wollheim, The Thread of Life 2 (1984).

11. John Locke, An Essay Concerning Human Understanding bk. II, ch. 27, § 9, at 127–28 (Peter H. Nidditch ed., 1979) (1689).

12. John McDowell, *Reductionism and the First Person,* in Dancy, *supra* Chapter 6, note 29, at 230, 245.

13. *Id.* at 233.

But this answer is unnatural, it will be said. Surely we do not have to die to be a person. Perhaps, however, we do; would an infinite symphony still be a symphony? Death, or at least its possibility, may be necessary to make us what we are. (Heidegger: only being-toward-death makes possible the wholeness of a human being.)[14] Perhaps it takes us as long as we live to be the persons we are. We hear a few bars of music. Is it a symphony? A symphony does not exist in any now. How long does it take, then, for music to be a symphony? It takes as long as the symphony takes.

Say a philosopher shows us two photographs. The first is of person A, at time 1, the second of person B, at time 2. He asks, "Are these the same?"

We say, "Well, A is lying in the street, while B is driving a car, so they are not the same in that sense. Is that what you mean?"

"No," he says, "you know very well that is not what I mean. I want to know if A and B are the same person."

"But I don't know whether I am looking at persons. They might be dummies or even drawings."

"Trust me," says the philosopher. "Each photograph shows a real person. Examine them closely. You can press this button to examine their bodies in minute detail. Press that button to hear their thoughts, memories, and so on, at the moment the photograph was taken—even their unconscious thoughts, if you like. Tell me whether A bears that degree of psychological connectedness to B which entitles us to call them the same person."

We should now reply: this philosopher hasn't understood what a person is. He hasn't understood that personhood takes time. How does the philosopher know that it is a *person* pictured in the two photographs? The answer is: the same way the sociologist knew that his videotapes showed innings of a *game*. To know these facts is to have *already* expanded the temporal horizons far beyond the frames of the pictures. That a game of baseball was played means that two teams played a number of innings, with three outs per inning, and so on. The sociologist's statement that each of his videotapes showed a game of baseball being played means precisely that if we unwound the temporal reel, as it were, we would see each of his innings within a larger temporal frame. But if we saw the innings in the full temporal extension that made them part of *a* game of baseball, then we would *already know* whether the two innings were innings of the *same* game.

14. Martin Heidegger, Being and Time 231–40 (J. Macquarrie & E. Robinson trans., 1962).

The point applies to persons. The philosopher's statement that each of his photographs shows a person means that if we unwound the temporal reel, as it were, we would see A and B living a certain kind of life. And of course if we unwound this reel to see that life in its entirety, that life without which there is no person, we would *already know* whether A and B are the same person. So we might say of both the sociologist and the philosopher that they are trying to specify what makes a game or person *the same* game or person over time, without having acknowledged the temporally extended criteria necessary to make a game or person *a* game or *a* person in the first place.

Obviously, recognizing temporal extension within the concept and being of persons does not resolve the more science-fictive scenarios that Parfit legitimately uses to highlight the problems of personal identity. To make a life into the unit of personhood does not solve, but merely reorients, the crucial question in such cases: we would have to specify what counts as being "born" and as "dying" in trying to decide whether, say, the severance of someone's corpus callosum had brought another "person" into being. And we would have to distinguish between, say, a person's really dying and his being "born again." But I think we would be able to say that when I face death, only superstitious or magical thinking would let me persuade myself that I will continue to live, whether in a far better place or in the person of my replica.

One who asks me whether I am the same person I was a few years ago, meaning by this question to ask whether my views or feelings have changed substantially in this period, either speaks idiomatically or else fails in some deep sense to understand what a person is. Certainly someone can ask me whether I am the same person whom he heard speak at such-and-such a place on such-and-such a topic a few years ago. Or he can ask me whether the values or beliefs closest to my heart have undergone significant change. But if he asks me whether I am the same *person* that *I* was a few years ago, then he has failed to understand something essential about the being of an I.

He is thinking about personal identity as a matter of whether I have remained the same *kind* of person over time, at the expense of considering what makes me *a* person in the first place. He has supposed that persons exist all at once at particular moments when in fact they exist only over a length of time—in the ordinary course, a lifetime.

So the way we solve the problem of the unity of the subject over time, in the case of persons, is by recognizing that human subjects occupy time as well as space. Persons do not exist at a given moment in time, any more than a country exists at a given point in space. Where does a country exist? It exists from border to border, from one end to another. So too with persons. To be a person is to live a certain kind of life, from one end to the other.

(But who is living this life, if being a person consists in living it? I am. To think that there is a self-contradiction here is like thinking we must be able to separate the dancer from a dance. Being the dancer of a dance consists in dancing it.)

It follows that a person never exists at a single moment. There is no such thing as a "present person." In this sense, we can never properly say of ourselves, "I *am.*" To be sure, it all depends on what the meaning of *am* is. There is never a moment of which one can say of a game that the game *is,* but still it remains possible to predicate games with present-tense verbs of being. ("This game is boring.") So too we can say, "I am boring." Moreover, as long we mean by "am" something like, "am in being," there is no difficulty even in saying "I am." A person *is,* but always and only in the sense of *being in being:* in progress, just as a symphony is always in progress, whenever a symphony is in being at all.

Some things, like a circle or a rock or a stereo, may be what they are all at once, in the present. This may be so even for some organic things. A tree may be this way. But not so persons. That is why "he is dead" and "the tree is dead" actually have very different logical structures. A dead tree is still a tree. But a dead person only *was* a person. A dead person is still a body, but a person no longer. "He is dead" means: one who was a person is no longer.

We might speak, then, of a speech-modeled conception of human identity, in which our being is what it is all at once, here and now, and would ideally be specifiable at any given moment by a full disclosure of our mental contents, a full speaking of our minds (a speaking of our minds that included the expression of every one of our then-present memories, desires, beliefs, dispositions, and so on, conscious and unconscious). Parfit's conception of human being is in this sense speech-modeled. By contrast, the temporally extended conception of human being would be "writing-modeled," because it requires that persons, to be persons, read from their past and write to themselves in the future.

The idea of human being as being-over-time completes the work necessary to situate commitment in human freedom. Living in the present is a radically inadequate expression of freedom for a being whose being is over-time. To be self-governing, a self whose being is over-time cannot be content to act on present will. He must attempt to put himself in a certain relation with his own temporally extended existence.

The ideal of freedom as acting on nothing other than present will is in the end unintelligible—and doubly so. The I who would be free in this way does not exist in the present, and the action he undertakes is always entrained in a temporal trajectory that extends into the past and future. I act here and now, but as my present consciousness is but a fragment of myself, so my present will is but a fragment of the self-governing agency that I bring to bear on my actions. To be self-governing is to give purpose and meaning to one's life. Freedom therefore cannot consist of acting, at each moment, on present desire or on one's best all-things-considered judgment. Freedom in the human sense is the struggle for authorship of one's being-over-time.

Which is to say: the state of grace worshiped by the model of speech, in which the self is governed only by its own present will or voice, is not fit for a human being. It is the state of grace hungered after by stray dogs. To be stray is an animal's freedom.

Many animals speak; man alone writes. Man alone is free to write—free to give himself texts. Animals act freely in the sense that they can act according to their present will. Man alone can give himself his word and hold himself to it over time, contrary to present will.

To be sure, only humans can build nuclear bombs, but it does not follow that to be fully free in a human sense, we must vaporize the planet. In other words, the fact that only persons can do a thing is ordinarily a non-starting premise for normative reasoning. But this only means: when it comes to deciding what to do with the freedom we have, the fact that one course of action is uniquely within human capability is not a very good reason to pursue it. When, however, it comes to understanding the nature of freedom as such, it is necessary to think through the distinction between persons and animals. Autonomy is something we recognize as a possibility of human existence, and not of animal; the nature of this freedom, if it exists, must therefore lie in some faculty that humans, alone among animals, possess (or at any rate possess to a substantially greater degree than do animals). A free will is usually said to be that faculty. But if what is meant by free will is the capacity to form a will and the freedom to act upon that will, then we have not distinguished human from animal freedom after all. The capacity to write better distinguishes human from merely animal being.

Obviously, a person can live, or be made to live, an animal existence. In other words, it is not the case that a person *needs* to exercise the freedom to write in order to remain alive. (But we should not be "reason[ing] the *need.*"

Doing so, says Lear, makes "man's life as cheap as beast's.") A person could even *commit himself* to living like a stray dog. Honoring this commitment would take considerable work; it is not easy for someone to keep himself disentangled from every temporally extended engagement that life throws his way. But this person, having committed himself to the freedom of being stray, would, despite himself, be living out a self-given commitment. He would have committed himself to having no commitments, a situation to be condemned not as illogical but as feckless. He would have failed to understand that such freedom as he has lies not in his strayness but in his living out this temporally extended commitment to being stray, a commitment he has given himself.

But isn't there value, all the same, in the reminder to live in the present? Kierkegaard, it will be said, was surely wise in observing that the "unhappy man" is "never present to himself," dwelling constantly in the past or future, always "remembering" or "hoping."[15] And isn't Kierkegaard's lesson one that we especially need to learn today, we who suffer from hyper-materialism, we who return home from the office one day to find ourselves old, our youth gone and our children grown?

The lesson to which this question points is not a lesson about living in the present. To "spend time" with one's children, for example, involves one in relationships as temporally extended, an activity as concerned with legacies and with creation over time as anything could be in a person's life. Merely to "enjoy" one's children, as modern childcare sometimes advises, would, if one took that piece of advice seriously, be a form of child abuse. What is really at stake when we think about how much of our lives to devote to our work, and how much to our "family life," is a judgment not about future-orientation versus present-orientation but about which temporally extended values or relations we want to live for. If a father never sees his children, there is no reason to say that he is not living "in the moment." He might well be living "in the moment"—at his office. And if he comes to feel that he has not lived any moment "fully" in the past twenty years, it is probably because he has lived *too much* in the moment, failing to think seriously about what he would have wanted those twenty years of his life to be *for.*

Here, then, is the root of our reason to follow through on our commitments. Having committed ourselves to x, we have a reason to x that someone not so committed does not. The reason is that we have (given ourselves) an ob-

15. Søren Kierkegaard, Either/Or 222–23 (Howard V. Hong & Edna H. Hong eds. and trans., 1987).

ligation to x. And the reason behind that reason is that, in making and honoring commitments, our freedom is at stake. The obligations we impose on ourselves by ourselves need not be moral in nature; they are obligations that exert force on us in the name of our freedom.

Why should a person ever consult a commitment entered into in the past in deciding what is right for him to do now? Because if *each* moment is "from now on," there is never an "on," and never a "from," but only a "now." We live through temporally extended courses of action. There is no escape from this. Self-government therefore requires that the self simultaneously be governing and governed. This is attainable only by one who lives out self-given commitments. Only when we do so are we free, in a human sense.

Because it demands, however, the continuing possibility of remaking, freedom is an incessant interplay between living out self-given commitments and re-writing these commitments. But we should not confuse moments of rupture, of emancipation from the past, with freedom itself. Freedom never is. It too can only be in being.

But perhaps it will be said that the question was not one of freedom but of practical reason. Why doesn't the self that wants to act rationally properly consult only its *present* preferences and judgment? The complete answer to this question is also available now.

The present-preferring self of the familiar rational actor model, who exists fully in this moment and whose coordinates are given by his present evaluative rankings of all possible states of affairs in the world, does not exist. He is another of these fleeting beings, these momentary time-sliced selves, that are figments of the imagination of modern thought. Restore time to this being, and the self who wants to act rationally will understand that he is always involved in a temporally extended agency the very engagement in which entails that he take seriously his past and future perspectives on what he is to do now. And once this temporal extension in his agency is conceded, it becomes possible for this rational self to take seriously the fact that he has given himself his word about something he was to do in future. It becomes possible for him to recognize obligations he has given himself. All this should not be thought of as a cost or drain on his otherwise rational behavior. On the contrary, only through this capacity of commitment can we achieve satisfying solutions to all the problems of intransitive preferences, preference-reversals, and reciprocal benefits discussed earlier. Commitment is necessary to make rationality reasonable.

But in the end, the commitmentarian self does not impose obligations on himself in the name of instrumental gain. He does so in the exercise of the capacity of taking hold of his temporally extended being—the capacity of self-law-giving without which he could not be free. He sees that present-preference rationality can be a threat to the passionate engagements, the investments of the self, the thrownness of his being, which he requires to be self-governing. He understands, in other words, that giving himself texts, and keeping his word, are necessary elements of his freedom.

Eight

POPULARITY

We don't believe in ourselves. Who speaks of the people, the national people, as a real subject, a "we"? Politicians. Ethnic cleansers. We know better. We know that the "one People" conjured up by the Declaration of Independence, the "We the People" in whose name the Constitution speaks, is and always was a mystical reification, a rhetorical trope, more brutal than it ever was beautiful.

A certain gap in our language is telling. *Individuality* refers to the status of being an individual, *personhood* (or, archaically, *personality*) to that of being a person. But there is no word designating the status or condition of being a people. To fill this gap I will use *popularity,* which was once synonymous with democracy itself, but which is now a fairly vulgarized term, a fate common to many of our words pertaining to the people.

Commitmentarian democracy holds that a people, understood as an agent existing over time, across generations, is the proper subject of democratic self-government. This proposition joins two ideas: that peoples, and not merely individuals, can be political agents; and that democracy is properly understood as a people's collective struggle for self-government. Hence commitmentarian democracy requires an answer to the claim that peoples do not exist. It requires an account of popularity—of what it means for persons to be a people.

The aim of this chapter is to offer not a comprehensive theory of popularity but only a rough working account. In defense of this modest ambition, observe that we lack anything like an agreed-upon comprehensive theory of personhood—of what it means to be a person—and yet this lack does not keep most of us from believing that persons exist or from feeling that we have a rough good sense of what they are. To come to the same good sense with respect to peoples would be a considerable advance.

One of the most influential recent statements of the imaginary quality of nations and national peoples is Benedict Anderson's deservedly acclaimed

Imagined Communities (from which some remarks on the modern sense of time were quoted earlier).[1] Anderson opens his book by juxtaposing modern nations with "primordial villages of face-to-face contact." In stark contrast to such primordial communities, the "members of even the smallest nation will never know most of their fellow-members, meet them or even hear of them." A nation, therefore, is an "imagined" community. Indeed it is doubly imaginary. It not only purports to unite in a communal life those who will never exchange so much as a single word with one another, but it is "always conceived as a deep, horizontal comradeship" among all citizens, in fantastic disregard of "the actual inequality and exploitation" prevailing among them.[2]

The fictitiousness of national peoples is a common thread that, for the past hundred and fifty years, has woven together ideologies that would otherwise seem profoundly antagonistic to one another. Anderson's analysis is congenial to a certain post-modern, all-identities-are-imagined school of thought, but it is equally compatible with—indeed it embodies, surprisingly and simultaneously—the foundational premises of both classical liberal and republican thinking.

Liberalism has always put "the people" in quotation marks, regarding with undisguised suspicion the idea of peoples as collective agents, governing themselves. True self-government, said Mill in a passage we have touched on before and will revisit later, is not government by the " 'people,' " but "the government of each by himself."[3] A century later, Hayek similarly decried the "anthropomorphism or personification of society," which led to such pernicious notions as "social justice" and collective responsibility for the outcomes of social institutions.[4] Accordingly, when Anderson exposes the imagined quality of the national "we"—in an analysis beginning with an image of a state of nature (the "primordial village") and ending with quotation marks around the words "our own"[5]—he recapitulates a classically liberal line of thought.

Yet this analysis also conforms to traditional republican thought. To be

1. Benedict Anderson, Imagined Communities (rev. ed. 1991); *see supra* at 35.

2. *Id.* at 6, 7.

3. John Stuart Mill, On Liberty 12 (E. Rappaport ed., 1978) (1859).

4. *E.g.,* Friedrich A. Hayek, 2 The Mirage of Social Justice: Law, Legislation, and Liberty 67–75 (1976).

5. The revised edition of *Imagined Communities* ends with the following passage: "From . . . accumulating cemeteries," "the nation's biography snatches . . . exemplary suicides, poignant martyrdoms, assassinations, executions, wars, and holocausts. But, to serve the narrative purpose, these violent deaths must be remembered/forgotten as 'our own.' " Anderson, *supra* note 1, at 206.

sure, republicanism is defined by a belief in political communities acting collectively, self-consciously, and self-determiningly. "According to the republican view," as Habermas puts it, "in the citizens' practice of political self-determination the community becomes conscious of itself, as it were, and acts upon itself through the citizens' collective will."[6] Nevertheless, putting the "we" of modern nations in quotation marks remains perfectly consistent with republican thinking, because republicanism has long been mistrustful of *national* peoples. From a classical republican perspective, the "People of the United States of America" is too big, too rent by inequality and self-interest, too individualistic, to permit the flourishing of an authentic political collectivity. Rousseau famously made inequality and self-interest incompatible with the flourishing of the body politic. (As soon as "private interests start to make themselves felt," the state "subsist[s] only in an illusory and ineffectual form.")[7] On similar grounds, Rousseau's legatees have frequently repudiated the "we" of modern nations as inauthentic, calling instead for forms of politics centered on the "working class," "organic groups," or other collectivities in which egoistic conflicts are to be finally transcended. Marx, for example, entirely agreed (and this is an agreement at once with Rousseau, with Mill, and with Anderson) that what is called "the People" in a nation like America is a wholly imaginary construct, a fiction intended to disguise the realities of egoism and exploitation.[8]

In other words, the idea of a national people, which was the very subject of political freedom as understood by the revolutionaries of the late eighteenth century, is a castaway of modern political theory. The recent boom in the study of nationhood only confirms how orphaned this world-historical phenomenon has been.[9] Today, the single political camp that would adamantly disavow Anderson's conclusions is the one occupied by the Le Pens, the Aryan Nationalists, the believers in ethnically pure and predestined nationalities. Long neglected by serious political and cultural thought, the

6. Habermas, *supra* Chapter 3, note 5, at 297.

7. Rousseau, The Social Contract, *supra* Chapter 2, note 1, bk. IV, § i., at 108–09.

8. Karl Marx, On the Jewish Question 24–33 (Helen Lederer trans., 1958) (1843).

9. The explosion of work on nationhood in the 1980s and 1990s testified by its very existence to how poorly studied the subject had previously been. For a small sample of the recent literature, see Anderson, *supra* note 1; Ernest Gellner, Nations and Nationalism (1983); Ernst Haas, 1 Nationalism, Liberalism, and Progress: The Rise and Decline of Nationalism (1997); Eric Hobsbawm, Nations and Nationalism since 1780 (1990); Tom Nairn, Faces of Nationalism: Janus Revisited (1997); and Charles Taylor, *Nationalism and Modernity,* in The Morality of Nationalism (Robert McKim & Jeff McMahon eds., 1997).

claims of national peoples have been left instead to the depredations of fascists and ethnic cleansers.

Where, perhaps, they belong. Nationalism has been one of the most fecund sources of war and atrocity in our time. Why seek to recover something of value from the pernicious idea of distinct national peoples seeking their own way in the world? Why not, with Habermas and so many others, embrace the inevitable disintegration of the modern nation-state[10]—and join the great leap forward to global democracy, administered through the wisdom of Belgian bureaucrats, multinational corporate managers, and supranational free trade tribunals?

To begin answering this question, distinguish between two different understandings of nationhood. I do not refer here to the familiar distinction, pursued by many of the new nationalism scholars, that contrasts a liberal-individualist nation with a nastier collectivist-authoritarian version.[11] According to this story, classical liberalism offers an understanding of the nation as a voluntaristic association of individuals, in principle open to anyone, serving wholly instrumental functions, primarily those of safeguarding property and overseeing the market, but also, more generally, enforcing the rights of free and equal individual autonomy for which liberalism stands. Democracy consists here principally of "electoral competition," to be regarded not as a means of collective self-determination but as a device for aggregating individual preferences and for protecting against abuses of office. In theory, the fundamental rights guaranteed by the constitution of a liberal state can be derived entirely a priori, from an original position, or from a-temporal postulates of equality and autonomy. Indeed, in theory, a liberal nation's constitution ought to be universal: valid not merely for this particular nation but for all the world. In short, liberal nationhood implies no real valorization of nations or nationality; on the contrary, just as Mill wished, individual self-government would be the true end of politics, and self-governing individuals would be citizens of the world.

When a bellicose Euro-Asian collectivist nationalism is impugned in favor

10. For Habermas's effort to "cut" the concept of "genuinely political freedom" from "its umbilical links to the womb of national consciousness of freedom that originally gave it birth," see Habermas, *Citizenship and National Identity* (1990), reprinted as Appendix II in Between Facts and Norms, *supra* Chapter 3, note 5, at 491–514 (quoted sentence appears on p. 495).

11. *E.g.,* Liah Greenfield, Nationalism: Five Roads to Modernity 11 (1992) (describing "the basic types of nationalism, which one may classify as individualistic-libertarian and collectivistic-authoritarian"); Haas, *supra* note 9, at 22–61.

of a peace-loving Anglo-American nation, the latter is usually associated with this liberal, individualist rendering of nationhood. But the contrast between individualist and collectivist conceptions of the nation is not the distinction I have in mind. The critical distinction is between two different *collectivist* understandings of popularity: a speech-modeled conception and a temporally extended conception. It is the speech-modeled conception that makes peoples seem as if they must be imaginary entities.

What is speech-modeled popularity? The most obvious example of a speech-modeled conception of popularity is also the oldest: the one that identifies national peoples through the sharing of a common tongue. Herder voiced this linguo-national idea two hundred years ago: "Denn jedes Volk ist Volk; es hat seine National Bildung wie seine Sprache."[12] *Sprache* must be understood here as referring to the spoken language, the vernacular, the common tongue of the common people. "It is a people in a body that makes a language," wrote Duclos in the mid-eighteenth century, in a work that influenced Rousseau. "A people is thus the absolute master of the spoken language, and it is an empire they possess unawares."[13] In linguo-nationalism, the spoken language is the people's special possession, it is the true *res publica,* which unifies, which makes the people *a* people.

This linguistic-based ethno-nationalism, acted out in repeated, massive, bloody episodes since the early decades of the nineteenth century, first in Europe and then beyond, is alive and well today.[14] It is visible in Western nations not only in the form of overexcited national-language campaigns, but also, more surprisingly, in some of the recent scholarship on nationhood, which can still proclaim, against all evidence, that "all members of a people . . . speak the same language."[15] What motivates the thought that speaking the same language can play so central a role in popularity?

Linguo-nationalism merely takes literally a looser, metaphorical demand that members of a people must "speak the same language." What is meant here is that persons, in order to be a people, have to share a common way of looking at the world and at themselves, a shared set of values, attitudes, un-

12. "Every people is a people; it has its own national development as it has its own language." Quoted in Aira Kemiläinen, Nationalism: Problems Concerning the Word, the Concept and Classification 42 (1964). As Anderson points out, Herder's remark, even in its own time and place, could be taken seriously only in "blithe disregard of some obvious extra-European facts." Anderson, *supra* note 1, at 66.

13. Quoted in Derrida, *supra* Chapter 4, note 1, at 169–70.

14. *See, e.g.,* Anderson, *supra* note 1, at 67–154; Hugh Seton-Watson, Nations and States: An Enquiry into the Origins of Nations and the Politics of Nationalism (1977).

15. D.J. Kotzé, Nationalism: A Comparative Study 4–5 (Henri Snijders trans., 1981).

derstandings, and interests. This was the demand that classical republicanism imposed on peoples. Habermas is once again penetrating: the "republican" "model," he writes, is that of a "homogeneous" group "sharing the same language or the same ethnic and cultural origins."[16] (Observe how in Habermas's formulation "the same language" presents itself, without explanation, as an apparently adequate substitute for "the same ethnic and cultural origins.") "The assumption of republican virtues," Habermas continues, "is realistic only for a polity with a normative consensus that has been secured in advance through tradition and custom."[17]

In other words, "speaking the same language" means in linguo-nationalism what it means in ordinary speech: possessing a like-mindedness; thinking alike. Thus the echo of Herder can still be heard when a writer as sensitive as the late Ernest Gellner tells us, as his best definition of nationhood, that members of a national people *" 'speak the same language' even when they do not speak the same language."*[18] Gellner means: they must share in a common way of thinking, whatever language they speak. Renan made the same point a hundred years earlier: "Ne peut-on avoir les mêmes sentiments et les mêmes pensées, aimer les même [*sic*] choses en des langages differents?"[19]

But why exactly is a homogeneous "normative consensus" considered so important to popularity, and why is speaking the same language its privileged marker? The answer is that popularity is here being constructed in accordance with the requirements of speech-modeled self-government. For persons to be a people on the model of speech, they must possess a common will. They must be able to speak with a single voice. And they must therefore enjoy a considerable degree of like-mindedness, of homogeneity, of fellow-feeling. For how could the voice of the people ever speak—how could there be a popular voice—if the members of this people did not even "speak the same language"?

Speech-modeled popularity, then, is the conception of popularity required by speech-modeled self-government. It is visible throughout republican political thought, where the ideal of a common tongue and vox populi is made essential to self-government and hence to freedom. But the same homogenizing, common-will conception of what it means for persons to be a people pervades liberalism too. Why?

Images of popular homogeneity have served a powerful function in liberal

16. Habermas, *supra* Chapter 3, note 5, at 500, 501, 504.

17. *Id.* at 473.

18. Gellner, *supra* note 9, at 109 n.1.

19. "Isn't it possible to have the same feelings and the same thoughts, to love the same things, in different languages?" Renan, *supra* Chapter 2, note 61, at 899–900.

thought: homogeneity is liberalism's dystopia, its *1984,* the nightmare that makes plain how valuable individuality and individual autonomy really are. Liberalism concurs with republicanism in believing that popularity lies in the homogenization of individuals and in their coming to possess a common will. The difference is that liberalism rebels against this scenario, while republicanism aspires to it.

As a result, in classical liberal thought, we constantly find the same duality of individuality and popularity described above, in which a collective identity forged through sameness is cast in opposition to individual identity.[20] Liberalism and republicanism are flip sides of a single coin. They emerge from the same conception of homogeneous, speech-modeled popularity, in which collective and individual will are engaged in mortal competition.

The possibility of written self-government depends on finding an alternative to the options created by this old dichotomy. Somewhere between autonomous individuality and homogeneous popularity, there must be room for a nation whose members struggle, despite and indeed because of their individual differences, to be the collective authors of their own foundational law. Room for a people of individualists. Room for *a* people—a collective, singular people—that does not speak and does not aspire to speak, not even at sublime moments of political transformation, with a single voice.

What is necessary, to make room for this kind of people, is an act of ethnic cleansing. But what needs to be ethnically cleansed is the concept of popularity itself. Without abandoning the idea of a people as a self-governing collective subject, we must clear out from this idea all the grand and brutal dreams of brotherhood in which speech-modeled nationalism has indulged. We are not brothers and sisters. We do not owe our popularity to any shared set of cultural, psychological, or biological characteristics that might confer upon us a unique national identity. We must give up altogether the search for this sort of homogeneous national identity, in which a certain set of values or traits is imagined as defining the unique and essential national character.

But what other sort of national identity is there? How can we speak of national identity—of a people, of a national "we"—in the absence of a unique

20. Thus Mill warns repeatedly and darkly against a pernicious "uniformity" spreading throughout England. England is in danger of becoming "another China," where people are "all alike," and where "Individuality" itself is extinguished. Mill, *supra* note 3, at 64–66. *See infra* Chapter 12. The same thought is suggested in Hayek's defense of liberalism as the only alternative to "tribal ethics." *See* Hayek, *supra* note 4, at 105, 134.

national character? And what can possibly entitle persons to be called a people if they do not at least feel a deep, identity-defining solidarity with one another?

This is like asking: what can entitle an individual to be called a person if he bears within him conflicting impulses, hopes, and fears? That which makes a people *a* people, that which gives a people the unity designated by the term "nation," is not to be found in the homogeneity that is supposed to allow its members to speak with one voice. The real unity of a people is simultaneously much larger and much reduced.

It is larger because it embraces past and future in a way that speech-modeled popularity cannot. The speech-modeled conception of popularity, like the speech-modeled conception of self-government, is profoundly present-oriented. To see this, return to Benedict Anderson's story of the imagined nation. Recall that the closest possible approach to real community, for Anderson, lies in "primordial villages" of "face-to-face" contact. At first blush, this hyper-nostalgic image of genuine community seems to protest against modernity; it seems to protest against the hugeness and alienation of modern societies. But this imagined community, this "primordial village" of "face-to-face" exchange, in reality perfectly expresses modernity's distinctive temporality—its insistence that authenticity and being can be found only in a here and now. For it is quite impossible to engage in face-to-face exchange *with the dead.* In the conception of community within which all of *Imagined Communities* unfolds, real community would be possible, if at all, only for those who *shared a present* with one another.

But the very idea of a nation, of a national people as a subject of self-government, contemplates an entity that extends across generations. This sort of people is ruled out in advance—it is *already* consigned to fiction and to unreality—by the terms of an analysis that can see genuine community, if at all, only in relations of "face-to-face contact" in the present. A people that wants what it wants here and now cannot have—itself.

I do not mean that a people imagining itself as a homogeneous unit can have no sense of its own historical existence. It can have such a sense, but only as a fantasy. Renan's famous formulation of the "essence" of nationhood precisely captured this combination of homogeneity and misperceived history: "Or l'essence d'une nation est que tous les individus aient beaucoup de choses en commun et aussi que tous aient oublié bien des choses."[21] So long

21. "Now, the essence of a nation is that all the individuals have many things in common and also that all have forgotten many things." Renan, *supra* Chapter 2, note 61, at 892.

as the nation is conceived, as Renan himself clearly conceived it (and as Anderson conceives it), in terms of cultural commonality and homogeneous interests, nationhood can be sustained only through a fantastic amnesia. This amnesiac image of a historically pure nation will not only suppress the intranational ethnic massacres of the past, as Renan pointed out, but will also support the ethnic massacres of the future, through which the nation seeks to reclaim the purity it never possessed.

These fantastic and violent dreams of ethnic purity would not be part of a genuinely temporally extended conception of popularity. In the latter, claims of popular unity and solidarity would be much reduced, but they would be reduced to their essence—reduced to writing. Suppose we defined popularity as follows. What makes persons a people is simply this: co-existence, over time, under the rule of a given legal and political order. A people, for purposes of democratic self-government, is the set of persons co-existing under the rule of a particular political-legal order.

Why should rule be accorded this definitive position? Because it is what makes a people *a* people over time. Not what makes a people the *kind* of people it happens to be at any given moment. Politics and law have no such privileged role in defining a people's general habits or characteristics. In that regard, politics and law are merely two cultural forces among many others. But politics and the rule that emerges from it are what make persons *a* people. Politics sires peoples.

Contrary to the dreams of speech-modeled popularity, what makes a people *a* people is not its language, its culture, or its distinctive character. These are the things that make a people the *kind* of people it happens to be. What makes popularity is the reach of a certain political-legal order. Of course there may be generalizations applicable in describing the members of particular nations. At some rough level of generalization, we could speak meaningfully of American values or American characterological traits. But it is perfectly possible in principle that every identifiable American value and characteristic might also turn out to be a Canadian value and characteristic. If this were so, would it follow that America and Canada were, despite appearances, *the same nation?*

All that separates these two nations, ultimately, is a border line, as fortuitous, as penetrable and yet as essential as is the physical boundary that separates one human being from another. It is in relation to this line, which demarcates the rule of a different political and legal order, that every claim of popularity, or of membership in this or that people, must be made. The ultimate rule of recognition, the one that determines whether a people exists, lies in the recognition of rule.

We must have done with the whole branch of political ethnography that investigates the existence of national identities by trolling for cultural homogeneity or by polling to see how people "define themselves." The existence of a people never depends on what anyone *says,* and above all not on what anyone says *here and now.* The speech-modeled conception of popular identity not only incorporates spurious and dangerous dreams of like-mindedness; it also rests on the same category mistake we observed in the case of personal identity. Speech-modeled popularity would decide whether persons are members of a people by reference to the *kind* of persons they happen to be (their cultural characteristics, their inclination to "self-identify" in particular ways, their like-mindedness, and so on), without having paid sufficient attention to what makes persons *a* people in the first place. It mistakes an inquiry into a people's widely shared traits of mind—which may or may not exist—for an inquiry into popularity as such.

But what is "rule," what is a "political-legal order," and what does it mean to "live under" or "co-exist under" such an order? I ought to offer definitions, but I can no more provide necessary and sufficient conditions of "rule" or "order," without which there can be no peoples, than I can for "mind" or "self-consciousness," without which there can be no persons. Instead I have only a warning: rule is here to be understood with considerable porousness and even reflexivity. That which rules can also be ruled by what it rules. And there is a wide variety of forms of co-existence or of "living under" that could qualify. But the implications and the soundness of this basic approach to popularity can be clarified in a number of ways.

To begin with, recognizing rule as definitive of popularity is to give popularity the required dimension of temporal extension. Law, we have seen, is necessarily temporally extended. A legal order cannot exist in a single moment. Hence a people consists not of a set of persons here and now, but of the temporally extended set of persons—past, present, and future—who will have lived under the rule of a particular political and legal order.

To be sure, this means that there may be no determinate fact at a particular moment concerning whether a certain group of persons is here and now a people, or whether a certain person here and now belongs to a particular people. A foreigner visiting America is subject to our political-legal order. He is not treated as a citizen, and this differential legal treatment means that American citizens do indeed constitute a people to which foreigners do not belong. (Because the legal order has constructed popularity in this way.) This is perfectly appropriate, because a moment's presence in a given territory need not be regarded as the kind of "living under" that would permit an individual to qualify as a citizen. But in a sense, every person who spends a year in America is for that year an American. There would be nothing incoherent, as a matter of logic or law, in recognizing every such person as a member of the American people. There is no fact of the matter about such things; the fact is dependent on the law and on events within a broader temporal horizon.

Moreover, to make peoples depend for their existence on the rule of a political-legal order allows for the possibility that there may be more than one political-legal order (and hence more than one people) in a particular place. There might, for example, be geographical sub-orders (cities or states) within an overarching, larger order. Or, in a particular society, different classes or castes of persons might be treated to radically differing political-legal rules. In either case, more than one people could co-exist within a national people. Similarly, given a sufficient development of international institutions, there may be places—perhaps Europe is becoming such a place—where supranational peoples exist even while national peoples remain in place. The possibility of multiple popularity in a single territory means, among other things, that a given people within a nation may achieve self-government for itself while denying it to others.

For example, if there was an American people that could count itself as self-governing two centuries ago, this people did not meaningfully embrace American blacks, Indians, women, poor persons, or Jews, many or most of whom were categorically excluded from participating in or holding basic rights under the regimes of the time. Today, the United States has carved out separate political-legal sub-orders for certain groups (some Indian tribes, Puerto Ricans, and so on) of such a nature that the popularity of these groups remains at least partly in play. The status of such groups is always poised in a condition of radical ambiguity, simultaneously calling for an end to the distinctions that separate them (integration into the national people) and for a recognition of their autonomy (as separate peoples in their own right).

The existence of more than one people within the same territory makes possible intra-national conflicts of democratic struggle, the most obvious and most extreme instance of which is secession. Liberal nationalism has very little to say against secession, so long as a free right of exit and migration are preserved. Speech-modeled popularity, by contrast, can mount a powerful argument against secession, but only by appealing to fictitious imaginings of pre-destined historical unities. But if peoples are understood by reference to political-legal orders, and if a given people has undertaken the temporally extended task of living under its own self-given commitments, such a people can legitimately deny secession to sub-peoples within its borders, not on grounds of pre-destined unity but on the ground that the national people has a right and a duty to ensure that every one of its members enjoys the protections of its commitments.

To recognize rule as definitive of popularity is also to recognize that peoples are born in chains. The rule that brings peoples into being will not have been self-rule. The American people was not created by the Constitution of 1789. It was created by English rule of the Atlantic colonies. Constitutional self-government does not create a people, any more than an emancipation proclamation creates persons. Constitutional self-government is not the process through which a people attains its being; it is the struggle through which a people attempts to seize its freedom.

To recognize rule as definitive of popularity is, finally, to change the subject of classical liberal and republican political thought. As we have seen, both these ideologies agree about the essential nature of political subjecthood. A political subject is defined by its having a will. Liberalism recognizes individuals as the true and only political subjects because it recognizes only individuals as having a will. Republicanism views peoples as possessors of a common, collective will. If, however, the freedom to write is the distinctive human and political capacity, then it becomes possible to define a political subject not as any being with a will but as any being with the capacity to give itself a commitment. In that case, it would be possible to say not only that persons are political subjects but that peoples are as well. For a people may have legible principles even if it does not have a voice or a will.

We do not have a collective or common will. We cannot help ourselves: we are self-interested; we want what is best for ourselves, and we typically want it now. But we are also capable of commitment. Commitments can be shared by those whose wills are widely divergent. They can even be shared by those who radically disagree about their meaning in this or that circumstance. The holding of common principles and the engagement in commitments by a large number of persons does not "constitute" those persons as a people. It is not even a necessary condition of their being a people. But if a sufficient number of individuals in a given people share the same general principles over a sufficient period of time, and if they are prepared to create and live under institutions that preserve these principles, then it becomes possible—even though there is substantial disagreement about the meaning of these principles—to speak of popular, national commitments to these principles. The disagreement about meaning precludes the possibility of governance by popular will, but it does not preclude the possibility of governance by popular commitment.

What basis is there, someone will ask, for ascribing principles or commitments to a people, rather than merely to persons? A "people" doesn't have principles, it might be objected; only individuals do. To say that a "people" commits itself to principles is (according to this objection) at best a figure of speech and at worst a lapse into mystification. Here quotation marks around the word *people* once again become appropriate, because the objection resurrects the line of thought that opposes popularity to individuality and hence questions the very existence of a people.

But why is subjectivity so confidently denied to peoples? True, a people contains all sorts of opposing wills and viewpoints, but so too the psyches of individuals contain all sorts of opposing impulses, views, and feelings—some of them even subject to stern suppression.

"But an individual's thoughts and feelings are linked together within one body," it will be said. True, but those of a people are linked together within a territory, within a society, within a legal order.

"But a person's mental operations are linked in a different way: by neurons that make them all part of a single consciousness." Perhaps, but what neurons do is communicate, and the various persons that make up a people can communicate among themselves too.

"But a person has a mind, don't you see? He decides. He acts. His inner conflicts are conflicts interior to a single consciousness. He has a will. He speaks, in the end, with one voice."

Does he? If so, then individuals certainly differ in that respect from peoples, who cannot speak with one voice. But a people can give itself purposes and act on them. A people can make decisions. If the citizenry of a given nation elects a new president, who has decided who the new president shall be? Someone might say that the individuals who voted for the winning candidate made the decision, but that characterization makes it sound as if those who voted for the winning candidate had exercised a special decision-making power not enjoyed by those who did not vote for the winner. Someone else might say that no one made a decision about the new president; there was only a result that followed upon millions of separate individual expressions of preferences (votes) combined with established rules for vote-counting.

Group decisional processes can always be redescribed in this way, as a series of coordinated, interdependent individual decisions, combined with vote-counting rules that are followed through another series of interdependent individual decisions. Such redescriptions are not false, but they leave something out. When a group of persons deliberates and votes, according to rules and conventions that this very group has given itself in the past, isn't it simpler, isn't it equally true and more complete, to say that the group made the decision?

To recognize a people as a subject persisting over time, despite the heterogeneity of its composition, is ultimately no more mystical than recognizing individuals as subjects persisting over time despite the heterogeneity of their composition. Mysticism in thinking about peoples is certainly possible, but so too is it possible in the case of individuals. The slip into mysticism is the same in both cases. It comes about when the attribution of subjectivity involves the suppression of heterogeneity and the substitution, in its place or behind it, of a timeless unitary soul. Our unity is contingent and historical. It is the product of rule—the rule of mind or of law—although we may be, if we are fortunate, in this porous, multiplicitous unity, both the rulers and the ruled.

There is and always will be something intensely self-delusive in the suggestion that "Americans" compose a single people engaged in a protracted, centuries-long struggle for self-government. This delusion invariably helps suppress everything we know about America's mistreatment of those excluded, now as well as then, from the Constitution's "People." The exclusion of a majority of persons from the constitution-making processes of the 1780s will always eat away at America's legitimacy.

But if a nation had to be born at a single founding moment, it could never be born at all. Peoples are not made, and constitutions are not made, in a moment. There was an American people in the 1780s that initiated the project of self-government through the Constitution. It consisted primarily of white, propertied, Christian males. This people did not exist as a natural kind. It owed its popularity to a certain invidious legal order. But this people did manage to institute self-government—for itself.

It goes without saying that individuals kept as slaves are no part of the self-government achieved by their masters. They are not bound by it. The masters' government has no legitimate authority over them.

Americans today cannot hide from the illegitimacy or the brutality of their constitution-making process. Indeed we are obliged to say something stronger. The people of America today *is* the people of white, propertied, Christian males who founded the Constitution in the 1780s, who gave itself self-government with one hand while branding slaves and felling the Indian tribes with the other. That people grew into this one; we are they.

This legacy is deeply ambivalent. It is infamous, but also promissory. Because it means, among other things, this: there is no longer a white or black people in America; there is no male or female people; there is no Christian or non-Christian people. At a constitutional convention in 1789, it was possible, even predictable, for a delegate to refer to the "hordes of Africans" "infest[ing] my region." And of course racists today can continue to speak of black Americans as a separate people—although it happens that the diatribe just quoted occurred in France, not America, and the reference was to Jews, not blacks.[22] Today we are all Jews and blacks; we are all minorities infesting a region that others wish they could have for themselves. We are all also members of a historical people, taking part in that nation's sins and glory. If popularity invites blindness to our exclusions and marginalizations, it is also the basis for making them visible, because it is what permits us to see these exclusions and marginalizations as *ours*. More than this: it is what permits us to see these exclusions and marginalizations *as* exclusions and marginalizations.

In the end, it doesn't matter what we say to ourselves. We have no more choice about the people into which we are born than we do about our family or body. While we speak, and regardless of what we say, a people is writing itself into history, the land its palimpsest, and we ourselves its characters.

22. *See* Paul Johnson, A History of the Jews 306 (1987).

Part III

CONSTITUTIONALISM AS DEMOCRACY

Nine

CONSTITUTIONALISM AS DEMOCRACY

Democratic self-government cannot be achieved, even in principle, by way of a politics of popular voice. It requires an inscriptive politics, through which a people struggles to memorialize, interpret, and hold itself to its own foundational commitments over time. I will call this idea: constitutionalism as democracy. The purpose of this and the final three chapters is to lay out the basic terms of constitutionalism as democracy: its theory of judicial review, its interpretive method, its fundamental rights.

Constitutionalism as democracy undoes all the theoretical perplexities that have so confounded contemporary constitutional thought. To begin with, it alone captures the meaning of the world-historical political innovation—written constitutionalism—that was created in America two centuries ago. It solves the counter-majoritarian difficulty. It explains the place of judicial review in a democracy. It makes sense of supermajoritarian amendment processes. Finally, it supplies a better account than we currently have of how a constitution *binds*—of how, in other words, constitutional law exerts legitimate authority over time.

Constitution-Writing

One venerable line of thought has maintained that the significance of the American Constitution's writtenness lay in the certainty and fixity it brought to constitutional law. Thus wrote Justice William Patterson in 1795:

> It is difficult to say what the constitution of England is; because, not being reduced to written certainty and precision, it lies entirely at the mercy of the Parliament. . . . [I]n England, there is no written constitution, no fundamental law, nothing visible, nothing real, nothing certain, by which statute can be tested. In America, the case is widely different. . . . The Constitution is certain and fixed. . . .[1]

1. Vanhorne's Lessee v. Dorrance, 2 U.S. (2 Dall.) 304, 308 (C.C. D. Pa. 1795).

We know better. Patterson was right that constitution-writing in America brought about a great political change concerning the limits of legislative power and the vulnerability of legislative acts to constitutional review. But this change was certainly not achieved through the "certainty and precision" of the constitutional text. The Constitution's central, sweeping terms are not precise ("commerce . . . among the states," the "equal protection of the laws"); even in its jurisdictional provisions, the certainty of the text has proved more seeming than real ("the judicial Power shall extend to all Cases . . . between a State and citizens of another state"). And as to fixity, one of the great departures of the United States Constitution from pre-existing constitutionalism was its introduction of a legalized amendment process.

The meaning of constitution-writing as it emerged in late-eighteenth-century America lay rather in a transformation that it expressed in the meaning of democracy itself. American constitutionalism rejected speech-modeled democracy in favor of something new: an unprecedented form of self-government in which a nation sought to write down and live under its own foundational law. The consciousness of this unprecedented shift was clear to those who debated the new Constitution in the 1780s.

Consider what a constitution *was* in the classical tradition, the background against which Revolutionary Americans quite self-consciously acted. In the classical tradition, a polity's "constitution" referred to nothing other than the ensemble of its established political institutions and laws. In this tradition, the "Spartan constitution" is a shorthand reference to Sparta's laws and to the arrangement of institutions through which political matters were dealt with there.

This way of thinking leads naturally to the idea of an "unwritten constitution," such as the "British constitution," referring to a set of laws, practices, and institutions supposed to govern, even if nowhere written down. An "unwritten constitution" need not be understood as just whatever laws or measures the current government adopts. On the contrary, the idea of an "unwritten constitution" made it possible, at least in principle, to condemn acts of state as "contrary to the constitution," or contrary to "the law of the land," where such phrases referred to longstanding customs and practices. Nevertheless, if the idea of an unwritten constitution allows for criticism of the currently prevailing norms of political order, it does so only by appealing to a past prevailing order, deemed to be of ancient, immemorial standing. Hence unwritten constitutionalism always identifies a polity's constitution with its governing laws and institutions, either those of the present or those said to have governed from time out of mind, and the immutability of these institutions is supposed to derive from their extra-political or supra-political source, whether this source is conceived as nature, ancient custom, divine will, or the genius of an inspired founder.[2]

Written constitutionalism is different. It introduces a new object, a constitution, into the political world: a manmade thing, whose material existence in the world, whose commitment to writing, ruptures the identity between a polity's "constitution" and its actual political-legal order, past or present. What force this rupture was to have, if any, remained unknown and unknowable at the time the constitution was made. But the rupture was a fact, forcing open a space that had not previously existed between constitutions and institutions.

This space was both textual and political. Textual because it was to be occupied by a writing. Political because this writing was to be found not in sacred tablets, not in nature, not in men's hearts, not in ancient custom or tradition, and not in the work of a single inspired founder. It was to be produced through a politics—specifically, through a popular, democratic, inscriptive politics.

Here, then, is the true revolutionary meaning of the American Constitution's writtenness. For the first time, *constitution-writing became a constitutive element of democracy itself.*

For two thousand years, Western political theory had analyzed the various possible *forms* that a polity's constitution might take, but it had applied no political typology—no politics at all—to a constitution's *formation.* In other words, those who classified constitutions according to whether they vested governance in the one, the few, or the many did not differentiate constitutions according to whether they had been *made* by the one, the few, or the many.[3] No linkage existed between constitutional form and formation, at least no linkage such that an ideal *democratic constitution* would have to have been itself the product of a *democratic politics.* On the contrary, politics could take place only when the constitution—the *politeia*—was in place. If, before America, political liberty was occasionally thought to require a "democratic constitution" (meaning government by the many or by the people), it was never thought to require a constitution *democratically made.*

The eruption of written constitutionalism in late-eighteenth-century America broke from this two-thousand-year history. It made constitution-formation—constitution-writing—a central component of the enterprise of

2. On unwritten constitutionalism of this kind, see J.G.A. Pocock, The Ancient Constitution and the Feudal Law 33–55 (1957); Gordon S. Wood, The Creation of the American Republic 1776–1787, at 259–68 (1969).

3. *See, e.g.,* Aristotle, The Politics 96 (Carnes Lord trans., 1984).

democratic self-government itself. This revolutionary democratization of constitution-writing announced itself in the very first paragraph of the very first page of *The Federalist.* Here is Hamilton's famous remark:

> it seems to have been reserved to the people of this country . . . to decide the important question, whether societies of men are really capable or not, of establishing good government from reflection and choice, or whether they are forever destined to depend, for their political constitutions, on accident and force.[4]

Observe that Hamilton's question is not whether a good constitution *includes* institutions of "reflection and choice." For all revolutionary Americans, it went without saying that a good constitution would include such institutions (which they would have called "republican," but which, for present purposes, we can call "democratic"). Hamilton's question was whether a good "political constitution" could be established *by* or "*from* reflection and choice," as opposed to by "accident and force." This was the question on which the world waited for America's answer.

The subject recurs again, much later in the same series of papers, but now with Madison writing:

> It is not a little remarkable that in every case reported by antient history, in which government has been established with deliberation and consent, the task of framing it has not been committed to an assembly of men, but has been performed by some individual citizen of pre-eminent wisdom and approved integrity.[5]

Madison's "deliberation and consent" obviously tracks Hamilton's "reflection and choice." Like Hamilton, Madison assumes that good government *includes* institutions of "deliberation and consent." In other words, Madison is not asking whether America ought to have a government *with* institutions of democratic deliberation and consent. That goes without saying. The question is whether "assembl[ies] of men," acting *through* deliberation and consent, can discharge "the task of framing" such a government. Revolutionary Americans knew it well: to make a good democratic constitution *democratically* would be—to make history.

To make a democratic constitution democratically would be to inaugurate a new form of democracy. Madison was clear about moving away from the

4. The Federalist No. 1 (Alexander Hamilton) at 1 (Clinton Rossiter ed., 1999).

5. *Id.* No. 38 (James Madison), at 199.

ideal (which he associated with ancient Greek democracy) of a politics of public assembly, where citizens heard oratory and delivered the voice of the people. A politics of voice and speech-making was for Madison (as it was for Plato) an invitation to political deception and even tyranny. Because of "the eloquence and address of the few," in "the antient republics, where the whole body of the people assembled in person," government tended to become rule by "a single orator . . . with as compleat a sway, as if a sceptre had been placed in his single hands."[6]

As to the motives behind Madison's rejection of the "pure" "democratic" ideal, there are a number of standard explanations. For example: Madison and the other Federalists, enlightened champions of individual liberty, were determined not to permit true majority rule.[7] Or: the Federalists, self-interested champions of the propertied class, were determined not to permit true majority rule.[8] For his own part, Madison offered an explanation in terms of the destructive consequences of faction, which required not a circumvention of majority rule, but rather an enlarging of majority rule across a large nation and the creation of intermediate, mutually checking representative institutions.[9]

But the debate over the Federalists' motives misses the central point. The very project of written constitutionalism was itself a decisive repudiation of speech-modeled self-government, replacing the politics of present popular voice with a politics of the written. From this point of view, the question of the Federalists' motives recedes. For in this antecedent repudiation of speech-modeled self-government, effected by written constitutionalism itself, the anti-Federalists—particularly in their calls for a Bill of Rights—were full participants. Through their demand for written constitutional rights, the anti-Federalists effected a displacement of present popular voice in favor of a popular writing just as much as Madison did.

Under the new constitutionalism, American democracy was to be, in its foundational principles and institutions, an act or project not of popular voice, but of *popular writing.* In constitutionalism as democracy, a constitution

6. *Id.* No. 58 (James Madison), at 328. Rossiter updates the orthography.

7. *See* Louis Hartz, The Liberal Tradition in America: An Interpretation of American Political Thought since the Revolution (1955).

8. *See* Charles Beard, An Economic Interpretation of the Constitution of the United States (1913); for a more recent and much more nuanced version of this position, see Jennifer Nedelsky, Private Property and the Limits of American Constitutionalism (1990).

9. *See* Federalist, *supra* note 4, No. 10 (James Madison), at 45–52.

is not a mere shorthand label for the actual institutions of governance, past or present (as is an unwritten constitution). Nor is it a mere procedural framework within which a democratic politics is to take place. Nor is it a divination of those sacred, unwritten, timeless rights that stand above all temporal power. Constitutionalism by popular writing is itself an exercise in and of self-government. American written constitutionalism holds that a people achieves self-government not by conforming governance to the authoritative democratic will at any given time, but by laying down and holding itself to its own democratically authored foundational commitments over time. That was and is the revolutionary meaning of the Constitution's writtenness.

The Counter-Majoritarian Difficulty

Constitutional law's so-called counter-majoritarian difficulty refers, it will be recalled, to the putatively "undemocratic" practice of allowing unelected, life-tenured judges to "thwart[] the will of representatives of the actual people of the here and now."[10] The "difficulty" is not that judges may occasionally depart from majority will (as legislators or presidents may also do). The difficulty is that constitutional law is *designed* to "thwart" the outcomes of representative, majoritarian politics. The difficulty, in other words, is nothing other than the problem that Jefferson, Rousseau, and so many others identified long ago: the problem of squaring written constitutionalism with the principles of democratic self-government.

Which is to say: the counter-majoritarian difficulty rests entirely on the speech-modeled notion, about which Bickel was just as explicit as Jefferson, that democracy ideally consists of governance by the will of the living. Restore time to self-government, and democracy can no longer be so understood. If democratic self-government involves a nation's generation-spanning struggle to live under self-given foundational law over time, apart from or even contrary to popular will at any given moment, the counter-majoritarian difficulty collapses.

Governance by majority will is not democracy. At best, majority rule can deliver willfulness and the tyranny of preference. But it cannot deliver self-government. It cannot deliver the political freedom of which humans alone are capable. For this, a people must attempt the reins of time.

If written constitutionalism is this attempt, then constitutionalism is not *counter* to democracy. It is *required* by democracy. It *is* democracy—or at least it ought to be, it promises to be, it holds itself out as the possibility of, democracy—over time.

10. Bickel, *supra* Chapter 1, note 16, at 16–17.

Judicial Review

But why should a judiciary—in particular, a judiciary composed of unelected judges—interpret the Constitution? In theory, all questions of constitutional interpretation could be put to a vote of the citizenry in electronic town meetings. Or perhaps Congress might be charged with final authority to decide constitutional questions. Or with a further twist: the judiciary could be vested with an original constitutional jurisdiction, subject to review by Congress or by popular vote. Out of all possible institutionalizations of the interpretive process, why should the judiciary have final authority, reversible only through onerous supermajoritarian acts of constitutional amendment?

The question could be put in terms still stronger: wouldn't the people, or the people's elected representatives, be a plainly superior interpreter of the people's own commitments?

Judicial review follows from the premises of written constitutionalism. Today the link between judicial review and the Constitution's writtenness seems to legal academics a non sequitur, but this connection was much better understood at the inception of American constitutional law. It formed the basis of the Supreme Court's famous opinion in *Marbury v. Madison,* written by Chief Justice John Marshall in 1803, in which the Court first authoritatively affirmed the power of judicial review. Marshall referred to the Constitution's writtenness no fewer than eight times in *Marbury.* The possibility of judicial invalidation of legislative acts was contemplated, he wrote, by all who "framed written constitutions." Even if not expressly set forth in the constitutional text, the "theory" of judicial enforcement of constitutional provisions was "essentially attached" to all written constitutions. "This theory is essentially attached to a written constitution, and is consequently, to be considered, by this court, as one of the fundamental principles of our society."[11]

These formulations are all but incomprehensible to contemporary legal thought. *Marbury,* we are told by our strongest constitutional commentators, "made a great deal of the fact that the Constitution is in writing—an obviously irrelevant circumstance."[12] "That the Constitution is a 'written' one yields little or nothing as to whether acts of Congress may be given the force of positive law notwithstanding the opinion of judges . . . that such acts are repugnant to the Constitution."[13] Historically, "the written quality of the Constitution counted a great deal," but "in theory, it would seem a mean-

11. Marbury v. Madison, 5 U.S. (1 Cranch) 137, 176–78 (1803).

12. Charles L. Black, The People and the Court 26 (1960).

13. William W. Van Alstyne, *A Critical Guide to* Marbury v. Madison, 1969 Duke L.J. 1, 17.

ingless circumstance."[14] Marshall's appeal to the Constitution's writtenness not only "beg[s] the question"; it "begs the wrong question."[15]

Some scholars seek to rescue *Marbury* by placing judicial review on the allegedly firmer footing of text and original intent. Article III of the Constitution, they say, vests the "judicial power" of the United States in the Supreme Court, and Article VI expressly denominates the Constitution "Law," indeed the "supreme Law of the Land." Because the "judicial power" is the power to say what the law means, the argument goes, the cumulative effect of Articles III and VI is to vest the Supreme Court with the ultimate power to say what the Constitution means.[16]

Against this argument, the reply has been that Article III merely creates a system of federal courts and says not a word about the fundamental question of judicial review. As to Article VI, the Constitution there declares the supremacy of federal over state law and commands state judges to enforce federal law, but once again says not a word about the dread power of any court to invalidate congressional legislation.[17]

Now, it is certainly possible to read Articles III and VI as countenancing judicial review. Marshall himself mentioned these textual arguments in *Marbury,* although they figure in his opinion as afterthoughts, as supplemental supports "not entirely unworthy of observation," rather than as grounds capable of bearing the weight of the decision. Is it embarrassing that an opinion so emphasizing the Constitution's writtenness should so neglect the Constitution's text? On the contrary: Marshall was right in according this secondary role to the textual arguments in favor of judicial review. The Supreme Court in *Marbury* could not have relied on these textual arguments without manifest circularity.

Articles III and VI do not provide for judicial review in language that defies any other reading. They must be *interpreted* so to provide. But the Court in *Marbury* could not logically have rested the judiciary's power to interpret the Constitution on an interpretation of Articles III and VI (or any other piece of constitutional text) without assuming for itself the very power that was in issue. To do so *would* have been to beg the question.

(Nor does originalism supply an escape route from this circularity. A court that relied on the records of the Philadelphia Convention or the *Federalist*

14. Henry P. Monaghan, *Stare Decisis and Constitutional Adjudication,* 88 Colum. L. Rev. 723, 770 (1988).

15. Bickel, *supra* Chapter 1, note 16, at 2.

16. *See, e.g.,* Raoul Berger, Government by Judiciary: The Transformation of the Fourteenth Amendment 355–56 (1977).

17. *See, e.g.,* Bickel, *supra* Chapter 1, note 16, at 5–12.

papers to conclude that Articles III and VI really were intended to provide for judicial review would be already engaged in the process of constitutional interpretation and hence would already be exercising the judicial power that was at issue in *Marbury.* Moreover, recourse to original intentions suggests that the democratic will at the time of the founding remains supreme and authoritative today. But the supremacy of *present* democratic will is precisely the question raised by the institution of judicial review. Thus an originalist defense of judicial review also begs the decisive question.)

It is logically impossible for a court to derive judicial review from the Constitution's actual provisions. Perhaps sensing this impossibility, and animated particularly by the seemingly anti-democratic nature of constitutional law, a minority of constitutional scholars have long decried the power that the Court announced in *Marbury.* To these enemies of "government by judiciary" (I refer to the title of Louis Boudin's magisterial study, not to Raoul Berger's later homonymous brief for originalism), the argument from writtenness is not only theoretically irrelevant but has been refuted by the court of history:

> At the time the great Chief Justice penned [his] famous words, mankind had had very little experience with written constitutions. . . . But since then the world went on a written-constitution basis, so to say, so that now there is practically no civilized country in the world, with the notable exception of Great Britain, which has no written constitution. . . . And practically each and every one of these written constitutions is a refutation of Marshall's basic assertion. . . . For under none of those numerous constitutions has the judiciary department the power to declare unconstitutional a legislative act of its own government as in contravention of its own constitution.[18]

The past fifty years have been kinder to Marshall's conclusions. With the notable continuing exception of England—an exception weakened, however, by the presence over poor England's head of the European Court of Justice—judicial review has in recent decades swept the "civilized" world. Indeed judicial review has become today practically a marker of a civilized polity, in the sense that its absence in a developing nation is often deemed a portent of authoritarianism, a chink in the rule of law.

This historical development cannot, however, establish the "essential attachment" between judicial review and written constitutionalism that *Marbury* claimed. Boudin was correct: a written constitution can indubitably exist

18. Louis B. Boudin, Government by Judiciary 8–9 (1932).

without judicial review. But Marshall was also correct, because *written constitutionalism*—which is to say, constitutionalism as democracy, constitutionalism as self-government on the model of writing—cannot exist without judicial review.

Constitutionalism as democracy begins with the memorialization of foundational commitments, but it requires more. It requires interpretation. As we have seen, all commitmentarian endeavor includes a commitment to an activity of ongoing interpretation. The cardinal rule of this interpretive task is that interpretation of commitments cannot be permitted to collapse into governance by the self's present will. In saying what commitments require, we are obliged not to rationalize our way, under the guise of "interpretation," to whatever we wanted to do in the first place.

But we all know what it is to be judge in one's own case. This is why individual morality is so consistently feeble. We all imagine ourselves committed to doing right, or at least to doing no wrong, and we all find ways to tell ourselves that what we want to do here and now conforms to this commitment. Who among us tells himself, at the moment of doing something really wrong, as opposed to a trivial indulgence, that he does wrong? Our tendency to rationalize, our capacity for self-deception, our general lack of character all conspire to make us highly unreliable interpreters of our own commitments.

In this regard, constitutional commitments have an advantage over individual commitments. Written constitutionalism creates the possibility of delegating the interpretive power to a body of persons neither institutionally beholden to popular will nor vested with the power that constitutional commitments exist chiefly to restrain. Speech-modeled self-government can grasp this obvious point, but cannot justify it. Speech-modeled governance moves toward unimpeachability as it increasingly conforms with the present will of the governed. By contrast, governance based on popular commitments becomes impeachable precisely when its interpretive questions are referred to the will of the people. For popular "interpretation" would inevitably collapse commitment into will.

If constitutional commitments are not to give way to governance by present political will, the power to interpret them must be assigned to a body insulated from that will. Why? One reason has to do with practical, consequentialist considerations. Referring questions of constitutional interpretation to majority will would make the present citizens judges in their own case, the result of which would be to make the Constitution's commitments about as reliable as a New Year's resolution. The image to bear in mind here is not Ulysses; the danger does not lie in the possibility of irrational popular passions. The real danger lies in the gradual erosion and ultimate dissipation of constitutional protection through little, incremental nibbling, as everyday rationality eats away at the enduring commitments for which so many died.

Moreover, if interpretation were vested in Congress or the president (or some combination of the two), the result would be an even more enfeebled constitution. It is too much to ask of anyone entrusted with immense power, or with control over a nation's treasure, to be the interpreter of the principled, institutional restraints on his power. Marshall made this familiar point in *Marbury*. To vest Congress with the interpretive power, he suggested, "would be giving to the legislature a practical and real omnipotence with the same breath which professes to restrict their powers within narrow limits."[19]

But there is another component to the necessity of judicial review, a nonconsequentialist component, that becomes explicable only in light of the extended temporality of constitutionalism as democracy. Just as the citizens living on a certain block in New York City lack the right to determine the meaning of the nation's commitments, so too do the citizens living on a certain day in 2001. If the people as a temporally extended whole could somehow declare at one moment, in one voice, its interpretation of its own commitments, this impossible declaration could be taken as supreme. But a temporally extended people cannot speak in such a voice. It can only inscribe itself, over time, into the world. Constitutional interpretation in written self-government must itself be a written project, an enterprise in which one text is intermeshed with another and another over a long period of time. It cannot be reduced to an authoritative, clarifying pronouncement by the people, even a pronouncement made in unison by every living citizen at a sublime constitutional moment.

Accordingly, both as a matter of practice and as a matter of right, constitutional adjudication cannot be done by popular vote (whether of the legislature or of the citizens themselves). Such a regime would collapse the distinction between enduring political commitment and momentary political will. Because this distinction is the foundation of self-government on the model of writing, some kind of judicial review is the first law of written constitutionalism. Constitutional interpretation cannot be vested in organs of government beholden to or expressing popular will.

To be sure, the problem of persons judging their own case can never be eliminated, only minimized. A judiciary invested with the power of judicial review will make decisions all the time involving its own powers. But short of a system in which the various officers are intricately permitted to decide

19. *Marbury*, 5 U.S. (1 Cranch) at 178.

only those questions of constitutional meaning that involve the rights and duties of other officers, which is probably impossible and certainly not an option within the American governmental structure, the judiciary's self-interest must be tolerated. Not simply because it is "the least dangerous branch," but because it is the only branch positioned to exercise the interpretive power in such a way as to avoid collapsing it into an exercise of present democratic will.

The point is not that written constitutionalism demands the particular institutional features of traditional American judicial review. Judicial life tenure is not necessary to constitutionalism as democracy. Neither is a nine-justice Supreme Court, rendering decisions by majority vote. Neither is the constitutional jurisdiction of the lower courts. But judicial review, in one form or another, is. Judicial review is an unwritten law of written constitutionalism.

Amendment

A second unwritten law of written constitutionalism: the Constitution must be open to revision. The people's freedom to write cannot be surrendered, certainly not by majority vote at a particular moment in time, nor even by a unanimous vote of the entire set of living citizens at a particular time. There can be no such thing, in constitutionalism as democracy, as a permanently entrenched written constitution. Nor can there even be a single permanently entrenched provision. The very principle that gives the Constitution legitimate authority—the principle of self-government over time—requires that a nation be able to reject any part of a constitution whose commitments are no longer the people's own. Thus written constitutionalism requires a process not only of popular constitution-writing, but also of popular constitution-rewriting.

Even the writing that sought to formalize this process of rewriting would itself be subject to rewriting. For any such formalized processes are subject to calcification and to capture by entrenched powers. Written constitutionalism always permits the possibility of legitimate rupture, of a revolutionary process of popular rewriting that takes place, in part or in whole, outside every existing political institution.

Nevertheless, a constitution may legitimately set forth a legally cognizable amendment process, even if the textually specified process cannot be exhaustive of all the possibilities of legitimate, revolutionary rewriting. In our Constitution, Article V sets forth the legally recognized amendment process. The obstacles that Article V erects in the way of amendment—for example, supermajoritarian votes in Congress to propose amendments, followed by supermajority approval in the states—are extraordinary. They create a process very difficult to negotiate successfully. From the point of view of speech-modeled, present-tense self-government, this onerous amendment process is as difficult to understand and to justify as judicial review. A really principled speech-modeler ought either to condemn the requirements of Article V or, at a minimum, to call for supplemental, majoritarian amendment processes (as, in different ways, Bruce Ackerman, Akhil Reed Amar, and Robert Bork all have done).[20] Indeed, as Amar and Bork would have it, amendment ought to be permissible whenever a majority genuinely wants it—a proposal that would abrogate constitutionalism in a speech-modeled effort to rationalize it.[21]

By contrast, written self-government does not demand that new constitutional principles be adopted whenever a majority so wills. It demands the creation of new constitutional commitments only when a people is prepared to make a significant *temporal* commitment to them. The burdensome, cumbersome proposal and ratification requirements of Article V supply one method to assure that this condition obtains. Supermajorities do not serve to confer greater legitimacy merely through greater numbers. (Consider that the existence of a minority veto, a necessary corollary of a supermajoritarian process, can operate precisely to undercut the legitimacy of the status quo.) Rather, the function of the supermajoritarian process is temporal.

Article V requires supermajority support at both the federal and state levels for a constitutional amendment. This is a process, as Ackerman has stressed, that itself occupies considerable political time and energy, requiring numerous electoral victories before, during, and even after the ratification period in order to be successful. In this way, Article V helps ensure that any constitutional change that succeeds is a change that the majoritarian process will continue to support for a substantial time to come. Of course this result is undercut, and the temporally extended amendment process perverted, when an amendment is accomplished only by a series of state votes drawn out seriatim over two hundred years.[22]

But even supermajority ratification can never fully legitimize a written constitution. Commitments take time. The most solemn act of memorialization, backed up by the unanimous vote of every citizen alive at the moment of proclamation, does not guarantee that a nation is in fact committed to the

20. *See* Bruce Ackerman, 1 We the People: Foundations 44–50 (1991); Amar, *supra* Chapter 3, note 52, at 1064–66; Bork, *supra* Chapter 3, note 53, at 117.

21. *See supra* at 64–65.

22. This is the state of affairs with respect to the 27th Amendment.

proclaimed purpose or principle. A constitution cannot claim the full authority of a popular commitment unless it succeeds over time: unless it takes and holds.

To recognize this fact is not too subversive. If in 1790, a year after the Constitution went into effect, Congress had declared war on England without serious provocation, would the states have been bound to send their men to this war? There is no way to answer such a question. Congress certainly had the power to declare war under the Constitution, yet so enormous an act by the fledgling government, if undertaken contrary to the majority will of the nation, would have jeopardized the entire constitutional structure. I don't mean merely that such a declaration of war would have risked, as a matter of historical fact, disobedience by the states. I mean that it would have been of genuinely uncertain authority, despite its warrant under the new Constitution. For in the period immediately after democratic enactment of a constitution, the constituted authorities have no better claim to authority than popular will, and if the government acts under that constitution in too blatant a disregard of popular will, its claim to authority is in jeopardy.

In the period immediately after ratification, only the weaker claims of speech-modeled authority can be made for a democratically ratified constitution. Ratification can at first supply only the authority of popular consent. If it should happen that popular will—or even indeed mere majority will—should turn against the constitutional order a day after enactment, the only remaining basis of constitutional authority would be a prudentialist appeal to the importance of stability. From the speech-modeled perspective, this is the permanent and indeed permanently worsening predicament of a written constitution's authority, whose legitimacy must progessively shrink as it grows more and more distant from the moment of popular will that ratified it.

But understood in the language of commitment, a constitution strengthens in its authority as it endures and as it is lived under. For this living-under is part of the realization, the coming into being, of its commitments. This does not mean we should stand by the Constitution because it is old. The Constitution's success for two centuries, its deep inscription into the life of the nation, is a mark that its commitments are ours.

How a Written Constitution Binds

A people's constituents at any particular period in time (its "generations," its citizens at a given moment) stand in a relation to the people as a whole similar to the relation that its geographical constituents (its states, its cities) bear to the people as a whole. The citizens here and now ought to regard themselves not as the bearer of the sovereign voice of self-government, but as participating in a temporally extended people whose commitments deserve respect regardless of present political will. The Constitution could impose a requirement on the nation contrary to the present will of *every single citizen,* yet this requirement could still be legitimately binding in the name of self-government.

We who live today could not achieve self-government by declaring new constitutional rules perfectly congruent with our present collective will (if we had a collective will). To suppose that we could is the mistaken premise of speech-modeled thought. We are beneficiaries of a history of self-government, and we are its trustees. It would be a great betrayal to jettison our constitutional history in favor of "our" freedom here and now. Our freedom is irreducibly temporally extended. A people must have law from the past, and it must project law into the future, to be self-governing. We can achieve liberty only by engaging ourselves in a project of self-government that spans time.

Thus the ultimate openness of constitutional commitments to revision does not make constitutionalism as democracy ultimately present-oriented. When a people decides between holding to its foundational law and embarking on a new constitutional path, it is not facing a choice between submission and freedom. Either course will be an effort to participate today in a temporally extended project, simultaneously involving both self-rule and self-submission. A democratic polity must be both self-*governing* and self-*governed.*

Thus the way a constitution ultimately binds the people as a whole is not the same as the way it binds individuals, presidents, or state legislatures. These parties have no authority to violate or revise the constitution at all. A constitution binds the people in a different sense; it does so as the spine of a book binds its pages. The Constitution is what continues to gather up generation upon generation of Americans into a single political subject. A written constitution's normative force depends ultimately on whether it works to recall a people to itself over time: a means by which a people re-collects itself and its fundamental commitments.

Because speech-modeled self-government cannot comprehend this struggle, it invariably disintegrates (as we have seen) the central elements of democratic legitimacy: legality, freedom, and justice. Constitutionalism as democracy rejoins these aspirations: it contemplates a nation pursuing justice and freedom by honoring its own higher law.

Ten

READING THE CONSTITUTION AS WRITTEN: PARADIGM CASE INTERPRETATION

This chapter is about reading the Constitution *as written*—as a project in temporally extended, commitmentarian self-government. When the Constitution is read this way, a distinctive interpretive method comes into view. I will call this method *paradigm case* interpretation.

A strange fact about contemporary constitutional law: it has no account of how to interpret the Constitution.

Just consider *Brown v. Board of Education.* No case this century is more respected, none more exemplary. You would think that scholars or at least judges must by now have some well-settled account of why, as a matter of interpretation, the case was rightly decided. Far from it. Constitutional thought has been scrambling to catch up with *Brown* since the day it was decided.

Many in the 1950s, including one of the most respected constitutional scholars of that period, condemned *Brown* as interpretively unjustified.[1] Today no academic or judge (with ambition) would do so. But the most prominent efforts to justify *Brown* in the language of constitutional interpretation are surprisingly obtuse and unsatisfactory.

One school of thought tries to claim *Brown* as an originalist decision, a claim with the disadvantage of being patently false—either to the facts or to originalism. Robert Bork is illustrative. A self-professed originalist, Bork concedes the "inescapable fact" "that those who ratified the [fourteenth] amendment did not think it outlawed segregated education or segregation in any

1. *See, e.g.,* Learned Hand, The Bill of Rights 54 (1958); Herbert Wechsler, *Toward Neutral Principles of Constitutional Law,* 73 Harv. L. Rev. 1, 34 (1959). Professor Gunther makes a persuasive case that Judge Hand would not have opposed *Brown* had the Court made clear that its rule barring segregation applied not merely to public schooling but to all state action. *See* Gerald Gunther, Learned Hand: The Man and the Judge 665–71 (1994).

aspect of life."[2] How then does Bork find it "clear" that *Brown* comports with the "original understanding"? As follows: "equality and segregation were mutually inconsistent, though the framers did not understand that." Faced with the choice between "equality and segregation," "it is obvious that the Court must choose equality," because equality was the "purpose that brought the fourteenth amendment into being . . . , and equality, not separation, was written into the text."[3]

The logic is simple enough: originalism is here made consistent with *Brown* by shifting ground from the framers' specific intentions to their general purposes. This shift is an old story; it has many proponents. But if this general-purpose originalism rescues *Brown,* it surrenders all the results originalists demand elsewhere in constitutional law. Originalists have insisted a thousand times that the Constitution was never intended to forbid the death penalty. But a general-purpose originalist could simply say, quoting Bork, that the death penalty and abolishing cruel and unusual punishment were "mutually inconsistent, though the framers did not understand that." Faced with this inconsistency, judges must choose abolishing cruel and unusual punishment, which was the "purpose that brought the Eighth Amendment into being" and was "written into the text." Even a Marxist judge could now be an originalist: "equality and [private property] were mutually inconsistent, though the framers did not understand that" either.[4]

Another common defense of *Brown* holds that by 1954 there had developed a national majority consensus against segregation, or, in a variation on this theme, that the Court was able to forge such a consensus through its own holding in *Brown.*[5] This argument, if it justifies *Brown,* would also justify

2. Bork, *supra* Chapter 3, note 22, at 75–76. There is little doubt on this score: the very Congress that framed the Fourteenth Amendment maintained segregated public schools in the nation's capital. John P. Frank & Robert F. Munro, *The Original Understanding of "Equal Protection of the Laws,"* 1972 Wash. U. L.Q. 421, 460–62. Eight ratifying, non-Confederate states either provided for segregated public schools in 1868 or permitted communities to segregate their schools if they chose. Richard Kluger, Simple Justice 633–34 (1976). Nor should it be imagined that the "original understanding" was "separate but *equal.*" Far from providing black children with tangibly equal facilities, five more non-Confederate states *excluded black children altogether* from public education. *Id.*

3. Bork, *supra* Chapter 3, note 22, at 75–76, 82.

4. For another heroic effort to make *Brown* safe for originalism, see Michael McConnell, *Originalism and the Desegregation Decisions,* 81 Va. L. Rev. 947 (1995).

5. Bickel, *supra* Chapter 1, note 16, at 241; Robert Post, Constitutional Domains: Democracy, Community, Management 47–48 (1995).

establishing Protestantism should the fundamentalists come to have, or to be on the verge of having, majority support. Yet another prominent justification of *Brown* rests on the claim that segregation was morally wrong,[6] which is at least true, but unhelpfully so, unless judges are to rule unconstitutional whatever they consider deeply immoral—progressive taxation, perhaps, or laws permitting abortion. *Brown*'s interpretive pedigree is so unsettled that one of the preeminent constitutional theorists of our day maintains that the case can be explained only by the operation of *unwritten constitutional amendments,* which, although no one knew it at the time, got into the Constitution in the 1930s or 1940s, only to be discovered (by this same theorist) some fifty years later.[7]

Practicing lawyers and judges, by contrast, are utterly unpuzzled by *Brown.* Not that they have done any better in explaining *Brown*'s interpretive rightness. But for them, *Brown* is a given, a fixed star, a source of law in whose light any governmental measure can be tested. Which makes the absence of an account of why the case was rightly decided all the more consternating. Having cut anchor from the original understanding, but refusing to set sail into pure moral philosophy, constitutional law remains baffled by its most exemplary decision.

The really remarkable thing in all this is that *Brown* is an easy case. Easy not only as a matter of justice, but as a matter of interpretation. No torturing of constitutional method, no obscure theorizing, no hidden amendments, are needed to account for *Brown.* All that is needed is the paradigm case method.

A warning. Sometimes we think that the ideal constitutional method, if only we could find it, would provide a kind of interpretive algorithm, putting to rest all the ideological contestation that has been part of constitutional law since its inception. The paradigm case method does not furnish such an algorithm. It does not even try to. The aim of constitutional interpretive method is not and cannot be to eliminate from constitutional law all matters of—interpretation.

The term "paradigm case" comes from a line of philosophical-jurisprudential thought concerning the meaning of rules and concepts. The basic idea is easily stated. Rules and concepts can take on meaning by reference to their "paradigm cases": their central or most clearly established instances. ("Case" here does not mean a lawsuit. It means an instance. But a legal case can be

6. *See, e.g.,* Ronald Dworkin, Freedom's Law: The Moral Reading of the American Constitution (1996).

7. Ackerman, *supra* Chapter 9, note 20, ch. 4.

a paradigm case, as we shall see.) "Paradigm cases" are so called because they do paradigmatic duty. They furnish fixed points of reference. They are the exemplars, the building blocks, out of which doctrine is to be built.

Constitutional law has always recognized—indeed in an important sense it begins with—a special category of *foundational paradigm cases*. An example. Imagine that Mississippi today passes a statute requiring all blacks (and only blacks) to be gainfully employed under contracts of at least one year's duration, while also excluding them from any employment other than that of "servant" or "laborer." Those found without written evidence of gainful employment, and those found following any "higher" occupation, are subject to arrest by "any white citizen." Now imagine that the Supreme Court upholds this statute under the Fourteenth Amendment.

What is wrong with this picture?

Is it that we cannot imagine an opinion rationalizing this result? But we can. The Court might announce that Mississippi's statute is subject only to "mere rationality" review, which is an extremely lenient test of constitutionality, and which is, with few exceptions, the almost universal test for validity under the equal protection clause. To be sure, everyone knows that mere rationality review is not supposed to apply to a law that discriminates on its face against blacks. But what underlies this fixed plank of equal protection doctrine?

As a matter of logic, it is easy enough to tell a story in which the Court reasons that equal protection jurisprudence will be much more predictable and consistent when the few exceptions to rational basis review are eliminated. Nothing in the "plain meaning" of the equal protection clause suggests a special test for racial discrimination. On what basis, then, do we claim to know that the Court's decision is categorically wrong? That it is as wrong as a constitutional decision can be?

Originalists may say that they have the answer. They would point out that upholding Mississippi's statute contravenes the original intentions. But *Brown v. Board of Education* did so too. The originalist answer is therefore unhelpful. It proves too much. It does not capture the specific sense in which a judicial decision upholding this hypothetical statute would be categorically different from the hundreds of other constitutional cases that have also departed from original understandings.

Moralists may also imagine that they have the answer. They would say that the Court's decision is so wrong because it is—so wrong. This answer too is unhelpful, and again because it proves too much. To repeat the question raised earlier: are judges to rule everything unconstitutional that they find morally wrong? (Or *deeply* morally wrong?) To be sure, the vast majority of

Americans would agree that Mississippi's hypothetical statute, together with the Court's decision upholding it, is a moral outrage. But to place the outrageousness of the Court's decision solely on that basis leaves something out. It leaves out the fundamental illegitimacy of the Court's decision, not only as a matter of morality, but as a matter of constitutional interpretation.

The specifically interpretive illegitimacy of the Court's decision consists in this: Mississippi has presented the Court with a paradigm case of what the Fourteenth Amendment prohibits.

What does it mean to say so? It means that Mississippi is trying to do what, under the Fourteenth Amendment, no state was ever to be able to do again. The significance of this kind of *never-again* is the first principle of the paradigm case method.

In 1865, the "reconstructed" Southern states began promulgating laws singling out blacks in matters of labor, land ownership, criminal penalties, and so on. "Virtually from the moment the Civil War ended, the search began for legal means of subordinating a volatile black population that regarded economic independence as a corollary of freedom and the old labor discipline as a badge of slavery. Many localities in the summer of 1865 adopted ordinances limiting black freedom of movement, prescribing severe penalties for vagrancy, and restricting blacks' right to rent or purchase real estate and engage in skilled urban jobs."[8] The hypothetical Mississippi statute described above—requiring blacks to be occupied solely as servants or laborers, requiring them to be under long-term contract as servants or laborers, and even subjecting them to arrest by "any white citizen" for violations thereof—exactly recapitulates provisions from the first of these "black codes."[9]

The black codes stand in a special relation to the Fourteenth Amendment. The struggle to abolish them was central to, motivating of, definitive of, the act of constitution-writing that eventuated in the Fourteenth Amendment.[10] Whatever else it might mean, whatever disagreements there might have been over general principles or other specific applications, all understood one thing: the Fourteenth Amendment abolished the black codes.

The paradigm case method holds that the meaning of the Fourteenth Amendment is secured, and its proper interpretation shaped, by this paradigmatic instance of its application. There are numerous other Fourteenth

8. Eric Foner, Reconstruction: America's Unfinished Revolution 1863–1877, at 198 (1988).

9. *See id.* at 199–200.

10. Note that many of the black codes were drafted in facially neutral language, apparently as a device to comply with the federal Civil Rights Act of 1866. *Id.* at 201.

Amendment paradigm cases as well (including those established by later judicial decisions), but the black codes exemplify a *foundational* paradigm case. Which is to say: the unconstitutionality of the black codes is as it were a *fact* about the Fourteenth Amendment's meaning.

It is not correct to say that the Fourteenth Amendment "can be interpreted," or "has always been interpreted," as abolishing black codes. This piece of the Fourteenth Amendment's meaning *precedes* interpretation. It is a given. It is a fixed point with which the task of interpreting the Fourteenth Amendment begins.

Why? The answer has nothing to do with general hermeneutic theory (although the idea of paradigm cases as *pre-interpretive* is consistent with a number of philosophical accounts of meaning). Rather, the answer has to do with the theory of constitutionalism as democracy.

Constitutionalism as democracy holds that self-government consists in a people's struggle to lay down and hold itself, over time, to its own political and legal commitments, apart from or even contrary to the popular will at any given moment. In self-government on the model of writing, the act of constitution-writing takes on a decisive importance.

As we have seen, the world-historical significance of American written constitutionalism was not to reduce constitutional law to clear, unambiguous texts—such a reduction never happened—but rather to *make democratic constitution-making part of democracy itself.* The interpretive task, therefore, is to honor the nation's acts of constitution-writing as acts of self-given commitment. This means:

(1) constitutional provisions are *not* to be interpreted merely as expressions of the democratic will of the ratifying moment, if there was such a will, whether this will is rendered in terms of specific "original intentions" or more general "original purposes";
(2) constitutional rights are *not* to be interpreted as mere procedural conditions for achieving governance by the democratic will of the present moment; and
(3) constitutional rights are *not* to be interpreted in terms of moral truths of putatively universal, a-temporal validity.

Proposition 1 rules out originalism as constitutional method; 2 rules out proceduralism; and 3 rules out philosophical moralism. Instead, the Constitution's provisions are to be understood in terms of the actual, historical struggles of a particular people to lay down and live out its own commitments.

The foundational paradigm cases are foundational, therefore, because they are nothing other than the core historical commitments memorialized by the act of constitution-writing in question.

It is a primary, definitive feature of the Fourteenth Amendment, for example, that it embodied at least this unabridgeable historical commitment: that black codes would not be legal any longer in any state in the union. If a court today were to formulate Fourteenth Amendment doctrine in such a way as to permit a reenactment of the black codes, the court would not have "interpreted" the Fourteenth Amendment at all. It would have surrendered the Amendment's core meaning. Under the guise of "interpretation," the court would have rewritten that amendment or unwritten it.

Surrendering the foundational paradigm case, the court would have dishonored the core commitment and thus erased an act of democratic constitution-making achieved at tremendous cost in blood and fortune. That is why the hypothetical Mississippi statute described above is *categorically* unconstitutional.

But someone will say: this is originalism all over again. The Constitution is interpreted here by reference to an original will. It is interpreted in accordance with what the framers or ratifiers would have said it meant.

The paradigm case method is not originalist. It is commitmentarian. The difference is that originalism defers (or is supposed to defer) to all the intentions or purposes that make up the original "understanding" or "will," whereas the paradigm case method picks out and privileges as foundational only the original commitments. This difference can be vividly illustrated by considering sex discrimination.

Take the question of whether the equal protection clause forbids a state to exclude women from the practice of law. It is as certain as such things can be that the Fourteenth Amendment was originally understood *not* to prohibit such a law. The amendment was understood to leave untouched most of the laws that we today would recognize as sex discrimination. An originalist equal protection jurisprudence would, therefore, have to uphold a state statute excluding women from the practice of law—as the Supreme Court did in 1873.[11] At a minimum, originalists would have to twist and torture their putative originalism (just as they are obliged to do in defense of *Brown*) in order to find a way to reconcile their method to contemporary sex discrimination doctrine.

But the original intentions concerning sex discrimination *are of no conse-*

11. *See* Bradwell v. Illinois, 83 U.S. (16 Wall.) 130 (1873).

quence in the paradigm case method. To be sure, the paradigm case method gives foundational significance to a piece of the original understanding. But only a piece—only the commitmentarian piece. Of the original understandings of the Fourteenth Amendment, only instances of what was to be *prohibited* can supply a paradigm case.

Why? Because only these understandings involved *commitments.* Not all understandings involve commitments. The original interpretation of the First Amendment presumably included an understanding that the Amendment did *not* prohibit Congress from inflicting cruel and unusual punishments on convicted criminals. But this understanding of what the First Amendment did *not* prohibit does not somehow involve a *commitment* to cruel and unusual punishments—as if the Eighth Amendment somehow repudiated or amended a commitment laid down in the First Amendment. An understanding that a constitutional right does *not* prohibit x involves no commitment in relation to x—neither in favor of it, nor against it. Hence the intention to leave sex discriminatory laws untouched, even if shared by every single framer and ratifier of the Fourteenth Amendment, involved no commitment toward such laws—neither in their favor nor against them.

It will be objected that I am engaging in a sleight of hand. No one supposed, it will be said, that the First Amendment had anything to do with cruel and unusual punishments. It is not as if the framers of the First Amendment considered and rejected a wording of that amendment that would have forbidden cruel and unusual punishments. But the Fourteenth Amendment's framers did in fact consider and reject proposals that would have explicitly protected women's rights. Hence the Fourteenth Amendment we actually have is properly regarded as embodying a commitment concerning state laws discriminating against women—a commitment to their permissibility.

There can of course be constitutional commitments to permit. The Constitution contains many of them. Every grant of power to Congress—for example, the power to regulate commerce among the states—is a kind of commitment to permit, in the sense that such provisions do not require but empower Congress to take certain actions (in the absence of a countervailing right). Another kind of commitment to permissibility can be found in provisions that bar Congress from interfering with state practices. An example is the international slave trade clause, which forbade congressional interference with state decisions concerning the "importation" of persons until 1808.[12]

12. Congress was barred from prohibiting the "Migration or Importation of such Persons as any of the States now existing shall think proper to admit" until "the Year one thousand eight hundred and eight." U.S. Const. art. I, § 9, cl. 1.

But one sort of provision that involves no commitment to x's permissibility would be a provision that merely leaves standing the pre-existing state of legal affairs concerning x. In such circumstances, there is no commitment toward x: neither in favor of it, nor against it, nor even to its permissibility. *To have no effect on something is to make no commitment concerning it.*

This proposition is central to the normative structure of commitment: beliefs about what a prohibitory commitment does *not* prohibit never involve, by themselves, a commitment. Say that I commit myself not to deceive some person A, and say that I have the following "original" understanding of my commitment: mere silence, even if misleading, can never count as deception. Say that I consciously considered committing myself against misleading A by silence as well as by deception, but I undertook, on reflection, only to commit myself against the latter. Have I, therefore, *committed* myself to the permissibility of misleading A by silence? Surely not. I might later decide that misleading A by silence is wrong even though it is not a form of deception; or I might decide that misleading by silence is a form of deception after all. But in either case, I have not somehow violated my commitment. The commitment is a commitment *against* deception; it is not a commitment *to the permissibility* of anything. I may never change my mind about the deceptiveness of silence, but I am free to do so, in the sense that taking this view does not violate my commitment. A self that makes a commitment is always free to conclude that its commitment requires more than was originally supposed; indeed this possibility is a defining feature of commitmentarian experience.

To hold that x is not prohibited by a given prohibitory commitment is simply to hold that the commitment does not apply to x. This understanding of *no-application* to x implies a result of *no-change* in the pre-existing normative state of affairs with respect to x. Commitment requires change. A result of no-change with respect to x means that there is no commitment toward x at all: neither in favor of it, nor against it, nor to its permissibility.

The paradigm case method recognizes foundational paradigm cases only in commitments. To be sure, a very different "paradigm case method" could be constructed for constitutional law that treated the entire set of original intentions as paradigmatic. (There would not be much sense, however, in calling this interpretive method "the paradigm case method," because it would already have a name: originalism.) Still another "paradigm case method" could be constructed that would treat only opinions written by Chief Justice John Marshall as paradigmatic. But the interpretive method I am describing is the one that follows from a commitmentarian conception of constitutional self-government. This method takes as foundational only *commitments*—and more specifically, only those commitments made in the course of the concrete historical struggles that actuated the nation's acts of constitution-writing.

Hence the paradigm case method does not defer, in interpreting a prohibitory commitment like the equal protection clause, to original understandings of what that clause did *not* forbid, for as to all such understandings, the clause would at most have left pre-existing law unchanged and hence would entail no commitments. While an originalist interpreter of the Fourteenth Amendment should in principle be bound by the original intention to permit sex discrimination, this intention counts for little or nothing in paradigm case interpretation.

In this way, the paradigm case method stakes out an interpretive position deeply at odds with all the contemporary schools of constitutional interpretation. It is all-but-universally understood in the constitutional literature that whatever one's view of the significance of original understandings (whether specific intentions or general purposes), all the original intentions or purposes have to be treated to the same analysis. Those who demand originalism in constitutional law and those who oppose it agree on this much. A judge found picking and choosing among the original intentions, based on their content, would be seen as shamming, as attempting to mask results arrived at through other means. By contrast, paradigm case interpretation explicitly privileges a portion of historical meaning and does so on the basis of its content. Paradigm case interpretation is historical, but not originalist.

In this respect, although contrary to constitutional scholarship, the paradigm case method is deeply consistent with actual constitutional practice. An asymmetry has long existed in constitutional law with respect to the "original understanding"—an asymmetry reflecting a profound ambivalence toward historical meaning. On the one hand, there can be no doubt that contemporary constitutional law is radically non-originalist. *Brown* alone is a sufficient citation for this point, but other major examples would include the unconstitutionality of sex discrimination and the tremendous expansion of Congress's commerce clause powers. Yet constitutional law has also remained profoundly shaped by and tied to certain pieces of historically established meaning. Equal protection law, for example, remains wholly structured—in its concept of suspect classes, its tiered levels of "heightened scrutiny," its focus on invidious prejudice—by the kind of discrimination perpetrated by the black codes. This structuring is historical; it reflects a continuing commitment to the foundational paradigm cases. The same pattern is visible throughout most of constitutional law. Core historical *applications* of a provision have characteristically remained intact, but original understandings of *no-application* have repeatedly been breached.

This ambivalence toward historical meaning is proper. Intentions do not bind. Commitments do. The foundational commitments behind most constitutional provisions continue to play a deep, structuring role in an otherwise radically non-originalist jurisprudence. The paradigm case method explains this asymmetry.

As noted above, in dealing with a constitutional *prohibition,* only instances of what the provision *prohibits* can count as a foundational paradigm case. Similarly, in dealing with constitutional grants of power, only instances of what the provision was to *permit* can count as foundational. And in the case of constitutional *requirements,* only instances of what the provision was to *require* can count.

The reason is the same in every case. A constitutional provision makes no change in the pre-existing legal order with respect to, and hence makes no commitment concerning, that to which it does *not* apply. For this reason, understandings of what a right does *not* prohibit involve no commitments and do not qualify as foundational paradigm cases. Similarly, a constitutional grant of power makes no change, and hence no commitment with respect to, that which it does *not* permit. And a constitutional requirement makes no change, and hence no commitment with respect to, that which it does *not* require.

Thus every constitutional provision has a floor, but no ceiling. Its core meaning is given by its core applications, but the *other* applications it might have—what *else* it prohibits, permits, or requires—remain open to future interpretation. This openness in constitutional law is sometimes condemned for imparting too much uncertainty into our basic legal order and for conferring too much discretionary power on the judges who interpret that order. But this openness is part of what it means to live by self-given commitments over time. It is part of the nature of a commitment that its full entailments can never be known until they have been lived out, and lived under, for an extended period of time.

I have spoken so far only of the *foundational* paradigm cases, the ones that lay behind the act of constitution-writing itself. Supplementing the foundational paradigm cases are others that come later. These post-enactment paradigm cases can be established by an intense political struggle (such as the struggle over the Alien and Sedition Acts in the late 1790s), or by longstanding practice. But by far the most abundant source of subsequent paradigm cases is those established by judicial precedent.

All judicial decisions are in a sense additional paradigm cases (of varying degrees of entrenchedness). This is why constitutional interpretation does not begin by skipping straight to the "founding" or to moral philosophy, as if one could interpret the Constitution without ever opening a case reporter. Why does commitmentarian interpretation elevate judicial decisions into paradigm cases? Because the precedentialist, common-law style of adjudication is the means through which a judiciary, holding certain results more or less constant, gives meaning to legal and political commitments over time.

To repeat: the full implications of a commitment are never known in advance. If I have a child, I inscribe myself into a complex network of commitments. When I try to interpret what these commitments require of me, it does little good if I refer to what I had in mind at the "founding" moment. For better or worse, I have to be prepared to discover, in the course of living out these commitments, that they require more than I might have originally supposed. Commitments have to be filled in and filled out through an ongoing task of interpretation. But in this ongoing interpretive process by which we live out our commitments, it is critical that *some* basic interpretation be given a chance to establish itself, to become part of our practices. Otherwise the commitments are never made real.

Some basic implications of the commitment, *some* line of approach toward its meaning, has to be held more or less constant, or else there is no lived commitment at all. If on Monday I interpret my commitments one way, on Tuesday completely differently, and so on, such that no particular interpretation is ever lived out for more than a day, then there is no actualized commitment over time. This is the ultimate basis of the doctrine of stare decisis in constitutional law. If a constitutional commitment is to be real, if it is to be a real part of the political life of a nation, there has to be a *holding*. Some results and some basic approach to its meaning must be adhered to for a substantial period of time.

This is not to say that every act of interpretation today must always conserve or "fit" the previously decided cases. There is no requirement that a constitutional decision "fit" with most or many of the precedents. On the contrary, a decision may properly break dramatically from the corpus of preceding decisions. Such breaks are justified when, for example, the precedent is judged to have failed to honor what was originally committed to writing in light of the *foundational* paradigm cases.

The paradigm case method explains not only the central role of precedent in constitutional law but the *method of interpretation* that applies to precedent as well. The interpretation of case law in our system is not, and has never been, intentionalist. Intentionalist interpretation finds its ideal in the consultation of "legislative history" to determine the lawmakers' true intentions (as revealed by their contemporaneous utterances). But judges nearly never consult the analogous "judicial history" of a case (bench memoranda, remarks at oral argument) to determine the intentions of the judges who decided it.

Instead, when interpreting the precedent, the later judges precisely follow the paradigm case method. They treat the case law as a fund of additional paradigm cases of varying degrees of significance. Among the decided cases, there will be some, and *Brown v. Board of Education* is again the usual example, that come to be deemed landmarks, carrying an extremely privileged interpretive position. Others are regarded as bearing lesser authority, but all are treated as paradigms, as points of reference creating frames of reference for further doctrinal elaboration. A judge's task respecting the constitutional cases of the past, in the common-law style, is precisely to discern and to work out, over time, the *commitments* that those cases paradigmatically embody.

But what does it mean for a judge to decide a lawsuit on the basis of past-established paradigm cases? How are judges supposed to decide a case like *Brown v. Board of Education,* which involves a law that was not among the foundational prohibitions and that was, in fact, originally understood to be constitutionally permitted? What is paradigm case interpretation?

Paradigm case interpretation is the effort to do justice to a text in light of its paradigm cases. To take the Fourteenth Amendment: starting with the black codes, judges are to derive doctrinal rules or principles that capture the paradigm cases—that explain, say, what it was about the black codes that makes them paradigmatic denials of equal protection—and then apply those rules or principles evenhandedly to subsequent cases, even if that means striking down laws supported by popular will, past or present.

This process is in fact exactly what has unfolded in equal protection law, although it took the justices considerable time to do it. Even in 1873, in the famous *Slaughter-House Cases,*[13] in which the Supreme Court all but eradicated one of the Fourteenth Amendment's principal guarantees,[14] the Court still

13. 83 U.S. (16 Wall.) 36 (1873).

14. The holding of *Slaughter-House,* which rejected a Fourteenth Amendment challenge to a livestock trade regulation, is not itself exceptional. But in reaching this result, the Court held in essence that the privileges or immunities clause of the Fourteenth Amendment—arguably the most important clause in the most important amendment ever added to the Constitution—made no change in preexisting law. "Unique among constitutional provisions, the privileges and immunities clause of the Fourteenth Amendment enjoys the distinction of having been rendered a 'practical nullity' by a single decision of the Supreme Court." Edward S. Corwin, The Constitution of the United States of America 965 (1953).

could not bring itself to transgress against that amendment's foundational paradigm case. The Court saw in the Amendment "one pervading purpose": "the protection of the newly-made freeman and citizen from the oppressions of those who had formerly exercised unlimited dominion over them." The Court offered a partial catalogue of those "oppressions":

> [Blacks] were [forbidden] to appear in the towns in any other character than menial servants. They were required to reside on and cultivate the soil without the right to purchase or own it. They were excluded from many occupations of gain, and were not permitted to give testimony in the courts of any case where a white man was a party.[15]

Although it recognized these paradigm cases, the *Slaughter-House* Court refused to extrapolate from them. The Court came close to holding that the *only* effect of the equal protection clause was to prohibit the black codes.[16]

The meaning of a constitutional provision, however, is never exhausted by its paradigm cases. The paradigm cases are the starting points of interpretation, not the end points. A few years later the Court moved slightly forward, confronting a state law that excluded blacks from jury service. Presumably because such statutes were common in the North as well as the South, and presumably because jury eligibility had long been denied to women, to persons without "freeholds," and so on, this bit of racial discrimination was thought by some to have remained constitutional despite the Fourteenth Amendment. But in *Strauder v. West Virginia*,[17] the Court struck it down—on the basis of paradigm case reasoning.

The Court, retailing the black codes once again, likened the jury exclusion to those codes in the following terms: "The very fact that colored people are singled out . . . is practically a brand upon them, affixed by the law, an assertion of their inferiority."[18] The Fourteenth Amendment, held the Court, stood against such laws. It conferred on blacks an "immunity" "from legal discriminations" "implying inferiority in civil society."[19]

This is classic paradigm case reasoning, extrapolating general principles from the foundational paradigm cases and applying those principles to the controversy at hand. Such reasoning, once begun, exerts a kind of hydraulic normative force. It pushes outward, in the well-observed common-law style, available for the next set of plaintiffs as a basis for argument. I do not mean

15. *Slaughter-House*, 83 U.S. (16 Wall.) at 70.

16. *See id.* at 83.

17. 100 U.S. 303 (1879).

18. *Id.* at 308.

19. *Id.* at 307–08.

this formulation of the judicial task to seem original or surprising. It describes, as I have said, nothing other than the common-law-like nature of constitutional interpretation.

If *Strauder*'s paradigm case reasoning was modest in many ways, it was profound from at least one point of view. *Strauder* illustrates why *Brown v. Board of Education* is so easy on the paradigm case method. Earlier I described some of the strangely unsatisfactory efforts to justify *Brown* that can be found in contemporary academic thinking. Consider then how *Brown* looks from the viewpoint of paradigm case interpretation.

According to the *Strauder* Court, not only the black codes, but all "legal discriminations" against blacks "implying inferiority in civil society" violate the equal protection guarantee. To repeat: this is classic, straightforward paradigm case reasoning. And is there any difficulty in seeing *Brown* as an elaboration on, and an application of, this straightforward reasoning? "To separate [black children] from others of similar age and qualifications solely because of their race," said the Court in *Brown,* "generates a feeling of inferiority as to their status in the community that may affect their hearts and minds in a way unlikely ever to be undone." Notice that the "inferiority" of which the Court speaks in *Brown* is not an academic inferiority (as if the evil of "separate but equal" lay in a communication of differing academic skills, so that separate but equal train cars would be unconstitutional only if they communicated differing railway passenger skills). The Court refers to "a feeling of inferiority *as to their status in the community,*" a formulation close to *Strauder*'s "inferiority *in civil society.*"

To be sure, *Strauder* does not logically compel the result in *Brown.* A discriminating lawyer in 1954 could have argued that "separate but equal" was not a "legal discrimination" against blacks. Or if it was, that this discrimination did not "imply inferiority." Or if it did, that this inferiority was not an inferiority in "civil society." Supporters of *Brown* have replies to all these points, but these thrusts or parries are beside the point. Particularly irrelevant is the claim made by *Brown*'s supporters that education had become a thing of newly fundamental civil importance by 1954[20]—a thought that, if it does some good for *Brown,* fails utterly to explain the numerous decisions that followed close on the heels of *Brown* in which the Court tore down America's racial separation regime in all its de jure forms, from segregated golf courses to public beaches.[21]

20. *See, e.g.,* Michael J. Klarman, *An Interpretive History of Modern Equal Protection,* 90 Mich. L. Rev. 213, 232–33 (1991).

21. *See, e.g.,* Gayle v. Browder, 352 U.S. 903 (1956) (buses); Holmes v. City of At-

The real issue is just this: whether *Brown* and all the decisions that extended it are difficult to account for as a matter of constitutional interpretation. Do they require, in order to be interpretively justified, the kind of tortuous accounts of interpretive method that began this chapter? The answer given by the paradigm case method is no. *Brown* requires just two pieces of reasoning, each of which is easily justifiable.

Brown first requires that judges formulate something like an anti-inferiorization or anti-caste principle for the equal protection clause. This is no more than what the Court did in *Strauder,* and what Justice Harlan did in his famous dissenting opinion in *Plessy v. Ferguson:* "[I]n view of the constitution, in the eye of the law, there is in this country no superior, dominant, ruling class of citizens. There is no caste here."[22] Justice Harlan's anti-caste principle may be viewed as a restatement of *Strauder*'s anti-inferiorization principle or as a modification of it. For present purposes, it doesn't matter. Either principle is a well-motivated reading of the abolition of the black codes.

Second, *Brown* requires that "separate but equal" be seen as a violation of this anti-inferiorization or anti-caste principle. As it clearly was. America's racial separation laws were untouchability laws. As Justice Harlan put it, they "proceed[ed] on the ground that colored citizens are so inferior and degraded that they cannot not be allowed to sit in public coaches occupied by white citizens"[23]—or to drink from the same water fountains, or to have intercourse with them. Untouchability is a universal marker of caste.

To be sure, the black codes do not *have* to be seen as Justice Harlan saw them. (That is why the result in *Brown* is not logically compelled.) The *Plessy* majority opinion itself offered an alternative interpretation of the meaning of the Fourteenth Amendment's foundational paradigm cases. The *Plessy* Court acknowledged the critical interpretive significance of the black codes, but redescribed these codes in an interesting way.

The Fourteenth Amendment, the *Plessy* majority stated, was written to protect members of "the colored race from certain laws . . . curtailing their rights in the pursuit of life, liberty, and property to such an extent that their freedom was of little value." Not all "distinctions based upon color" were thereby ruled out, for not all such distinctions were so "onerous," or so "curtailed [blacks'] rights," "that their freedom was of little value." So long as Louisiana

---

lanta, 350 U.S. 879 (1955) (golf courses); Mayor of Baltimore v. Dawson, 350 U.S. 877 (1955) (public beaches and bathhouses); Loving v. Virginia, 388 U.S. 1 (1967) (miscegenation).

22. 163 U.S. 537, 559 (1896) (Harlan, J., dissenting).

23. *Id.* at 560.

provided blacks with equal accommodations, the equal protection clause was satisfied.[24]

Plessy too, therefore, was an example of paradigm case reasoning. But a very bad example.

The *Plessy* reading of the paradigm cases fails strikingly to capture the black codes themselves. Consider the exclusion of blacks from, say, the profession of medicine. The right to practice medicine is not necessary to give one's freedom value. The exclusion of blacks from the professions was unconstitutional because of the kind of *inequality* to which it subjected them, not because it rendered their freedom "of little value." Or again, consider the common black code provision imposing on blacks greater criminal penalties than those imposed on whites for the same offenses. In what way does this discrimination render blacks' freedom "of little value"?

In effect, the *Plessy* Court tried to read the black codes in terms of a *liberty* principle, when the much more powerful interpretation, indeed the only acceptable interpretation, reads them in terms of an *equality* principle. We are here looking at the black codes as the paradigm case of the equal protection clause; *Plessy*'s attempt to paint those codes as violating a liberty principle fails entirely to do justice to the text in light of its paradigm cases.

The paradigm case method captures *Brown* the way it ought to be captured: as an easy case, not only as a matter of morality, but also as a matter of interpretation. *Brown* was rightly decided because ending segregation was a matter of living up, at long last, to the nation's constitutional commitment to end the legalized degradation of blacks.

A more general lesson: every commitment, personal or political, raises the possibility that we may be obliged to give up practices that seemed perfectly reasonable to us, perfectly natural, at the time we embarked on the commitment. No matter how widely held, no matter how intensely felt, the original understanding that the Fourteenth Amendment permitted racial segregation deserves no interpretive deference. The foundational paradigm cases of a constitutional right are absolute, but what *else* it prohibits is always a matter of interpretation, reserved for the future to decide.

I want to emphasize it: the paradigm cases will far more often be of service in ruling *out* a proposed interpretation of the Constitution. They will rarely rule a single interpretation *in*. The reason is that the interpretive task called for by the paradigm case method—the task of extrapolating principles from

24. *Plessy*, 163 U.S. at 544–45.

paradigm cases and applying those principles to new facts—irreducibly requires the exercise of judicial, normative, evaluative judgment. This is why constitutional law has always been and always will be so dependent on the wisdom, the values, the instincts, the qualities of feeling, and the ideologies of our judges. The intrusion of all this into constitutional law is no reason for cynicism or despair. For this is just where all the considerations of rightness in the largest sense—whether of morality, of structure, of workability, or of justice—come into play.

The paradigm case method regards the Constitution not as the voice but as the word of the people: as a commitment the nation has given itself, binding even against a contrary popular will in future. In this way it integrates legitimacy's three principal ingredients. It integrates the rule of law and the aspiration to justice within a single project of democratic self-government. The next chapter offers further illustrations.

Eleven

SEX DISCRIMINATION AND RACE PREFERENCES

This chapter applies paradigm case reasoning to two more topics in equal protection law. A brief discussion of sex discrimination will illustrate how the paradigm case method deals with extensions of equal protection law beyond the paradigmatic category of race. For a second and more detailed illustration, I will consider a topic much more controversial in constitutional law: minority race preferences.

The previous chapter raised but did not discuss the question of how judges should decide the constitutionality of laws discriminating against women. As noted, the "original understanding" on this point is almost diametrically opposed to the law that we have today. *Bradwell v. Illinois,* which upheld in 1873 a state statute excluding women from the practice of law, was almost certainly consistent with the Fourteenth Amendment's original understanding.[1] Today, however, such an exclusion would be considered grossly unconstitutional. As with *Brown v. Board of Education,* many think that contemporary sex discrimination doctrine is therefore something of a cheat or a fraud—a good result, perhaps, but unjustified as a matter of constitutional interpretation.

Stipulate for purposes of this discussion that the men who ratified the Fourteenth Amendment would not have voted for it had they understood it to abolish the system of legalized sex discrimination then in place throughout the United States. Stipulate that they believed, to quote one of the concurring opinions in *Bradwell,* that women's "natural and proper timidity and delicacy . . . evidently unfits [*sic*]" them "for many of the occupations of civil life." That women's privileges and immunities were those of "the domestic sphere," those attached to "the noble and benign offices of wife and mother." That such was the "law of the Creator."[2] To men who held this view, there would

1. 83 U.S. (16 Wall.) 130 (1873). *See, e.g.,* Eleanor Flexner, Century of Struggle 146–48 (1975).

2. *Bradwell,* 83 U.S. (16 Wall.) at 141 (Bradley, J., concurring). As late as 1948, the

have been nothing illogical in concluding that laws denying women some of the rights accorded to men do not violate the Fourteenth Amendment. Sex discrimination by no means violates the "plain meaning" of the equal protection clause (or the privileges and immunities clause or any other provision of the Fourteenth Amendment). But then, nothing violates the plain meaning of the equal protection clause, because the "equal protection of the laws" has no plain meaning in the dictionary-definition sense that seekers of plain meaning typically have in mind.

Despite all this, contemporary sex discrimination doctrine presents no serious difficulties for constitutional interpretation. Within the framework of paradigm case reasoning, sex discrimination is an easy case. To begin with, as discussed in the last chapter, the original understanding that the Fourteenth Amendment did *not* forbid sex discrimination is not entitled to interpretive deference because it involves no commitment. It is an understanding of the text's *inapplicability*—an understanding that the Fourteenth Amendment had no effect on sex discriminatory laws—and such understandings have no commitmentarian weight.

Accordingly, the interpretive question is whether the Fourteenth Amendment, read in light of its paradigm cases of racial discrimination, also condemns sex discrimination. And it is undeniable that every one of the arguments used in *Bradwell* to defend sex discrimination—natural unfitness for higher occupations, dependence on others for protection, divine will—could have been made with equal force to defend racial discrimination. Indeed, such arguments were staples of the defense of slavery.

Undoubtedly, there were countless respects in which the discriminating lawyer of the late nineteenth century, or even of this century, could differentiate between sex discrimination and race discrimination. The claim is not that the unconstitutionality of race discrimination *logically compels* the unconstitutionality of sex discrimination. The point is simply to show how easily contemporary sex discrimination doctrine holds up as an interpretation of the Fourteenth Amendment, when that amendment is read in light of its foundational paradigm cases. Once bare references to original intentions are ruled out, it is almost impossible to give a good reason for upholding sex discrimination under the Fourteenth Amendment that could not also be turned into a good reason for upholding racial discrimination.

On what ground, other than an originalist ground, may states or judges deem women properly confined to "domestic" work that could not also have

---

Supreme Court held that a state "could, beyond question, forbid all women from working behind a bar." Goesaert v. Cleary, 335 U.S. 464 (1948) (Frankfurter, J.).

been applied to blacks? If a judge can hold that excluding women from the practice of law does not deny them equal protection because women's unfitness for practicing law is given by biology, by natural psychological differences, or by "the law of the Creator," why couldn't the same judge uphold a law excluding blacks from the practice of law on the same grounds?

The question is not whether sex discrimination is "analogous" to racial discrimination. The question courts must answer is: what constitutes a denial of the equal protection of the laws? The doctrinal principles and rules that they set out in answering this question—"a statute violates the equal protection guarantee if it . . ."—must first and foremost capture the black codes as paradigmatic instances. But after such principles and rules are formulated, judges must apply them even-handedly, striking down all laws that transgress them, regardless of past or present popular will. To pick up the thread from the previous chapter, once the black codes (and *Brown*) are read to stand for an anti-caste or anti-inferiorization principle, where is the difficulty in concluding that governmental sex discrimination is also unconstitutional?

We might put the point as follows. The desire to have in one's society a class of persons born for subjection and service is perfectly natural. Having such a class around is satisfying in the extreme (unless one happens to be a member of it). Indeed it satisfies so many interests, material and psychological, that it has served the world over, from time immemorial, as a universal engine of social order. It just happens that this desire cannot be made the basis of law—not here, not ever again, not after the enactment of the Fourteenth Amendment. Such is the Fourteenth Amendment's core principle, read in light of its paradigm cases. Applying this principle consistently, apart from or even contrary to the will of the nation at any given moment, is the prerogative—more than that, the duty—of a court charged with the task of reading the Constitution as written. And applying this principle consistently, a court should without hesitation conclude that the nation's regime of sex discrimination was just as unconstitutional as was the nation's regime of racial discrimination.

Perhaps, however, someone may object that this result does not follow from what was said about the black codes in the previous chapter. On the contrary (it might be said), to read the abolition of the black codes in anti-inferiorization terms implies no more than that laws treating *blacks* as inferior will be unconstitutional. This view would explain and justify the result in *Brown,* but it by no means explains or justifies the Court's holdings that laws discriminating against women are unconstitutional. Hence the paradigm cases furnish no basis for concluding that sex discrimination is unconstitutional.

Paradigm cases, however, are never free-floating. They are paradigm cases *of* a textual guarantee. The judge's task is not to offer an interpretation of the paradigm cases in the abstract; it is to interpret those cases as paradigm cases *of* the constitutional proposition committed to writing. Looking at the black codes in the absence of the constitutional text, a judge could conceivably read them to stand for the following principles: that no state in the former Confederacy could pass any laws governing civil rights; that if a state denied to blacks any rights afforded to whites, that state must also apply the same denial of rights to all other racial or ethnic minorities within its jurisdiction; and so on.

Similarly, looking at the black codes in the abstract, it would be conceivable to say, as the Supreme Court came close to holding in the decades immediately following the Civil War, that a statute violates the equal protection clause "if and only if it discriminates against negroes."[3] Such a rule might capture the foundational paradigm cases, but it would not do justice to the text. The equal protection clause does not provide that states shall not "discriminate against blacks" or "deny blacks the equal protection of the laws." It provides that states shall not "deny to any *person* within its jurisdiction the equal protection of the laws." And the plain meaning of "person"—yes, the plain meaning of it—rules out a certain view that might otherwise be a conceivable extrapolation from the abolition of the black codes: namely, that women are simply not protected by the equal protection guarantee.

By demanding that justice be done to the *text,* the paradigm case method captures the significance of plain meaning in constitutional interpretation. By demanding that judges do justice to a text *in light of its paradigm cases,* the paradigm case method captures this significance better than any literalist or so-called textualist jurisprudence can. The only real "plain meaning" the Fourteenth Amendment has—in its equal protection or privileges and immunities provisions—is not textual but historical: the abolition of the black codes. But the plain meaning of "person" forbids judges from using the black codes to conclude that the equal protection clause simply does not cover women, because whatever else "person" might mean, it certainly refers to women as well as men.

By itself, let me stress, this point is not remotely sufficient to warrant any conclusions. The fact that a man driving a car at a hundred miles per hour is a person does not mean that his equal protection rights are violated if he gets

3. *See* The Slaughterhouse Cases, 83 U.S. (16 Wall) 36, 83 (1873) ("We doubt very much whether any action of a state not directed by way of discrimination against the negroes . . . will ever be held to come within the purview of this provision.").

a ticket. The word "person" does not indicate in any way what counts as an equal protection violation. The word simply indicates who is entitled to the equal protection of the laws—all persons.

Consider one final objection. Someone might observe that even current equal protection doctrine permits states to respect differences between men and women in ways that would not be permitted in matters of racial discrimination. After all, public bathrooms may be segregated by sex, but not by race. Hence it is plainly not true that states violate the equal protection clause whenever they distinguish between men and women in a fashion that would be unconstitutional were the state distinguishing between blacks and whites. Thus the fact that denying blacks rights enjoyed by whites is unconstitutional cannot logically compel the conclusion that denying women rights enjoyed by men is unconstitutional as well.

The practice of sex-segregating bathrooms should not be dismissed as trivial, given the history and meaning of the practice of race-segregating bathrooms in this country. But the objection offered at the end of the foregoing paragraph—that the unconstitutionality of governmental sex discrimination is not logically compelled by the unconstitutionality of race discrimination—*should* be dismissed as trivial. Few results in constitutional law are logically compelled. It is always a matter, as I have said, of doing justice—to a certain text, in a certain light (the light of its paradigm cases). Constitutional interpretation is irreducibly normative. The foundational paradigm cases give a decisive structure to constitutional law, but this structure must still be elaborated, and in this elaboration there is no escaping the exercise of normative judgment. Nor is there a reason to want to escape from such judgment, which is a necessary part of giving any commitment meaning.

An anti-caste reading of the equal protection clause is not undermined by sex-segregated bathrooms. On the contrary, the constitutionality of sex-segregated public bathrooms confirms, rather than calls into question, the basic principle at stake. Racial segregation of public bathrooms was a deliberate effort to legalize a caste-like untouchability for blacks. Are bathrooms segregated by sex in order to legalize female inferiority?

The judgment that does *not* see an invidious untouchability in sex-segregated bathrooms, but does see one in race-segregated bathrooms, is in some ways complex and in some ways simple. It is a judgment no doubt reflective of, and contingent on, the entire history of race and sex relations in this country. But however that may be, the constitutionality of sex-segregated bathrooms reaffirms the basic proposition that state action will and should be struck down whenever it is found to treat women as men's legal inferiors. And this proposition in turn reflects and reaffirms the anti-caste or anti-inferiorization reading of the Fourteenth Amendment's paradigm cases discussed above.

Ultimately, the question is whether we are obliged to regard contemporary sex discrimination doctrine as an act of well-intentioned interpretive illegitimacy. According to paradigm case reasoning, the answer is no. The unconstitutionality of governmental sex discrimination follows as easily from the Fourteenth Amendment's paradigm cases as does the unconstitutionality of racial segregation. Preventing the law from embodying men's desire to have in women a class of persons inferior to them, born to serve them and to be dependent on them, is a matter of doing justice to the nation's commitment never again to treat any class of persons as a subordinate or servile caste.

Turn now to race preferences. Following general usage, "affirmative action" will refer here to minority race preferences, but the term is of course a euphemism. It testifies to a certain hypocrisy surrounding this entire subject, a hypocrisy well represented on both sides of this debate. Exhibit A: "I oppose affirmative action because it's bad for minorities." Exhibit B: the word "diversity." Exhibit C: "Affirmative action is not contrary to merit; it's part of merit." Exhibit D: "the fact that he is black and a minority has nothing to do with this in the sense that he is the best qualified at this time."[4]

Hypocrisy, however, is a small price to pay for our principles.

Were there foundational paradigm cases involving the use of minority race preferences? As a matter of fact—although this is a fact widely ignored today—the framers of the Fourteenth Amendment often gave express race-based preferences to minorities in the allocation of governmental benefits. For example, in 1866, the Thirty-Ninth Congress (the body that framed the Fourteenth Amendment) passed a statute appropriating money for the "relief of destitute *colored* women and children." In 1867, the Fortieth Congress (the body that drove that amendment down the throat of the bloody South) provided relief for destitute *"colored"* persons in the District of Columbia. Throughout the Civil War period, Congress enacted special appropriations and specially protective procedures for the *"colored"* soldiers and sailors of the Union. Moreover, Congress in this period enacted, just as it had before and would continue to do thereafter, substantial blood-based preferences for American Indians.[5]

4. *Excerpts from News Conference Announcing Court Nominee,* N.Y. Times, July 2, 1991, at A14 (quoting President George Bush).

5. *See* Act of July 28, 1866, ch. 296, 14 Stat. 310 at 317; Resolution of Mar. 16,

But not one of these laws is a foundational paradigm case, because, once again, paradigm cases of constitutional rights must be instances of what the right forbids, not what it permits. Apparently, a majority of the body that framed the Fourteenth Amendment saw no conflict between the principles for which they fought and minority race preferences, but this original understanding is not conclusive. It does, however, have some importance. It reminds us that on the issue of affirmative action, the usual putative alignments of judicial outcomes and methodologies are askew. The judges and scholars who most prominently oppose affirmative action, saying that "the government may not make distinctions on the basis of race," are the very same ones who supposedly champion the jurisprudence of original understanding.[6] But here, without excuse, without a word of explanation, they adopt a highly unoriginalist position, and they ought at least to be candid in doing so.

All the foundational paradigm cases concerning race—and *Brown v. Board of Education* as well—involve the deliberate *disfavoring* of blacks, not the deliberate favoring of them. So the foundational paradigm cases do not establish that affirmative action is unconstitutional. Nor, however, do they establish that affirmative action is constitutional. How, then, would a judge proceed?

I have said that the paradigm case method, properly executed, is as concerned with precedent as it is with the foundational period. So in this more detailed illustration of paradigm case reasoning, we will begin with current doctrine. In 1995, in *Adarand Constructors, Inc. v. Pena,* the Supreme Court held that all governmental affirmative action measures would henceforth be evaluated under *"strict scrutiny."* This term refers to a "standard of review," a certain kind of test that judges apply to determine the constitutionality of a law or other governmental action. Strict scrutiny is the most exacting level

---

1867, No. 4, 15 Stat. 20; Resolution of June 15, 1866, No. 46, 14 Stat. 357, 358–59; Resolution of Dec. 21, 1865, No. 1, 14 Stat. 347 (authorizing expenditure of $500,000 "for the immediate subsistence and clothing of destitute Indians"). *See generally* Jed Rubenfeld, *Affirmative Action,* 107 Yale L.J. 427, 430–32 (1997); Eric Schnapper, *Affirmative Action and the Legislative History of the Fourteenth Amendment,* 71 Va. L. Rev. 753 (1985).

6. Adarand Constructors, Inc. v. Pena, 515 U.S. 200, 240 (1995) (Thomas, J., concurring). Justices Thomas and Scalia, together with Robert Bork, have all condemned the use of minority race preferences—indeed they have described judicial support of affirmative action as an example "the politics of ultraliberalism . . . driving the law"—without ever confronting or explaining the fact that this position contradicts their often-expressed dedication to the original understanding. Bork, *supra* Chapter 3, note 22, at 107. For further citations, see Rubenfeld, *supra* note 5, at 430.

of equal protection review that exists under current doctrine; it requires that a governmental measure be struck down unless it is "narrowly tailored" to "further a compelling governmental purpose."[7] Strict scrutiny is very difficult to survive; indeed, it is almost always fatal. Under *Adarand,* the Supreme Court and the lower courts have invalidated affirmative action programs all over the country.[8]

What does the paradigm case method say about "strict scrutiny" and its application to affirmative action programs? The answer is that there are two quite different ways to understand strict scrutiny, and that the paradigm case method rejects one understanding but supports the other.

One natural way of understanding strict scrutiny is to see it as a balancing test—a cost-benefit, justificatory balancing test. From this point of view, strict scrutiny serves to test whether a given intrusion into individuals' constitutionally protected interests is justified by extremely important countervailing interests that could not have been served through any measure less invasive of the constitutional interests at stake. This is exactly how the Court presented strict scrutiny in *Adarand.*

Justice O'Connor's opinion for the Court in *Adarand* reasoned as follows:

> [W]henever the government treats any person unequally because of his or her race, that person has suffered an injury that falls squarely within the language and spirit of the Constitution's guarantee of equal protection. . . . The application of strict scrutiny, in turn, determines whether a compelling governmental interest justifies the infliction of that injury.[9]

Race-based classifications, says the Court in this passage, invariably inflict a constitutional "injury"—a square violation of "the language and spirit" of the equal protection guarantee. Yet this "injury," this violation of the equal protection norm or principle, does not end the inquiry. The violation is a cost to be factored into a larger constitutional calculus, a cost that will be deemed "justifie[d]" if the governmental interests at stake are sufficiently weighty.

The paradigm case method wholly repudiates this strict scrutiny balancing test.

When government "squarely" violates "the language and spirit of the Con-

7. 515 U.S. 200, 235 (1995).

8. *See, e.g.,* Shaw v. Hunt, 517 U.S. 899 (1996) (invalidating majority-minority voting district); City of Richmond v. J.A. Croson Co., 488 U.S. 469 (1989) (striking down the use of race preferences in governmental contracting); Hopwood v. Texas, 78 F.3d 1547 (5th Cir.), *cert. denied,* 518 U.S. 1033 (1996) (striking down affirmative action program in university admissions).

9. *Adarand,* 515 U.S. 200, 229–30.

stitution's guarantee of equal protection," the government has acted unconstitutionally—period. There can be no further inquiry into whether the violation is "justified" by the social benefits it might produce. Why? Because of the foundational paradigm cases.

The inviolability of these cases introduces a certain absolutism into constitutional law, a certain invulnerability of constitutional rights to cost-benefit calculations. In paradigm case reasoning, it cannot be the case that the judiciary's most exacting "level of review" still leaves room for constitutional violations to be excused when the government is pursuing "compelling" state interests.

Imagine that Mississippi passes a statute consigning all non-whites to menial employment. State lawyers come to court armed with empirical data demonstrating that Mississippi's measure will reduce violent crime and thereby save x lives every year. Do we know that these data are false? Stipulate that they are accurate. Do we know that a more narrowly tailored or less restrictive measure could achieve the same reduction in crime or the same saving of lives? Stipulate that there is no equally effective, more narrowly tailored measure. Reducing violent crime and saving lives are undoubtedly compelling governmental interests, but Mississippi's measure does not become one iota more constitutional. The reason is that we deal here with a paradigm case of unconstitutionality, which no cost-benefit calculus can rationalize away.

To say that black codes are categorically unconstitutional is to rule out the justificatory cost-benefit strict scrutiny embraced in *Adarand*. It is to say: these laws are unconstitutional *even if* they would make the nation as a whole richer, happier, or better off in relation to some putative state interest, including a "compelling" one. The foundational paradigm cases cannot be viewed as instances in which there were no governmental interests arguably outweighing the liberties at stake. On the contrary, in their own time and place, all the practices that America committed itself never again to tolerate—certainly the black codes, and even slavery itself—could have been defended, indeed were defended, as necessitated by the most compelling of governmental interests. If there was ever a time when black codes could have been claimed to be necessitated by compelling state interests, it was the period directly after emancipation.

Many readers will wonder about this conclusion. Isn't it easy, after all, to imagine cases in which constitutional rights must yield in the face of legitimate countervailing interests? Surely we all know that constitutional law can never be absolute. Even racial segregation is justifiable if one constructs a hypothetical the right way: for example, couldn't prison authorities constitutionally segregate inmates by race, just for a few days perhaps, if such segregation were the only way to avoid a race riot? Isn't this precisely the sort of case in which strict scrutiny would serve very well to distinguish constitutional from unconstitutional governmental behavior?

The answer is yes: a prison could be temporarily racially segregated to avoid a riot, and such a case is perfectly suited for strict scrutiny. But this hypothetical would still not support the propriety of the justificatory balancing test described by Justice O'Connor in *Adarand.* Strict scrutiny *is* appropriate in the prison segregation case, and it *does* provide a ground for upholding such segregation, but only if we understand strict scrutiny very differently than did the Court in *Adarand.*

Here is how the *Adarand* cost-benefit version of strict scrutiny would analyze the prison segregation case. Segregation inflicts a clear constitutional "injury" on the inmates, because "whenever the government treats any person unequally on the basis of his or her race," the government "squarely" violates "the language and spirit of the Constitution's equal protection guarantee." On the other hand, avoiding a riot is a "compelling" governmental interest. If the only way to avoid such a riot is to segregate by race, then the infliction of a constitutional injury—in other words, the violation of the otherwise applicable equal protection principle—will presumably be "justified."

This is the line of reasoning, so natural, so seemingly sensible, that the paradigm case method condemns. Why? Because, by a parity of reasoning, the Court should also be prepared in principle to uphold slavery if a state could "justify" its action by showing that slavery would save lives. No American court should be open to such an argument. Abolishing slavery, it may be worth recalling, did cost lives, hundreds of thousands of lives.

Those who feel the pull of cost-benefit balancing in constitutional law will not want to accept this conclusion. They will say that even the judgment that abolishing slavery was worth a war is itself a cost-benefit calculation. The paradigm cases, they will say, do not rule out cost-benefit analysis. They are simply cases where very great costs were deemed to be worthwhile. Imagine, therefore, a much more "trivial" infringement of equal protection: a law requiring blacks to shine white people's shoes.

Stipulate that the purpose of this law is to inflict on blacks an inferiorized lower-caste status. The law is unconstitutional *period.* If the state's lawyers come to court with data showing that treating blacks this way will in fact reduce violent crime and hence save lives, their showing is out of order, their data wholly irrelevant. The Fourteenth Amendment does not permit racial subjection in American society, regardless of whether society would be more peaceful as a result. That is the Fourteenth Amendment's core meaning, as I have said, when the paradigmatic abolition of the black codes is seen to exemplify a commitment against caste.

But how then can prison segregation ever be constitutional, and how can strict scrutiny be an appropriate test for determining whether such segregation is constitutional?

Here we arrive at the second way to understand strict scrutiny. Suppose the question the judge is trying to answer is whether the prison authorities' segregation order *had the purpose* of treating black inmates to an inferior legal status. Why is the judge asking this question? Because the judge, reflecting on the black codes and *Brown,* understands the equal protection clause to stand against every deliberate governmental effort to treat blacks as untouchable or otherwise to subject them to an inferior status. If invidious purpose is central to a finding of unconstitutional racial discrimination, then strict scrutiny makes considerable sense.

When, as in the shoe-shining example mentioned a moment ago, we stipulate that state action *has the purpose* of embodying in law the degraded or untouchable status of colored people, strict scrutiny will not be called for. The law is unconstitutional, period. That is why *Brown* could strike down "separate-but-equal" without any application of strict scrutiny: as the Court would later say of racial miscegenation laws, separate-but-equal was a measure "designed to maintain White Supremacy,"[10] and it was therefore unconstitutional without any further inquiry. But where a judge confronts a racial classification whose purpose is controverted, a judge trying to determine purpose will find strict scrutiny very useful.

Any time prison authorities in this country treat prisoners differently on the basis of race, there is powerful cause to suspect the operation of an invidious discriminatory purpose. Strict scrutiny is the appropriate test for judges to employ if the state is to be given an opportunity to dispel this suspicion. Where a prison segregation order is genuinely narrowly tailored to achieve a compelling interest such as avoiding a riot, the segregation order should be upheld, because the suspected invidious purpose has been negatived. By contrast, if the segregation order required black inmates to live in worse conditions, or (say) to shine white inmates' shoes, or to be segregated from whites when there is no plausible reason to fear violence, then a judge should reject the state's claim that the segregation order was adopted without prejudice. This is just what strict scrutiny calls for.

On this view, strict scrutiny does not serve as a cost-benefit justificatory test. It serves as a test to smoke out invidious purposes masquerading behind

10. Loving v. Virginia, 388 U.S. 1, 11 (1967).

claims of legitimate state interests. This smoking-out view of strict scrutiny is well known to equal protection jurisprudence. Almost twenty years ago, John Hart Ely described the function of strict scrutiny as one of "flushing out" impermissible state motivations.[11] Judges too have described strict scrutiny in similar terms. Contrast the *Adarand* formulation quoted above to the following passage from a 1983 opinion on affirmative action, an opinion that also happens to have been written by Justice O'Connor:

> Absent searching judicial inquiry into the justification for such race-based measures, there is simply no way of determining what classifications are "benign" or "remedial" and what classifications *are in fact motivated by illegitimate notions of racial inferiority*. . . . [T]he purpose of strict scrutiny is to *"smoke out"* illegitimate uses of race.[12]

This earlier presentation of strict scrutiny is consistent with the paradigm cases. Cost-benefit strict scrutiny is not. Cost-benefit strict scrutiny is concerned with *conceded* violations of a constitutional norm (the question is whether this violation is "outweighed" or "justified" by countervailing benefits). Smoking strict scrutiny is concerned with *concealed* violations. On the cost-benefit view, strict scrutiny applies after it is conceded that government has squarely violated the language and spirit of the equal protection guarantee. On the smoking-out view, the question to be decided is whether the state has violated the language and spirit of the equal protection guarantee.

As a result, in smoking strict scrutiny, there is never any call for balancing. If the court determines that government acted with an impermissible racist purpose, the government has acted unconstitutionally, and its measure cannot be saved by a justificatory balancing of interests. If the court determines otherwise, then there is no infliction of a constitutional "injury," and hence once again no occasion for balancing. The difference is critical, as we will see in a moment, when we return to affirmative action. First, however, a few more general observations need to be made about what "purpose" means and about the place of purpose in equal protection jurisprudence as a whole.

In principle, in appropriate cases, the purpose behind a challenged state action could be revealed by discovering the decisionmaker's actual motivations

11. Ely, *supra* Chapter 3, note 41, at 146 ("[F]unctionally, special scrutiny, in particular its demand for an essentially perfect fit, turns out to be a way of 'flushing out' unconstitutional motivation. . . ."). Ely also uses the case of a temporary prison segregation to make his point. *Id.* at 148.

12. Richmond v. J.A. Croson Co., 488 U.S. 469, 493 (1995) (plurality opinion).

at the time of the challenged action. But *purpose,* as I will use the term, is not identical to *motive.* A law with an invidious purpose may not have been enacted with invidious motives. This means three things.

First, a law can purposefully violate certain persons' constitutional rights even though the legislators sincerely believed that they were acting to *help* these persons. A law barring women from any occupation other than mother and housewife would purposefully consign women to largely menial work and deny them access to higher-status and more powerful occupations. These consequences are in no sense inadvertent or accidental. It is the law's purpose to achieve these consequences. Hence this law would purposefully inflict upon women a legally inferior, subordinate status even if the actual, sincere motivation of the legislators was to protect women and children. Another way to put the same point: a law's "ultimate" or "further" purposes are irrelevant if the law's "immediate" purpose is impermissible.

Second, purposes may be unconscious. A government employer might unconsciously distinguish among equivalently qualified candidates on the basis of their skin color. If asked, "Why (for what purpose) was B denied the job?" this employer would sincerely say that B was rejected because B was less qualified than W, when in fact B was denied the job because he was black. This sort of unconscious discrimination is to be contrasted with a situation in which the employer makes decisions solely on the basis of legitimate hiring criteria, with the unintended consequence that members of one or another racial group happen to fare disproportionately well or ill. The latter case is a case of non-purposive disparate impact: the hiring decisions were made not *because* of, but at most *in spite* of, their racial consequences. By contrast, in the unconscious racism case, hiring decisions are in fact made *because* of skin color. Unconscious discrimination therefore counts as purposive discrimination (as I use the term), even though the actor was not conscious of his purposes, and even if he acted with the "best of intentions."

Finally, the purpose assigned by a judiciary to a law is always ultimately a construct, not reducible to the actual "subjective" states of mind of the legislators. What were the subjective motives of the Louisiana legislators who enacted the separate-but-equal statute upheld in *Plessy*? This was the law of which Justice Harlan famously wrote: "Every one knows that the statute in question had its origin in the purpose, not so much to exclude white persons from railroad cars occupied by blacks, as to exclude colored people from coaches occupied by or assigned to white persons." Justice Harlan also described the statute as "proceed[ing] on the ground that colored citizens are so inferior and degraded that they cannot be allowed to sit in public coaches occupied by white citizens."[13] These are attributions of purpose. Does their validity depend on Justice Harlan's having correctly characterized the states of mind of (the majority of) Louisiana's legislators?

No. We can accept Harlan's observations as valid even though, for all we know, every member of Louisiana's august legislature was paid for his vote, in which case it might plausibly be said that the legislators had acted without any thought about what they were doing. Another way to put the point is to say that a reasonable citizen in 1896 would have understood the statute's purpose exactly as Justice Harlan understood it, regardless of the legislators' actual motivations. In *Plessy,* it would probably not have made any difference whether this fictive "reasonable citizen" was imagined as black or white, but if this line of reasoning were to be formalized, it would be necessary to take much greater care in determining the attributes—geographical as well as racial—of the "reasonable citizen."

Reasonable black citizens today might judge the Confederate flag atop a South Carolina state house as a purposeful celebration of that for which the Confederacy fought, including white supremacy and black enslavement. Reasonable American citizens of any skin color, I imagine, might see it the same way. But if "the reasonable citizen" were (improperly) identified with the average-white-citizen-of-South-Carolina, we could well get a different answer.

Let me stress that the question here is not whether reasonable citizens (black or white) might feel pain or insult on seeing the Confederate flag. That effect is almost certain, and that effect alone should be reason enough for reasonable citizens and legislators of any color to vote to remove the flag. But if the question were solely one of effects, almost every governmental action would be subject to constitutional attack, because almost every such action is felt to be painful or insulting by someone. Welfare laws strike many people as insulting, but it is very difficult to believe that this is the *purpose* behind welfare laws, conscious or unconscious. The point, however, is not only to distinguish between effects and purposes; it is also to see that the correct legal determination of a law's purposes is necessarily a constructed thing, which can in appropriate cases be independent of the legislators' motivations.

As to the place of purpose in equal protection law as a whole, it is important to see that the demand for a purposivist equal protection jurisprudence, a demand rooted solidly in the paradigm cases, is not a call for some sort of doctrinal overhaul. On the contrary, almost everywhere *except* in the affirmative action arena, equal protection law already embraces the proposition

13. Plessy v. Ferguson, 163 U.S. 537, 556–57, 560 (Harlan, J., dissenting).

that an invidious discriminatory purpose must be present before there can be a finding of unconstitutional racial discrimination. The Court has "repeatedly" and expressly affirmed the "principle that an invidious purpose must be adduced to support a claim of unconstitutionality."[14] Thus harm to minorities is not a ground of unconstitutionality under the equal protection clause unless government acted *"because of,"* rather than merely *"in spite of,"* these harms.[15] The Court has referred to the requirement of "invidious purpose" as a "basic equal protection principle."[16]

And this principle cannot be reconciled with current affirmative action doctrine. It turns out, unsurprisingly, that the *Adarand* ruling (according to which all affirmative action measures must be subjected to strict scrutiny) depends on the cost-benefit, justificatory view of strict scrutiny embraced in that case. If strict scrutiny were returned to the smoking-out function that it is properly (and was formerly) understood to play, *Adarand* would have to be reversed.

To cut to the chase: there are three basic arguments *against* affirmative action that could conceivably claim consistency with the paradigm cases. But none of them is ultimately tenable. I will consider them in turn.

1. *The Harm-to-Minorities Argument.* "Every state action that stigmatizes racial minorities and promotes notions of racial inferiority, violates the equal protection clause. This is the lesson of the black codes and *Brown v. Board of Education.* Affirmative action has these consequences, no matter how 'benign' the motives behind it might be. Hence affirmative action is unconstitutional—or at least unconstitutional in the absence of exceptional and compelling justification in a particular case."

Affirmative action unquestionably stigmatizes. That is why institutions that practice it do not publicly identify the affirmative action hire or admittee. Moreover, affirmative action unquestionably promotes notions of racial inferiority in the minds of some who are inclined to embrace such notions. Supporters of affirmative action do not help their cause when they deny or minimize these harms, which may in some contexts be very substantial.

These harms to minorities have repeatedly served in the justices' opinions as the principal basis for strictly scrutinizing affirmative action programs. Thus strict scrutiny has been said to be necessary to assure that the racial classifications in affirmative action plans do not "foster harmful and divisive

14. Mobile v. Bolden, 446 U.S. 55, 63 n.10 (1980).

15. Personnel Adm'r v. Feeney, 442 U.S. 256, 279 (1979).

16. Washington v. Davis, 426 U.S. 229, 240 (1976).

stereotypes without a compelling justification."[17] Time and again, the justices have rested the need for strict scrutiny of affirmative action on the ground that the "unintended consequences" of minority preferences "can be as poisonous and pernicious as any other form of discrimination."[18]

But "unintended consequences" are precisely not *purposeful.* Accordingly, strict scrutiny of racial classifications cannot be predicated upon them. To be sure, in cost-benefit thinking, it makes perfect sense to demand strict justificatory scrutiny of affirmative action because of its *inadvertent* promotion of stereotypes of racial inferiority. But as we have seen, the equal protection guarantee, interpreted in light of its paradigm cases, does not admit this kind of cost-benefit analysis. Once strict scrutiny is restored to its smoking-out function, which alone is consistent with the foundational paradigm cases, strict scrutiny of affirmative action programs is not allowable on the ground that they inadvertently "foster harmful and divisive stereotypes."

But couldn't opponents of affirmative action deny this view? Couldn't they argue for a principle that bars all state practices that *have the effect* of stigmatizing or of promoting racist thinking, regardless of whether these effects are purposeful?

The answer is no. This *effects-test* principle is foreclosed to opponents of affirmative action. For two reasons. First, consider that standardized tests also stigmatize. That is why universities do not disclose their results. More crucially, standardized tests have the effect of stigmatizing *racially.* That is, they promote notions of racial inferiority in the minds of those inclined to embrace such notions. Indeed standardized tests have probably done more to promote notions of racial inferiority in this country than affirmative action could ever do.

But affirmative action's opponents never oppose standardized tests. On the contrary, affirmative action's opponents invariably champion standardized testing as an appropriate, non-discriminatory selection procedure with which affirmative action interferes. Hence opponents of affirmative action cannot lay claim to the effects-test principle. The reason is that they do not believe in this principle. They would be the last to say that the Constitution

17. Bush v. Vera, 517 U.S. 952, 984 (1996) (plurality opinion). For other examples, see *Adarand,* 515 U.S. 200 at 229 (quoting Fullilove v. Klutznick, 448 U.S. 448, 545 [1980] [Stevens, J., dissenting]); *Croson,* 488 U.S. at 493 (plurality opinion).

18. *Adarand,* 515 U.S. 200, 241 (Thomas, J., concurring) ("[R]acial paternalism and its unintended consequences can be as poisonous and pernicious as any other form of discrimination. So-called 'benign' discrimination teaches many that because of chronic and apparently immutable handicaps, minorities cannot compete with them without their patronizing indulgence.").

should void (or should subject to strict scrutiny) every governmental measure that inadvertently causes harm to minorities.

But perhaps someone genuinely dedicated to the effects-test principle will say that standardized tests are indeed unconstitutional. Many friends of minority interests have suggested an effects-test or disparate-impact principle for equal protection law that would call into question the constitutionality of all governmental measures, including the use of standardized tests, that adversely affect minorities. But consider: welfare laws throughout this country also stigmatize, and they have also tended to promote invidious racial stereotypes. Would proponents of minority interests want to see welfare invalidated as well?

Neither the supporters of affirmative action nor its opponents would actually want to see a pure effects-test imported into equal protection law. What they probably imagine is that, with respect to legislation they disfavor, the bad effects would always be seen to outweigh any benefits gained. That is always how it is with balancing tests: they are appealing to everyone, because everyone imagines that the interests of most concern to him are more important than the competing interests. Balancing tests justify everything, which is to say they justify nothing.

The Fourteenth Amendment's paradigm cases have nothing to do with governmental measures inflicting *inadvertent* harm upon minorities. The black codes were instances of deliberate racial inferiorization, of a purposeful effort to inflict a second-class status or citizenship on a racial minority. And so was the apartheid regime struck down in *Brown* and subsequent cases. To be sure, if state action has disparate adverse effects on a racial minority, these effects can be evidence of an invidious purpose. But inadvertent racial consequences, without more, are not a ground of unconstitutionality. Not every bad law is unconstitutional. The harms that affirmative action may do to its intended beneficiaries are significant factors to be taken into account by anyone considering whether to support an affirmative action plan at any given institution. I myself oppose affirmative action in many contexts because of these harms. But this is a policy question, not a constitutional question. The fact that state action has adverse consequences for a given racial minority does not make the state action unconstitutional unless the action was undertaken *because of* those consequences.

As noted above, this point is firmly established throughout equal protection law. For example, zoning laws or laws requiring standardized tests in employee or student selection procedures cannot be constitutionally challenged on the basis of their disparate, harmful effects on racial minorities, unless it can be shown that these laws were adopted in order to produce such effects. This "basic equal protection principle"[19] cannot be reconciled with striking down affirmative action (or subjecting it to cost-benefit strict scrutiny) on the basis of its "unintended consequences."

Opponents of affirmative action will almost certainly respond to this reasoning with incredulity. "You're missing the whole point," they may say. "Affirmative action explicitly classifies on the basis of race or color. Standardized tests do not. Welfare does not. Government must be color-blind. So long as state action is color-blind, it is perfectly constitutional unless it was actually adopted for non-color-blind purposes. But affirmative action is not color-blind. No further inquiry into its purposes is necessary."

Remember: the only argument we are considering at this point is the harm-to-minorities argument. According to this argument, affirmative action is unconstitutional or at least deserving of strict scrutiny because it has the effect, even though inadvertent, of stigmatizing racial minorities and of promoting notions of racial inferiority. This argument does not sustain a categorical color-blindness position.

The harm-to-minorities argument makes inadvertent racial consequences the issue, and as the example of standardized tests shows, color-blindness is no safeguard against such consequences. Color-blind measures can be just as racially stigmatizing; they can promote notions of racial inferiority just as much as color-conscious measures can. If inadvertent racial harms trigger strict scrutiny, then equal protection law should *not* adopt a blunderbuss rule to the effect that all racial classifications are subject to strict scrutiny. Non-race-based state action (such as the use of standardized tests) should be equally subject to strict scrutiny where it demonstrably causes equally great if not greater racial stereotyping. Defended in terms of inadvertent harm to minorities, a rule that all racial classifications are subjected to strict scrutiny is not narrowly tailored; it is at once substantially overbroad and underbroad. In other words, current strict scrutiny doctrine, so defended, cannot survive strict scrutiny. It might be the first example in the nation's history of a constitutional doctrine unconstitutional under itself.

It is, in fact, quite astonishing for affirmative action to be singled out as the one context in which inadvertent harm to minorities is treated as a ground of unconstitutionality (or as a trigger of "strict scrutiny"). In case after case, where disparate but inadvertent racial harms work *against* minorities, these harms have been treated as constitutionally unproblematic. But when

19. Washington v. Davis, 426 U.S. 229, 240 (1976).

the law finally began to treat minorities with special *favor,* inadvertent racial harms became a ground of unconstitutionality.

Affirmative action cannot be deemed unconstitutional on the basis of its *unintended* harms to minorities without a fundamental overhaul of what is meant by an equal protection violation. If inadvertent harm to minorities were really the test of unconstitutionality, not only standardized tests but half the criminal law and a great deal more would become unconstitutional or at least subject to strict scrutiny. Needless to say, this is an overhaul of equal protection doctrine that the opponents of affirmative action would be the last to accept. More important, this overhaul is not warranted by the paradigm cases. The abolition of slavery and the black codes should not be read as prohibiting *inadvertent* promotion of racial strife or racial stereotypes. Indeed they cannot be so read. For this was a consequence that the Thirteenth and Fourteenth Amendments may *themselves* have had.

If the claim were that the true purpose behind a particular affirmative action plan was to harm or to stigmatize minorities, the situation would be different. But this sort of claim is almost never made. Whether affirmative action is successful in helping blacks and other minorities is an open question. But because affirmative action's harms to minorities are conceded to be inadvertent, the harm-to-minorities argument fails.[20]

2. *Color-Blindness.* "Any governmental measure classifying persons on the basis of the color of their skin is unconstitutional. This is the great lesson of the black codes and of *Brown.* No matter how benign may be the purposes behind affirmative action, racial preferences must be held unconstitutional because they are not color-blind."

Here the opponents of affirmative action begin to draw more strength from the Fourteenth Amendment's paradigm cases, so many of which involve racial or color-based classifications. But the color-blindness principle, while consistent with the paradigm cases, does not satisfactorily capture these cases. It does not do them justice.

20. This is not to justify paternalist statutes that "help" a class of persons by denying them the right to make certain decisions for themselves. Paternalist legislation—for example, preventing women from practicing law on the ground that they will be better off in the home—can well be unconstitutional. But the definitive feature of paternalist legislation is that it takes away from the "helped" persons a right or privilege they would otherwise have possessed and, typically, that others continue to possess. Standard affirmative action programs are not and need not be paternalist. So long as an affirmative action plan permits persons to decline, if they wish, to identify themselves as a member of a beneficiary class, there is no paternalism.

A simple illustration: consider an employer whose workers are exposed to some degree of potentially harmful radiation. Say that this radiation is more harmful to those with darker skin color. We could specify that this employer is a public agency, so that constitutional norms apply as such, but it hardly matters for purposes of this illustration. The employer adopts a policy requiring its employees to wear protective gear. Because the potential harmfulness of the radiation differs according to skin color, the policy differentiates among employees based on their skin color. Is it plausible to see in this policy a perpetration of the evil represented by the black codes?

Perhaps a proponent of color-blindness will answer that the employer's policy is not comparable to the black codes (or to affirmative action) because the policy is *rational.* Skin color here happens to be rationally related to a perfectly legitimate interest that the employer is trying to pursue: protecting workers' health. Thus the radiation policy is not discriminatory, but the same cannot be said for the black codes and affirmative action.

This is the rational-basis answer. It suggests that distinguishing among persons on the basis of their skin color is wrong if but only if there is no rational basis for doing so. The notion is that in most cases, there will be no rational basis for making skin-color distinctions. The radiation case is then presented as the exception that "proves the rule": an unusual situation where skin color happens to present a rational basis for treating people differently.

There are two reasons why this rational-basis answer is unavailing. First, skin color may well be rationally related to any number of legitimate goals that a university or an employer is trying to pursue through affirmative action. There is no rule of law—certainly no constitutional rule—according to which the only legitimate interest a university or employer can pursue is that of selecting and educating the best performing students or the highest scoring job applicants.

The second reason is still more important. The rational-basis answer surrenders the paradigm cases. There is no difficulty formulating legitimate educational interests to which maintaining segregated schools in the 1950s would have been rationally related. In fact it seems quite plausible that desegregation made some students' educational experiences not only difficult but even traumatic. The black codes themselves could have been defended in large part as rationally related to a number of legitimate state interests, such as increasing the happiness of the greatest number, maintaining peace in the aftermath of the Civil War, or ensuring that blacks were not harmed by a too-sudden influx of freedom.

Perhaps it will be said, however, that the employer's radiation policy is not merely rational. The radiation policy (it might be said) is narrowly tailored to achieve the compelling interest of protecting workers from the carcinogenic effects of radiation. By contrast, affirmative action and the black codes are not narrowly tailored in this fashion.

This is the strict scrutiny answer. If strict scrutiny were rigorously applied here, the hypothesized radiation policy would presumably be impermissible. Like almost all workplace safety regulations, it would presumably be significantly overbroad, underbroad, or arbitrary at the margins. But strict scrutiny should *not* be applied to the radiation policy unless there is strong reason to believe that the policy is a mask for something more invidious. Otherwise, strict scrutiny could be advocated here only by resurrecting the cost-benefit justificatory version of that test that we have already rejected. If we stipulate that there is no invidious racial purpose whatsoever behind the radiation policy, then there is no place for strict scrutiny. So long as we stipulate that there is no invidious racial purpose behind the policy, the skin-color distinction in this hypothetical strikes us as innocuous because it *is* innocuous. Even though it differentiates among persons on the basis of a biological characteristic with which they were born, it does not violate any serious norm, just as a policy requiring certain persons to wear glasses when driving does not violate any serious norm.

Which is only to say: color-blindness as such is not a plausible equal protection principle. It is not plausible to claim that there is a great evil in a mere color classification as such. It is not plausible to interpret the evil of the black codes in such terms. Everything depends on what is done with or through the color classification, and for what purpose it is done. What the black codes *did to blacks* was evil. The color classification as such, in the abstract, was not. Otherwise one is obliged to say that apartheid perpetrates the very same evil against whites as it does against blacks, a position that is logically coherent, but that is also *blind*—not only to color, but to the distinctive injury and injustice that apartheid regimes inflict.

The appeal today of color-blindness as a constitutionally mandated bright-line rule is so widespread that this critical point will seem simplistic or tendentious. But the reasoning is quite straightforward. The same reasoning would be instantly recognized as valid virtually everywhere in equal protection law other than the superheated zone of affirmative action.

Imagine that California passed a War on Poverty Initiative, which provided that poor persons (defined by some measure of personal and familial income) could no longer attend university, practice law or medicine, or enter fancy restaurants except as employees. We would all, presumably, instantly regard such a law as an instance of invidious discrimination. But just as obviously, we do not on this basis generate a rule of *wealth-blindness* that would apply to laws *favoring* the poor. California's War on Poverty does not demonstrate that government may never properly classify on the basis of wealth (or may never do so unless its measure can satisfy strict scrutiny). Welfare laws all over the country routinely classify on the basis of wealth, and such laws are held neither to violate the equal protection clause nor to trigger strict constitutional scrutiny. The evil of the War on Poverty does not lie in its classification. It lies in the way that classification is being used.

What is the difference between our actual poor laws and the hypothetical War on Poverty Initiative? Just this: welfare classifies on the basis of wealth *in order to give the poor benefits denied to the better-off,* whereas the War on Poverty Initiative classifies on the basis of wealth *in order to deny the poor rights enjoyed by the better-off.* In other words, the classification as such is not remotely determinative of whether a law perpetrates invidious discrimination. Everything depends on what is being done, to whom, and for what purpose.

All over our legal system, groups are permitted to be singled out for *benefits* (think of veterans' benefits or the special compensations afforded to the handicapped), when laws singling out the same group for *unfavorable treatment* would be automatically and properly subjected to rigorous constitutional scrutiny. From abusive instances of discrimination *against* certain classes of persons, it is the height of illogic to extrapolate a general principle of mandatory *group-blindness,* so that laws helping that class become categorically impermissible too. Isn't it just a little strange that of all groups who have been the subject of discrimination, racial minorities should be singled out as the one sort of group who may not be singled out for benefits?

But it will be said that race is different. Even if group-blindness is not the rule for most other classifications, it will be said, group-blindness must be the rule with race. Classifications on the basis of wealth, veterans' status, disability, and so on, are not themselves invidious. They are invidious only when used in an invidious fashion. By contrast, it will be said, the mere decision to treat persons differently on the basis of skin color is inherently invidious and illegitimate.

The thought may be appealing, but its logic doesn't hold. That is the lesson of the radiation policy discussed a moment ago. If an employer treats its employees differently on the basis of skin color, we cannot know whether this is invidious without knowing what the policy is and what the relevant circumstances are. A doctor who subjects members of one racial group to different diagnostic exams may be acting invidiously, or he may be acting with eminent good sense. Treating persons differently on the basis of race or skin color simply isn't "inherently invidious," whatever that might mean.

In this light, we can specify how color-blindness fails to do justice to the paradigm cases. The color-blind proposition comes down to this: farmers, veterans, the poor, the handicapped, huge corporations—all these minority groups may be singled out for special governmental benefits, but *racial* minorities may not be. Color-blindness always presents itself in the name of consistency, but in actuality color-blindness asks us to make an exception. In the case of *racial* minorities, there is to be an exception to the otherwise almost universal rule that minorities can be constitutionally singled out to receive special governmental benefits.

Which is to say: racial minorities are unequal to other minorities under current law. Under the name of the equal protection of the laws, racial minorities are denied the *equal protection of the laws.* This is the actual position of current equal protection doctrine.

Blacks, for example, do not enjoy the same equal protection that, for example, veterans and the handicapped enjoy. While all three groups are protected to some degree against discrimination against them, veterans and the handicapped may also constitutionally be singled out for special legislative benefits, in the form of job preferences, accommodations, and so on. Blacks may not.

Something has gone profoundly wrong in constitutional interpretation when the Fourteenth Amendment is read, as it is today, to make racial minorities virtually the only minorities in our entire legal system that cannot be singled out for favorable treatment. To call this result a disgrace may be too strong. But such an interpretation fails profoundly to do justice to the paradigm cases, every one of which involves ensuring that blacks receive as much legal protection as others do.

3. *The Harm-to-Whites Argument.* "Forget categorical color-blindness. Forget unintended harms to minorities. Affirmative action deliberately inflicts harms on white persons because of their race. To penalize any individual because of his race precisely recapitulates the evil of the black codes. That is why affirmative action is properly held unconstitutional under the equal protection clause."

Ultimately, the harm-to-whites argument is the simplest and the strongest constitutional argument against affirmative action. Affirmative action plans do not treat whites equally. They are not fair to the individual whites who lose out on a coveted position because of a racial preference. Doesn't affirmative action therefore deny whites the equal protection of the laws?

If so, we are going to have to rethink all the measures described a moment ago that single out other minority groups for benefits. Does it violate my equal protection rights when poor persons or farmers are granted governmental benefits, but I am not? When prestigious universities grant a special admissions preference to the children of alumni, do the rest of us (as potential applicants or parents of applicants) conclude that these universities are discriminating against us? Giving benefits to one group does not necessarily imply, normatively or logically, invidious discrimination against others.

To be sure, race has a special, central status in equal protection jurisprudence in a way that wealth and alumni-lineage does not. So it is always possible in theory for someone to say the Fourteenth Amendment must be read to single out race in this special way, categorically forbidding governments to engage in racial classifications.

But if we do not want to rationalize, if we want to let go of all the hypocrisy that runs through the affirmative action debate, we will say this: the special, central status of race in our constitutional history lay in its use as a marker of caste. As we have seen, a color-blind principle—singling out racial minorities as virtually the only minorities in the entire legal system who cannot be singled out to receive governmental benefits—does not do justice to the paradigm cases. Only the anti-caste principle does.

And if so, then it is hard to see affirmative action as violating the Fourteenth Amendment. If there is a colorable case to be made that affirmative action in America has treated whites as an inferior caste or has deliberately subjected them to a lower-class social status, I have not heard it. If there is a colorable case to be made that selecting one justice of the Supreme Court in part on the basis of his black skin subjects whites in this country to a second-class citizenship, I have not heard it. Justices of the Supreme Court have notoriously been selected in part on the basis of their geographical origins, their ethnic affiliations, their religion, and so on. Do we conclude in such circumstances that the rest of us are being treated as inferior orders of being?

Why was it that Congress in 1867, even while promulgating the Fourteenth Amendment, could allocate special welfare benefits to the "destitute colored" population of the District of Columbia? This congressional action, without dredging up originalist rhetoric or logic, can still remind us, if we need reminding, that helping a long-suffering minority just doesn't belong in the same sentence with the vicious discriminations instantiated by the black codes. It is not the kind of invidious discrimination that we enacted the Fourteenth Amendment to prohibit.

Settled or unsettled, the debate over affirmative action is today less burning than boring. Perhaps this is as it should be. The real denial of equal protection in this nation occurs outside the narrow confines in which affirmative action is debated. When a class of persons is too pervasively and too disproportionately unprotected from criminality—from murder, child abuse, assault, the drug trade, and on and on—there comes a point when the nation's commitment to equal protection has been dishonored.

The criminalization of a third or more of the young men of a particular race in this country is no accident. It is another of this nation's inheritances. Individual responsibility for criminal conduct, which I do not at all mean to question, is not the issue here. The issue is this: no one can fail to see that we are failing to give a large number of our citizens the equal protection of the laws. We are failing to protect them from the kind of rampant criminality that would draw many of us, if we were in the same place, into its devices.

Assuming that there is no racial purpose behind this lack of protection, then the latter is not an instance of racial discrimination. But the controversy over affirmative action should not cause us to forget that there is more to the equal protection of the laws, and more to the Fourteenth Amendment, than discrimination. A certain minimum of legal protection in the most literal sense, a certain degree of protection from criminality (where such protection is possible), is a necessary condition of being a free citizen. If and when the Supreme Court acts on this recognition, it will have to order remedies sure to prompt an outcry. The charge will be that the Court is engaging in judicial activism and acting contrary to the original intentions. This charge will be correct.

Twelve

THE RIGHT OF PRIVACY

The last two chapters dealt with interpreting a written constitution. A different question concerns *unwritten* constitutional rights. Such rights are well established in American law. The most prominent example is the subject of this chapter: the "right of privacy."

Roe v. Wade[1] is the most famous of privacy cases, but the reach of this unwritten right is not limited to abortion. American courts also consider the right of privacy to protect, among other things, contraception,[2] marriage,[3] interracial marriage,[4] divorce,[5] the refusal of life-sustaining medical treatment,[6] and the right to send a child to private school.[7] But there is no accepted constitutional definition of privacy, nor even an authoritative articulation of the principle for which these cases stand. This is hardly surprising, given the notorious porousness of the public-private boundary and the embarrassments suffered by virtually every effort to police this boundary. Privacy in American constitutional law is perpetually in search of an explanation of itself.

Nevertheless, a certain aspiration is evident often enough in the privacy cases and the surrounding literature. The right of privacy seeks to name a space in which individuals would be free from law. For consenting adults, nothing would be required or forbidden in this space, this domain of "private

1. 410 U.S. 113 (1973).
2. *See* Griswold v. Connecticut, 381 U.S. 479 (1965).
3. *See* Zablocki v. Redhail, 434 U.S. 374 (1978).
4. *See* Loving v. Virginia, 388 U.S. 1 (1967).
5. *See* Boddie v. Connecticut, 401 U.S. 371 (1971).
6. *See, e.g.,* In re Guardianship of Estelle M. Browning, 568 So. 2d 4, 11 (Fla. 1990); *cf.* Cruzan v. Director, Missouri Dep't of Health, 457 U.S. 261, 279 (1990).
7. *See* Pierce v. Society of Sisters, 268 U.S. 510 (1925). *Pierce* was decided well before the contemporary "right of privacy" had been articulated, but the case is now authoritatively regarded as a privacy decision. *See, e.g., Roe,* 410 U.S. at 152.

life," which ideally the state could not police or penetrate at all. On this picture, the right to privacy is, as Brandeis put it, the right to be let alone. What does constitutionalism as democracy—constitutionalism on the model of writing—have to say about this unwritten right of privacy?

To recognize privacy's unwrittenness is to acknowledge, as *Roe*'s critics have always said, that the right of privacy neither appears in the Constitution nor is plausibly derived from an interpretation of any of the rights that are enumerated in the text. (I refer here only to the right of privacy at issue in such cases as *Roe v. Wade,* and not, for example, to the protection against unreasonable searches or seizures expressly guaranteed by the Fourth Amendment.) All the belated efforts to find a "textual home" for *Roe,* for example in the due process clauses or in the religion clauses,[8] do nothing to change this. On the contrary, they merely reemphasize the embarrassing sense of artifice, of post-hoc rationalization, that has accompanied the right of privacy since the Supreme Court first discerned it in the "penumbras" and "emanations" of the Bill of Rights.[9]

Just to be clear: to acknowledge privacy's unwrittenness is not to agree with those who say that the right of privacy lacks a defensible basis in the constitutional text. Those who condemn *Roe* on this ground run together two very different claims: first, that the right of privacy is unenumerated; second, that there is no defensible basis in the Constitution's text for the existence of unenumerated constitutional rights. The first claim is correct; the second is not. The Bill of Rights and other amendments contain more than one provision perfectly plausibly read to establish that the enumeration in the Constitution of certain rights should *not* be construed to deny the existence of others. For example, the Ninth Amendment: "The enumeration in the Constitution, of certain rights, shall not be construed to deny or disparage others retained by the people." To be sure, the Ninth Amendment does not compel acknowledgment of unenumerated constitutional rights. One can read its words otherwise. Nevertheless, the Ninth Amendment most definitely negates the claim that unenumerated constitutional rights lack any defensible textual warrant. On the contrary, a court that recognizes the existence of unenumerated constitutional rights acts well within the bounds of defensible, plausible textual authority.

But the Ninth Amendment, even taken for all it is worth, can establish

8. *See Roe,* 410 U.S. at 153 (due process); Ronald Dworkin, Life's Dominion: An Argument About Abortion, Euthanasia, and Individual Freedom 160–68 (1993) (religion).

9. *Griswold,* 381 U.S. at 483–85.

only that the enumerated rights are not exhaustive. As to the actual *content* of any other rights "retained by the people," the Ninth Amendment offers no guidance whatsoever, no proposition to be interpreted. As a result, even though unenumerated rights have a defensible textual basis, every time such a right is posited by a judge (or anyone else), there has to be some extra-textual account of its constitutional status—some extra-textual account of why this particular right counts, even though unwritten, as a constitutional right. And such an account has to answer to all the demands of legitimacy imposed by constitutionalism as democracy when unelected judges render constitutional decisions for the nation.

Some accounts of unwritten constitutional rights cannot satisfy these demands. For example, "natural law" accounts of unwritten constitutional rights, although they might claim support in the original understanding of the Bill of Rights, cannot satisfy the essential tenets of constitutionalism as democracy. Not only is originalism rejected by constitutionalism as democracy, but so too is the whole idea that a democratic polity is constitutionally bound by any "natural," pre-political, or otherwise *immemorial* law. The only constitutional law binding on a democracy that seeks to be the author of its own fundamental legal and political commitments is law that derives from the nation's own acts of *memorialization*.

How then can there be any unenumerated constitutional law in constitutionalism as democracy? The answer is that there can be very little. Constitutionalism as democracy is very broadly opposed to judge-made "fundamental rights" not derivable from any of the nation's written constitutional commitments. Little room for extra-textual constitutional law exists on the model of writing.

But not no room. There are, at the extreme limits of what a democratic government might try to do with or to its citizens, certain *unwritten laws of written constitutionalism,* and a right of privacy is among them. But the principle of inviolable individual liberty for which this right of privacy stands cannot be grasped by the classical liberal formulations—not, for example, by John Stuart Mill's principle of self-regarding acts, nor by any principle of individual autonomy, nor by a principle of reasoned neutrality among competing conceptions of the good. Explaining these conclusions, together with the right of privacy that results when the right to be let alone is severed from the classical liberal framework, is the burden of this final chapter.

Abortion furnishes a good starting point, in part because *Roe v. Wade* is the most famous of privacy cases. But *Roe* is by no means a foundational paradigm case. It has no foundational authority, and no serious inquiry into the right of privacy can simply take *Roe* as given. Even so, without presupposing *Roe*'s givenness, abortion still provides the most useful context in which to begin setting out the main points I want to make.

What was said about *Brown v. Board of Education* at the beginning of Chapter Ten applies doubly to *Roe:* there is an astonishing absence, both in the doctrine and the scholarship, of anything like a satisfactory account of this famous constitutional decision. Why does a woman have a constitutional right to abort a pregnancy? There is no well-accepted answer. Sometimes abortion is said to be fundamental because it implicates the right to "control one's own body"; or because it involves a "personal," "family" decision with which the state has no business interfering; or because reproduction is central to a person's "self-definition." But these explanations are completely unsatisfactory.

A vast number of laws impinge on my "right" to control my own body. Robbery laws prevent me from using my body to steal; narcotics laws regulate what I can put into my body. Similarly, "personal" or "family" matters are routinely subjected to state regulation. Wife-beating is illegal; so is marrying more than one person. And if there were really a general right of "self-definition," nearly every law would be constitutionally suspect.

For a long time, many supposed that the best philosophical explanation of the "right to be let alone" must be that it protects any action that does no harm to others. The enormous weaknesses of a harm principle, however, are an old story. On the one hand, so-called harmless conduct nearly always imposes some costs on some others; on the other, many laws that are central to contemporary Western legal systems would violate the harm principle, at least in its conventional formulations. To give just one example, there is a serious disjuncture between the venerable harm principle and *anti-discrimination* laws. From the libertarian perspective that underlies the harm principle, I do not "harm" someone merely by refusing to hire him or sell him my property. Accordingly, my refusal to deal with a person because of his skin color should inflict no legally cognizable "harm" on him. I will say no more at present about the well-worn harm principle. The great text that most famously argues for that principle—Mill's *On Liberty*—will be discussed below.

Instead, I want to suggest a wholly different way of looking at *Roe v. Wade,* a way of looking at the right of privacy that not only avoids all the difficulties noted in the last two paragraphs, but also captures the extraordinary nature of anti-abortion laws far better than does a principle of bodily control, a harm principle, a principle that the state cannot regulate "personal" and "family" matters, or a principle of self-definition. All these principles share the same methodological approach to privacy problems: they focus on the prohibited conduct (say, abortion) and try to determine whether this prohibited conduct has something special or fundamental about it—its relationship to the body, its personalness, its centrality to self-definition, and so on—that somehow render it beyond the law's legitimate reach.

An eloquent illustration of this way of looking at privacy can be found in the Supreme Court's 1990 *Casey* decision, which reaffirmed *Roe v. Wade:*

> Our law affords constitutional protection to personal decisions relating to marriage, procreation, contraception, family relationships. . . . These matters, involving the most intimate and personal choices a person may make in a lifetime, [are] central to personal dignity and autonomy. . . . At the heart of liberty is the right to define one's own concept of existence, of meaning, of the universe, and of the mystery of human life. Beliefs about these matters could not define the attributes of personhood were they formed under compulsion of the State.[10]

It is child's play to point out the weaknesses in this rhetoric. The state routinely regulates individuals' "personal decisions relating to marriage, procreation, [and] family relationships." The law tells us, for example, how many spouses we can have, what gender of person we can marry, what duties we owe to our spouses and children, even whom we can have sex with. Far from having little or no power to intrude on the "private" sphere of family life, the law constructs what is and is not a permissible family. Moreover, the most basic of all laws, the law against homicide, denies to individuals the freedom to live by whatever "concept of existence," or of "the mystery of life," they choose.

But suppose we looked at anti-abortion laws from a very different perspective. Suppose we shifted our focus from what this law *proscribes* (the act of abortion) to what it *prescribes*. A law forbidding a pregnant woman to have an abortion differs profoundly from virtually every other prohibition in our entire legal system in one specific sense. It not only is proscriptive (banning abortion), but also has the most invasive, far-reaching prescriptive, indeed *conscriptive* effects. It compels this woman to bear a child. It forces motherhood upon her.

It is impossible to name a single prohibitory law in our legal system with greater affirmative, conscriptive, life-occupying effects than those imposed by a law forcing a woman to bear a child against her will. This woman is physically taken over for a purpose dictated to her by the state, and this taking-over can be expected to last not merely nine months but for many years

10. Planned Parenthood v. Casey, 505 U.S. 833, 851 (1992).

thereafter. Her body, her mind, and her *time* will be substantially occupied by the task that the state has forced upon her. She has been instrumentalized, impressed into state-dictated service. It is no exaggeration to say that a law forcing women to be mothers is a totalitarian intrusion into their lives.

From this perspective, *Roe v. Wade* brings into a view what I will call an *anti-totalitarian* right of privacy. The anti-totalitarian right of privacy is not a matter of individual autonomy in the familiar sense of that term. The anti-totalitarian right of privacy is simply not implicated, for example, by a law that prohibits polygamy, even though such a law: legislates morality; regulates "personal" or "intimate" behavior; is non-neutral among competing conceptions of the good; criminalizes "victimless" conduct; prevents individuals from pursuing happiness in their own fashion; and forbids conduct deemed by some individuals to be central to their "identity," religious faith, or self-determination. The anti-totalitarian right to privacy is implicated only when a law does much more than prohibit. It is violated only when a law substantially takes over an individual's life: impressing that life into service, directing it along a state-chosen path, dictating the course of a person's future. Anti-polygamy laws do not have this effect. They rule out a liberty, but force no one into a life-script of the state's choosing. By contrast, a law forcing you to marry would violate the right of privacy I am describing. A law prohibiting you from working more than ten hours a day in this or that job does not implicate the anti-totalitarian right; a law forcing you into a particular occupation would.

It might be wondered, however, whether this anti-totalitarian right of privacy genuinely provides a satisfactory account of *Roe v. Wade*. First of all, how can I say that an anti-abortion law forces motherhood on women when, in most cases, a woman could avoid this result either by refraining from sex (unless she is prepared to bear the issue) or, after delivery, by releasing any unwanted children to adoption services? And what of the fetus's right to life?

I will defer these questions for a time. My purpose in discussing abortion to this point has been merely to lay out the basic structure of an anti-totalitarian right of privacy, so that readers would have some sense of what is at stake as they read the ensuing discussion. I will offer an answer to the difficult questions just posed, but it would be pointless to do so now, without having first said a good deal more about the anti-totalitarian principle itself. Where does this principle come from? What is its claim to constitutional status? And why is it preferable to more familiar liberal principles of individual autonomy or governmental neutrality?

Revisiting *On Liberty* will make it possible to answer these questions. Mill's classic work is central to this discussion not only because the values of privacy and individuality are elaborated there with canonical force. It is central because certain powerful contradictions trouble this text, contradictions that, despite the extraordinary fame of Mill's book, are almost always overlooked. These contradictions are not fortuitous. They generalize very broadly across liberal theory as a whole. And they point, when worked through, not to the harm-based principle of individual autonomy for which *On Liberty* is so well known, but rather to a very different principle. They point to the anti-totalitarian right just described.

On Liberty begins with an epigraph taken from von Humboldt: " 'the grand, leading principle, towards which every argument unfolded in these pages directly converges, is the . . . essential importance of human development in its richest diversity.' "[11] Mill will return, as the book progresses, repeatedly to the theme of human diversity.[12] Why?

All of *On Liberty* is haunted by a specter: of social uniformity, of popular standardization. This nightmare is captured for Mill, in a magnificent burst of ethnocentrism, by the country of China. "We have a warning example," he writes, "in China," where "conformity" is the "ideal," where everyone is "alike," and where all have remained "stationary" in this alikeness "for thousands of years." Once such conformity sets in, the members of such a society have no further hope of improvement, unless enlightened foreigners take a hand: "if they are ever to be farther improved, it must be by foreigners."[13]

But instead of improving the East, the West is emulating the East. England is in danger of becoming "another China." Already Englishmen have begun to "resemble one another" to a startling degree. There is a "despotism" afoot in the West rivaling that of the East, a "despotism of Custom," through which the "public" "endeavors to make everyone conform to the approved stan-

11. John Stuart Mill, On Liberty [1859], in On Liberty and Considerations on Representative Government lviii (R.B. McCallum ed., Oxford 1946) (quoting Wilhelm von Humboldt, The Sphere and Duties of Government).

12. For example, Mill praised von Humboldt for being one of the "very few" to have discerned the crucial value of "individual vigour and manifold diversity." *Id.* at 50–51. Mill defended the freedom of speech and thought in terms of the "advantage[s]" of a "diversity of opinion." *Id.* at 40. Europe's imperium is "wholly indebted" to its "remarkable diversity of character and culture." *Id.* at 64. And of "unspeakable importance" is "diversity in education." *Id.* at 95.

13. *Id.* at 64.

dard." European society in general is falling prey to this standardization. Europe as a whole, warns Mill, is "decidedly advancing towards the Chinese ideal of making all people alike."[14]

What is responsible for this Orientalization of the white man's civilization? The threat is coming not from the East, but from within European society itself. The responsible force is nothing other than the enlightened spirit of modern "philanthropy," "liberalism," and "democracy." Yes, all these things are criticized by name in *On Liberty.*

In the first pages of the book, Mill tells a story about "European liberalism," which had always believed that "democracy," when finally achieved, would spell the end of tyranny. "In time," however, "a democratic republic came to occupy a large portion of the earth's surface"—this European narrative turns out to be a story about the United States—as "one of the most powerful" of the world's nations. Democracy became "a great existing fact," and this fact revealed a truth that had remained "concealed" so long as "popular government was a thing only dreamed about."[15]

"It was now perceived that such phrases as 'self-government' and 'the power of the people over themselves' "—Mill puts these terms, as mentioned earlier, in quotation marks—"do not express the true state of the case." The " 'people' " (more quotation marks) is a fiction, and so is the concept of popular " 'self-government.' " "The 'people' who exercise the power" are not the same as the people "over whom it is exercised." And "the 'self-government' spoken of is not the government of each by himself, but of each by all the rest."[16]

With these formulations, Mill articulates a liberalism decisively shorn of "the People," freed from the twines of republicanism with which the American and French Revolutions had interwoven it. Mill here proclaims his dedication to the individualism with which liberal philosophy would come to be identified. Mill will not speak here of *a* people, the genuine collective article, but only of *"the"* people. The English definite article, *the,* is of course ambiguous in number, not differentiating between singular and plural; and "people" is similarly ambiguous, usable both in the singular and plural (either referring to *a* particular people or operating as the plural of "person"). But Mill is not ambiguous: his "the 'people' " is definitely plural; its pronomial object is "them" or "those," its copula "are" (" 'the power of the people over *themselves*' "; "[t]he 'people' who exercise the power *are* not always the same

14. *Id.* at 62–65.
15. *Id.* at 2–3.
16. *Id.* at 3.

people with *those* over whom it is exercised"). There is no such thing, in Mill's introduction to *On Liberty,* as "*a* people." The phrase "*a* people" is a mystification; it would not "express the true state of the case." Individuals exist; they are capable of self-government. "The 'people,' " collectively, are not. There is no popular "self" that could govern itself. There are only persons, some exercising power over others.

As a result, Mill argues, contrary to the hopes of "European liberalism," the so-called power of the people over themselves did not end tyranny. Instead it made possible, for the first time, a new form of tyranny, "the tyranny of the majority."[17] This tyranny is not exercised only by state actors and other "public authorities." That would be a "vulgar" misconception, which would miss the new and real danger that democracy creates. For "when society itself is the tyrant," there comes into being a new form of despotism that goes beyond all "legal penalties." "[W]hen society itself is the tyrant—society collectively, over the separate individuals who compose it—its means of tyrannizing are not restricted to the acts which it may do by the hands of its political functionaries."[18]

This new form of despotism Mill calls "social tyranny." It is the "tyranny of the prevailing opinion and feeling," which is "more formidable than many kinds of political oppression," more formidable than the mere "tyranny of the magistrate."[19] "In our times," writes Mill, "from the highest class . . . down to the lowest, every one lives as under the eye of a hostile and dreaded censorship."[20] This dreaded censorship goes beyond legal sanctions. The hostile, panoptic "eye" of which Mill writes, sounding almost like the Foucault of *Discipline and Punish*—a Foucault who, as we will see, is relevant in more ways than one to the present discussion—this "eye" is concerned not only with what individuals do in public but also with what they do in their own homes, "leav[ing] fewer means of escape, penetrating much more deeply into the details of life, and enslaving the soul itself."[21]

This "despotism of custom" will, if unabated, eventually destroy—indeed it is already destroying—England's "greatness." Social tyranny "maims" individuals. It deforms their "souls." It crushes "Individuality." It seeks, Mill says, drawing on another stock Chinese image, to "maim by compression, like a Chinese lady's foot, every part of human nature which stands out."[22]

17. *Id.* at 4.
18. *Id.* at 4, 8.
19. *Id.* at 4.
20. *Id.* at 54.
21. *Id.* at 4.
22. *Id.* at 62, 66.

Roughly the second half of *On Liberty* consists of Mill's prescription, his antidote to the poison of uniformity. Obviously Mill does not propose anarchy. Where, then, does society's jurisdiction over our conduct end and individual sovereignty properly begin? Mill's famous solution lies in the principle of "self-regarding" acts. The "Individual is sovereign," he writes, over all "conduct which affects himself only":[23]

> As soon as any part of a person's conduct affects prejudicially the interests of others, society has jurisdiction over it. . . . But . . . when a person's conduct affects the interests of no person besides himself, or needs not affect them unless they like . . . there should be a perfect freedom, legal and social, to do the action and stand the consequences.[24]

A "perfect freedom, legal *and social*": this "and social" reemphasizes that Mill is concerned here with more than the "tyranny of the magistrate." "Protection, therefore, against the tyranny of the magistrate is not enough: there needs protection also against the tyranny of the prevailing opinion and feeling." It is to combat such legal *and social* tyranny—to mark "the limit to the legitimate interference of collective opinion with individual independence"—that Mill articulates the principle of self-regarding acts.[25]

Everyone knows the tired arguments surrounding this principle. If I take an action that you find deeply immoral, doesn't my action hurt you—doesn't it cause you the psychic and sometimes physical pain of moral offense? Or suppose I indulge in a dissipating hedonism; might I not leave my children uncared for? Might I not influence others by setting a bad example? Mill himself raises all these obvious objections, but he remains resolute in his answer. For a person's action to fall into society's jurisdiction, it must be "directly" "harmful" or "damaging." There must be "direct harm to others." There must be "definite damage, or a definite risk of damage." Without such direct and definite harm, the consequences are too "minor"—too merely "inconvenient"—to say that others' interests or those of society as a whole have really been "prejudicially affected."[26] On the contrary, the influx of "genius, of mental vigour, and moral courage" that will be found in a society that respects "Individuality" will far outweigh the "minor" indignities that might be caused by "eccentric" self-regarding conduct. "Precisely because the tyranny of opinion is such as to make eccentricity a reproach, it is desirable, in order to break

23. *Id.* at 9, 11. Mill adds, of course: "or, if it also affects others, only with their voluntary, undeceived consent." *Id.* at 11.

24. *Id.* at 67.

25. *Id.* at 4–5.

26. *Id.* at 67–73.

through that tyranny, that people should be eccentric. . . . [T]he amount of eccentricity in a society has generally been proportional to the amount of genius, of mental vigour, and moral courage which it contained. That so few now dare to be eccentric, marks the chief danger of the time."[27]

I do not intend to pursue here the old arguments about liberalism's inability to define a concept of "harm" sufficient to its purposes. Rather I mean simply to hold up next to each other the two halves of *On Liberty*—its diagnosis and its prescription. For when these two halves are brought together, we will find that the entire classical structure of Mill's argument is held together, if it can be said to hold together at all, by three startling internal paradoxes that the old arguments have overlooked.

First paradox: what kind of conduct is involved when the "despotism of custom"—which Mill carefully distinguishes from the tyranny "of the magistrate"—does its work? We know that "social tyranny" is stunting England's greatness and maiming its individuals. But what kind of conduct does this "social tyranny" consist of?

It consists, precisely, of *self-regarding* conduct.

Social tyranny imposes no force, neither of arms nor of law, on anyone. "Social tyranny" involves no "physical force," as "legal penalties" do; it consists solely of "moral coercion."[28] But this means that social tyranny, despite its "coerciveness," does no "direct harm." It does no "definite damage." It censures; it "reproaches." At worst it "shuns."[29] The first half of *On Liberty* is entirely devoted to making us see that *the expression of opinion*—of "public opinion," of "collective opinion," of the "prevailing opinion and feeling"—is inflicting the most grotesque and profound harms not only on society as a whole but also on the individual soul. Yet we are never supposed to see (Mill himself perhaps does not see) that these harms, this "maiming" of society and individuals, disproves the case for individual sovereignty over self-regarding acts. For once again, Mill's central claim in making that case is that the mere expression of an individual's opinions, like other "self-regarding" conduct, does not do harm, or at least that the effects of such conduct are so "minor," so merely "inconvenient," or so on-balance wholesome, that no interference with it can be justified.

Of course, Mill does not call for "social tyrants" to be jailed. He does not fall into so obvious a trap. But the fact that he does not call for legal sanctions

27. *Id.* at 59–60.
28. *Id.* at 8.
29. *Id.* at 54.

against social tyranny only confirms the point just made. Those who impose on us the despotism of custom are themselves engaged in the putatively non-regulable conduct that liberalism is supposed to protect. What is floridly called "social tyranny," what is most threatening to individual autonomy, in fact turns out to be itself an exercise of individual autonomy—by the intolerant. But this means that the argument for a liberty to engage in self-regarding acts is self-exploding, because it depends on the recognition that the conduct it is designed most centrally to protect—the expression of opinion—is not self-regarding at all.

A self-contradiction? Yes, but a logical one. The reason behind it is this: the greatest threat to individuality proves, at bottom, to be individualism. Liberalism—the individualist, Millian liberalism that we admire so much, and that, let me say straight out, I do not for one moment suggest that we merely abandon—is itself the source of the standardization that liberalism fears. Mill makes this point as plain as day, if one attends carefully to what he says.

In what respect, exactly, are Englishmen becoming more and more alike? Listen to Mill's answer:

> Comparatively speaking, they [Englishmen] now read the same things, listen to the same things, see the same things, go to the same places, have their hopes and fears directed to the same objects, have the same rights and liberties, and the same means of asserting them. . . . [T]he desire of rising becomes no longer the character of a particular class, but of all classes.[30]

Second paradox: John Stuart Mill raising an alarm at the prospect of all individuals obtaining the "same rights and liberties, and the same means of asserting them." John Stuart Mill, in *On Liberty,* raising an alarm at the increasing liberty of Englishmen, from all classes, to "read the same things," to "listen to the same things." Now we know what is responsible for "enslaving the soul[s]"[31] of Englishmen: the culprit is the *freedom of speech and press.* What, chiefly, fills the heads of Englishmen with their received, conformist opinions? Mill's answer: "newspapers."[32]

30. *Id.* at 65.

31. *Id.* at 4.

32. "And what is a still greater novelty, the mass do not now take their opinions from dignitaries in Church or State, from ostensible leaders, or from books. Their thinking is done for them by men much like themselves, addressing them or speaking in their name, on the spur of the moment, through the newspapers." *Id.* at 59. Here Mill joins in a line of thought, familiar to English conservatism since the late

The passage block-quoted above must be placed next to others from *On Liberty* to see just how contrary it is to what we have every right and reason to expect from Mill. For example, in Mill's discussion of the "almost despotic power of husbands over wives," the same language of equalizing rights and remedies will reappear, but now in a much more familiar, more favorable, more Mill-like light. "[N]othing more is needed" to cure husbandly abuse, Mill argues, "than that wives should have *the same rights,* and should receive *the protection of law in the same manner,* as all other persons."[33] In other words, just as Derrida's pharmacology would have it,[34] the antidote is the same as the poison: what Mill holds most dear—giving to everyone the same rights and the same means of asserting them—turns out to be that which brings about the standardization he most fears.

At the same time, with England's increasing homogeneity, resulting from its increasing liberalization, *On Liberty* arrives at its third paradox. Listen carefully to Mill's words as he describes the "Chinese ideal" of uniformity that has begun insidiously to take hold of England. The Chinese, Mill writes, "have succeeded beyond all hope in what English philanthropists are so industriously working at—in making a people all alike."[35] To repeat: "making *a people* all alike."

Suddenly it is *a people* of whom Mill speaks: in the singular, and without quotation marks. As *the* people (plural) increasingly "resemble one another," "*a* people" comes closer to reality. *A* people, in the sovereign national singular, springs into being with popular standardization. Which means that popular self-government, which was supposed to be a falsehood—because there was no such thing as *a* "people"—can become a reality after all. *A* people can have *a* will, and this popular will just might be made to govern. This is no grammatical slip or fortuity. The possibility of *a* people coming into being, with *a* will that is made to govern, is precisely the danger that Mill has been warning against all along: the danger of society being ruled by "the will of the public."

> [A]s the very idea of resisting the will of the public . . . disappears more and more from the minds of practical politicians; there ceases to be any

---

eighteenth century, deriding the proliferation of popular newspapers. For a brilliant discussion, see Don Herzog, Poisoning the Minds of the Lower Orders (1998).

33. *Id.* at 94 (emphasis added).

34. *See* Jacques Derrida, *Plato's Pharmacy,* in Dissemination 61 (Barbara Johnson trans., 1981).

35. Mill, *supra* note 11, at 64.

> social support for nonconformity—any substantive power in society which, itself opposed to the ascendancy of numbers, is interested in taking under its protection opinions and tendencies at variance with those of the public."[36]

Such is the threatened outcome when liberal rights—the freedom to read and to listen to what one pleases, the right to have and to act on one's own opinions so long as one does no harm to others—become popular rights, belonging not "to a particular class, but to all classes." From the proliferation of these rights, there comes into being "a people," not only with a "collective opinion" both standardized and standardizing, but also with a "public will," which increasingly governs public and private life.

Third paradox: proclaiming *individuality,* liberalism produces *popularity.* Professing the fictitiousness of peoples, liberal liberty breaks down the ascriptive, status-based distinctions formerly separating class from class, man from woman, man from man, thereby making it possible for "*the* people" to become "*a* people," with a popular will that might be made to govern. Liberal individuality creates the possibility of republican popularity—and fears what it has created.

What are we to make of these paradoxes? The contradictions that structure *On Liberty* arise for a reason. Mill was, as usual, ahead of his time: he had identified a danger peculiar to modern societies that would not be clarified until the next century. The right to engage in self-regarding acts was to meet this danger, but it could not do so, because that right services an ideal of individual autonomy, and individual autonomy, as *On Liberty* says quite explicitly, is itself a precipitant of the danger that the right was supposed to meet.

This danger I will refer to as that of *totalitarian* power. Call power totalitarian if, extending far beyond ordinary legal prohibitions, it exerts or seeks to exert a much more affirmative, managerial, dictatorial and minute control over individuals, a power to standardize or as it were write the scripts of individual lives. This is the threat against which *On Liberty* repeatedly warns, a threat posed, as Mill said, not by mere prohibitory laws, but by an entire societal apparatus that "leaves fewer means of escape, penetrating much more deeply into the details of life, and enslaving the soul itself."[37]

The terrain Mill charted in such formulations would be explored much later by Michel Foucault, who in a sense merely elaborated on *On Liberty*

36. *Id.* at 65.
37. *Id.* at 4.

when he warned against regarding power in modern societies merely as a prohibitory force, "whose function is repression." The power to be reckoned with in modern societies, for Foucault as for Mill, is more *productive* than *prohibitory*. It is a power, deployed through a variety of practices, to monitor, discipline, shape and normalize lives, to produce individuals from within. "What makes power hold good, what makes it accepted, is simply the fact that it doesn't only weigh on us as a force that says no, but that it traverses and produces things, it induces pleasure, forms knowledge, produces discourses. It needs to be considered as a productive network that runs through the whole social body. . . ."[38]

Now, if this productive, normalizing power is the threat to be resisted, it is natural to think of individual autonomy as the appropriate starting point, if not indeed the endpoint, of resistance. Mill thought so. But the thought is a blind alley. Invoking individual autonomy to solve the problem of forced conformity in democratic societies invariably generates the first of *On Liberty*'s paradoxes, in which the true threat to each individual's liberty to engage in self-regarding conduct turns out to be nothing other than others' self-regarding conduct. That paradox is completely generalizable: whenever individual autonomy is said to be that which the tyranny of the majority threatens, the true threat to individual autonomy will turn out to be individual autonomy itself.

An illustration. Homosexual sex is a clear instance of the kind of conduct that the concept of individual autonomy is supposed to vindicate. Individual autonomy need not be understood here solely by reference to Mill's principle of self-regarding acts. Many have argued against anti-homosexuality laws on the basis of a principle of individual self-determination or self-definition.[39] Indeed, before the United States Supreme Court in *Bowers v. Hardwick*[40] brought such decisions to a halt, it was possible for a lower court to read *Roe* and the other privacy cases as standing for a right, as the Supreme Court itself would put it, "to define one's own identity," which protected homosexuality just as it protected decisions concerning procreation.[41] Some commentators enthu-

38. Michel Foucault, *Interview—Truth and Power,* in Power/Knowledge: Selected Interviews and Other Writings 1972–1977, at 119 (C. Gordon ed., 1980). *See also, e.g.,* Michel Foucault, Discipline and Punish 183–99 (1977).

39. Professor Tribe made this argument over twenty years ago. *See* Laurence Tribe, American Constitutional Law J. 15–13, at 943 (1st ed., 1978).

40. 478 U.S. 186 (1986) (rejecting a right of privacy challenge to the prohibition of homosexual sodomy).

41. BenShalom v. Secretary of the Army, 489 F. Supp. 964 (E.D. Wis. 1980) (holding that the military could not discharge a soldier because of her homosexuality); *see*

siastically supported this result, arguing that homosexuals could not be discriminated against in the workplace because such discrimination would violate their right of "self-definition":

> Ideally, the law should . . . recognize a public right of employees to work in a sexually pluralistic environment . . . , a workplace atmosphere that allows all people to explore and express their sexual identities. . . . [P]ersonal identity has an interactive and communicative component. The emancipatory potential of the case can only be fully realized when its logic is extended to the communal aspects of working life.[42]

The argument is well-meaning, but hopelessly self-contradictory. The author fails to notice that, precisely because of the "communal" and "interactive component" of "personal identity," intolerant heterosexuals can equally insist that *their* identity (and hence their right of privacy) would be violated by laws establishing a "sexually pluralistic environment" in which homosexuals were free to "explore and express their sexual identities." Indeed they can claim that their self-definition is violated simply by having to labor in the same workplace, or live in the same community, as homosexuals. Intolerance is never mere spitefulness; as everyone knows, it is also a putative exercise in self-definition and self-determination. The principle of self-determination cannot resolve a conflict in which it figures equally on both sides.

Liberalism needs to portray the conflicts in which it wants to intercede as conflicts between "man" and "state." When problems of liberty are so conceived, there is no contradiction in the liberal demand for individual autonomy. And in the political circumstances of liberalism's birth—circumstances that included, principally, resistance to tyranny in its classical, monarchic sense—it may have been possible to understand the problem of liberty in this way. But when liberalism directs itself against democracy, which brings with it, as Mill was hardly the first to see, a different form of tyranny—the "tyranny of the majority"—the analysis falters. In circumstances of "majority tyranny," every contest in which liberalism wants to intercede *on behalf of* individual autonomy is in fact a contest *between* or *among* individual autonomies. The

---

Roberts v. United States Jaycees, 468 U.S. 609, 618 (1984) ("the ability to define one's own identity" "is central to any concept of liberty"). In *Hardwick,* the dissenting justices reaffirmed this self-definitional view of the right of privacy: "We protect the decision whether to have a child because parenthood alters so dramatically an individual's self-definition." 478 U.S. at 205 (Blackmun, J., dissenting).

42. Karl Klare, *The Public/Private Distinction in Labor Law,* 130 U. Pa. L. Rev. 1358, 1387–88 (1982).

individualist—the non-conformist—threatens the self-determination of the intolerant majority just as they threaten his, and the law that imposes conformity on the individualist, while suppressing *his* self-determination, is an exercise of *theirs*.

To be sure, we often fail to see this obvious contradiction within the logic of self-determination. We say, for example, that someone's interest in making others conform to his values does not count as a legally cognizable interest, or that it does not count as part of his self-determination, or that if he and other like-minded persons pass a law forcing conformity on others, this collective political exercise does not count as an act of individual self-determination. But such propositions cheat. They are not warranted by the concept of self-determination, individual autonomy, or neutrality (the concepts that are supposed to be doing the work). The fact is that many individuals' "identity" or self-understanding is wrapped up with the idea of living in a particular kind of homogeneous society or community. The efforts of such individuals, legal or non-legal, to preserve their homogeneous values are just as much an exercise of self-determination as is the effort of an "individualist" to resist them. In other words, a liberal regime based on the ideal of individual autonomy has no principled reason to prefer the autonomy of the iconoclast over that of the intolerant. What liberalism calls a threat to individual autonomy in such cases is nothing other than an exercise of individual autonomy—by the intolerant.

But this is not all. If we only said that the value of individual autonomy figures on both sides of conflicts such as the one over homosexuality, we would leave out another point of still greater importance. We would entirely miss the force of Mill's insight—and this was the source of the second paradox noted above—that the democratic proliferation of individual autonomy rights is itself a primary cause of the homogenization with which Mill was concerned. Mill made this observation, but offered no analysis or explanation of it. He could not. For Mill, liberal individual rights were to be the antidote to the poison of Oriental conformism seeping into Western society. What can he say when liberal individual rights turn out to be the carrier of this poison, if not the poison itself?

It is not so puzzling that the proliferation of a right to make one's own choices, to act on one's own preferences, to "define one's own identity," might serve as a vehicle of homogenization. We know this phenomenon. We feel it when we are obliged to define ourselves by choosing which car to buy. If this illustration trivializes, consider sexuality. Foucault's elaboration of the paradoxical lines of thought initiated in *On Liberty* illustrates how the entire struggle for sexual self-definition—the entire idea that we have "sexual identities," whether homosexual, heterosexual, or something else, deeply needing to be "explored and expressed"—can itself be a vehicle for the standardization that it is supposed to resist.

Foucault denies the claim, commonplace since Freud, that sex occupies a biologically or psychologically privileged status in human identity—that sex holds, if only we could unravel its secrets, "the deeply buried truth about ourselves."[43] The twentieth century's "sexual liberation" movement was not the emancipatory struggle it imagined itself to be. It was, according to Foucault, part and parcel of a profound development occurring throughout modern Western society, traceable to the confessional practices of medieval Christianity, through which we have come, almost obsessively, to seek the fundamental truth about who we are and who we might be in our "sexuality" and our "sexual identities." Freud, on this view, did not break revolutionarily from Victorian "sexual repression"; on the contrary, Victorianism and Freudianism are both manifestations of a "centuries-long rise of a complex deployment for compelling sex to speak, for fastening our attention and concern upon sex." "What is peculiar to modern societies"—and Foucault is here describing not merely twentieth-century Western societies, but the supposedly sexually repressive cultures of the nineteenth century as well—"is not that they consigned sex to a shadow existence, but that they dedicated themselves to speaking of it *ad infinitum,* while exploiting it as *the* secret." "[I]n the West, the project of a science of the subject has gravitated, in ever narrowing circles, around the question of sex."[44]

Homosexuality again provides a case in point, illustrating how nineteenth-century sexual "repressiveness" in fact assigned to sexuality an unprecedented importance in individual's lives, sexualizing personal identity itself. "As de-

43. Michel Foucault, 1 The History of Sexuality: An Introduction 69 (1980). For a good short discussion, see Charles Taylor, *Foucault on Freedom and Truth,* in Foucault: A Critical Reader 69 (D. Hoy ed., 1986).

44. *Id.* at 35, 70, 158. Foucault's conclusion is memorable:

> Perhaps one day people will wonder at this. They will not be able to understand how a civilization so intent on developing enormous instruments of production and destruction found the time and the infinite patience to inquire so anxiously concerning the actual state of sex; people will smile perhaps when they recall that there were men—meaning ourselves—who believed that therein resided a truth every bit as precious as the one they had already demanded from the earth, the stars, and the pure forms of their thought. . . .

Id. at 157–58. "The irony of this deployment"—these are the book's last words—"is in having us believe that our 'liberation' is in the balance." *Id.* at 159.

fined by the ancient civil or canonical codes, sodomy was a category of forbidden acts." But in the nineteenth century, writes Foucault, homosexual sex came to be seen as somehow definitive of the entire personality, the identity, of "the homosexual":

> The nineteenth-century homosexual became a personage, a past, a case history, and a childhood, in addition to being a type of life, a life-form. . . . Nothing that went into his total composition was unaffected by his sexuality. . . . It was consubstantial with him, less as a habitual sin than as a singular nature. The sodomite had been a temporary aberration; the homosexual as now a species.[45]

This is why the concept of a sexualized personal identity and the concomitant "right" to such an identity cannot be the solution to the problem of homosexuality in modern society. This concept and this right *are* the problem. To accept the notion that acts of homosexual sex are definitive of the "personhood" of "the homosexual" is not to fight heterosexism, but to play into its hands. Are acts of homosexual sex "self-defining"? Do they mark a person as a particular kind of being—a "homosexual"? To say so is not emancipatory. It is, rather, part of the culture through which a heterosexist society produces heterosexuals and vilifies—"inverts."

The real challenge in conflicts such as the one over homosexuality is not to give more respect to an "identity" that has been insufficiently accredited. On the contrary, the challenge presented, as Mill and Foucault both suggested, is to resist the complex network of forces that attempt to impose particularized "identities" upon us. Women do not need to be told about this; the desire to specify a set of feminine identities has organized one of the most obvious and potent of these networks for a long time. (Another example: the specification of negro identities. Another: the Western tendency, indulged in by Mill, to imagine an exotic, conformist Orient.) Today's partisans of identity politics remain hopelessly caught in this old cage, licking the boots of the warden with every call for recognition of a "feminine" morality, a "black" linguistics, a "gay" jurisprudence, a "Native American" understanding of time, and so on.

Against the danger of totalitarian power, resistance does not begin with an individual's right to be self-determining, to live the particular life of his choice. It begins rather with the right of each person *not to have a particular life imposed upon him*. We arrive in this way at the anti-totalitarian right of privacy sketched at the beginning of this chapter. To have a life imposed upon

45. *Id.* at 42–43.

you in the pertinent sense—the totalitarian sense—is to be impressed into service, to see your life occupied and taken over, as a woman is taken over when motherhood is forced on her against her will.

Here is a virtue of an anti-totalitarian right: by contrast to the usual liberal formulations, it states a right that people can and do actually have. Consider the "right to pursue the occupation of one's choice." This is a formulation prototypical of the rhetoric of individual autonomy and self-determination; this right is even guaranteed by certain contemporary European constitutions. But this right is a fantasy. No one has ever had it. No state has ever recognized it. To begin with, in every society there will be some occupations—say, burglary or prostitution—that are unlawful for everyone. Moreover, among the lawful occupations, some will be monopolized, while others will be subject to legal eligibility requirements that many people cannot pass. And then there is the uncomfortable fact that some people are physically unable to pursue the "occupation of their choice." But the idea of a right to "occupational autonomy" contains one kernel of truth. In one sense there is such a right, and it is recognized, albeit implicitly, by every modern democracy in the developed world: *the right not to be forced into an occupation dictated by the state.*

Without even citing the *Republic,* we can have no difficulty imagining how this right might be violated. Perhaps everyone at the age of seventeen might have to undergo a battery of examinations, with each person assigned, on the basis of the results, to the occupational category best utilizing his talents. The power to write citizens' life-scripts in this fashion would be a totalitarian power. Hence the anti-totalitarian principle stands against it. It does so, however, without the false logic of individual autonomy, which at best falls into self-contradiction and at worst reentrenches the problem it is meant to solve.

The *logical* structure, then, of the anti-totalitarian principle is arrived at: (1) by recognizing, with Mill, the possibility of lives being taken over from within, through exercises of power "penetrating . . . deeply" and affirmatively "into the details of life"; and (2) by recognizing further, with Foucault, that this possibility calls for a shift in focus from proscription to prescription, from the individual who finds that the particular life he would choose for himself is forbidden to him, to the individual who finds that a life is being forced upon him. The *normative* premises, however, behind the anti-totalitarian principle follow from the theory of self-government that has been the subject of this book.

Self-government on the model of writing is, as I have said, the freedom to live by commitments of one's own authorship. This is not a freedom of self-determination or self-definition. There is no such thing as the right of each individual to define his own identity. No one has ever had this right. No one could do it even if he had the right. We come into our subjectivity far too formed, too constructed by family, by society, by history, by genetic coding, to indulge in dreams of self-definition. The absence of willed or chosen self-definition obtains not only for such physical facts as skin color, but just as much for those more psychological attributes of the self that those who like to think of identity in terms of self-definition invariably regard as central. Who among us chooses, for example, his beliefs about religion? The notion that American constitutional law secures a "freedom to believe or disbelieve as one chooses" misstates the relationship of will to faith. Few people choose the God they believe in. No one chooses the God he does not believe in.

A commitmentarian self does not seek to be self-defining or self-determining. This self understands the role of inheritance in what we are. But within the constraints imposed by biology, history, society, and family, we may yet be free, if we are fortunate, to give meaning to our lives. We may be free to make our own monuments, to give ourselves purposes, to be the authors of commitments by which we live. This freedom does *not* imply living according to the commitments of our choice, meaning the commitments we would most prefer, the ones we would choose for ourselves if we were entirely free to choose. That would be to recast commitmentarian freedom in the rhetoric of individual autonomy. Law does *not* violate an individual's commitmentarian freedom when it prohibits conduct that he deems central to the one life or life-script he most wants to pursue. Law violates this freedom only when it makes an individual live out a script of someone else's authorship.

A person unable to pursue the one occupation he most prizes is not deprived of the freedom to be the author of his own life. That would be like saying that a writer who cannot today write *Moby Dick* (because it's been done, or because it would be a copyright violation) cannot be an author at all. But a person forcibly assigned to a state-dictated occupation is necessarily forced to live out commitments of someone else's making; he is pressed into a life the fundamental commitments of which are of someone else's authorship. As a result, the anti-totalitarian principle reflects an absolute requirement of individual freedom within the theory of commitmentarian self-government.

More than this, the anti-totalitarian right of privacy reflects a requirement of *political* freedom within the theory of commitmentarian self-government. Totalitarian power reverses the essential democratic relationship of authority between citizens and state. A totalitarian state is one that seeks to produce citizens according to *its* designs, whereas democracy requires just the reverse. When individuals are subject to totalitarian power, when their futures are taken over and affirmatively dictated, when they are instrumentalized and impressed into service by law, they have become the objects, not the agents, of government. They have become no longer the authors, but the conscripts, of their law.

Democracy on the model of writing requires a certain space to be maintained between state and society. A democratic state cannot be permitted either to take over the institutions that mediate between individuals and the state or to take over individual lives directly. The danger of a state that erases this space does not lie in its intrusion into zones of life that are somehow "private" by nature or by timeless moral truth. The danger of such a state lies in its attempt to strangle the future, to freeze the processes of change, to eliminate the political openness of the time to come. Democratic self-government requires not only a people that honors its own self-given commitments but a people that maintains its independent authority to reexamine, to remake, to rewrite these commitments over time. Totalitarian power, regardless of whether it conforms at any given moment to popular will, is precisely that power which seeks to bring democracy-over-time to an end. Individuals whose lives are scripted by the state cannot be the authors of their state.

Totalitarianism is therefore antithetical to democracy—to democracy-over-time, to constitutionalism as democracy. An anti-totalitarian limit on political power is a condition necessary to the continuance of the very project (the temporally extended project) of constitutionalism as democracy. It is, in this sense, an unwritten law of written constitutionalism.

This is the constitutional case on which alone an unenumerated right of privacy can legitimately rest. If a right is necessary to the very project of constitutionalism as democracy, then alone does it have a claim to constitutional status even though nowhere enumerated in the constitutional text. But for just this reason, the anti-totalitarian right that I am describing departs from the Millian and Foucauldian lines of thought that brought this right into perspective. The right of privacy is not Millian: it is very far from a perfect freedom, legal and social, to engage in self-regarding acts. Nor is it Foucauldian: Foucault's controversial, wholly decentralized, almost subjectless conception of power provides no basis (and was not intended to provide a basis) for a *constitutional* principle. The anti-totalitarian principle I have described is more limited. It is concerned with *state* power; it responds to the specific threat of a democratic state attempting to exercise a scripting or conscripting power over its citizens' lives incompatible with the project of democracy over time. As will be seen more clearly below, I am by no means dismissing the complex operation of social norms and practices that concerned both Mill and Foucault. But it is only when a law (or some other state action) backs up such norms and practices, throwing the state's coercive weight behind them, that the right of privacy I describe will be implicated.

This point can best be clarified by offering some illustrations of the anti-totalitarian right of privacy in operation.

I begin with the so-called right to die, which ensures that terminally ill patients may refuse or terminate unwanted life-sustaining medical technology, and which highlights acutely the deficiencies of individual autonomy accounts of privacy. The "right to die" is doctrinally problematic because, among other reasons, of the difficulty of distinguishing cases of "ordinary" suicide, which are not understood to involve the exercise of a constitutionally protected right. (Assisted suicide continues to be a crime in most states, and the suicide himself, even if he is not criminally liable, remains liable to other kinds of legal restraint, such as involuntary civil confinement.) The numerous American courts upholding a privacy right to refuse life-support machinery have invariably and gamely sought to distinguish suicide,[46] but their autonomy-based rhetoric makes the distinction impossible to draw. After all, if the decision to live or die is so fundamental that individuals must be allowed to make it for themselves, then it is difficult to see why the "right to die" is not generally available to all competent adults.

The juridical logic deployed to explain away this difficulty has been less than satisfactory. It has been said, for example, that a terminally ill patient's termination of life-sustaining medical treatment "may not properly be viewed" as suicide, because "if death were eventually to occur, it would be the result, primarily, of the underlying disease."[47] This is like saying that throwing oneself out of a window cannot properly be viewed as suicide, because if death were to occur, it would be the result, primarily, of the underlying pavement. Should a murderer kill by disconnecting a hospital patient's life-support machinery, his lawyers would be laughed out of court if they claimed that there had been no homicide because death was primarily the result of the victim's underlying medical condition. One who terminates life-support machinery kills; one who terminates his own life-support machinery

46. *See, e.g.,* Rasmussen v. Fleming, 741 P.2d 674, 685 (Ariz. 1987) (upholding the right to refuse life-sustaining treatment, but distinguishing suicide); In re Gardner, 534 A.2d 947, 955–56 (Me. 1987); Superintendent v. Saikewicz, 370 N.E.2d 417, 426 n.11 (Mass. 1977).

47. *Conroy,* 486 A.2d at 1224.

kills himself. Nothing is gained by denying this fact. Nor is the analysis improved by saying that the person terminating medical treatment lacks a "specific intent to die," because he "may fervently wish to live, but to do so . . . without protracted suffering."[48] At bottom, this is only to say that the patient, if he could escape his actual condition, would have no wish to die. But that is true in cases of "ordinary" suicide too; someone throwing himself off a bridge also "may fervently wish to live, but to do so . . . without protracted suffering."

The patient exercising his "right to die" is indistinguishable from cases of ordinary suicide so long as the focal point of analysis is the proscribed act. The prohibited act—the decision to cause one's own death—is the same in both cases. But the analysis changes altogether when the focus shifts from what is prohibited to what is affirmatively brought about. From this perspective, the dissimilarities between the two situations become much more apparent. For a patient attached to medical machinery in a hospital room, to be compelled to remain in this condition is in fact to be forced into a highly particularized, totally dependent, and rigidly standardized life. This person's body is so far expropriated that the most elemental acts of existence—breathing, eating, circulating blood—are thrust on him by external mechanisms. He has become a kind of living marionette. The right of privacy I have described invalidates any law that has this effect on a person's life.

By contrast, the "ordinary" suicide suffers no such thoroughgoing occupation of his life or take-over of his body. An avenue of escape is foreclosed to him, to be sure, and he may suffer excruciating unhappiness as a result. But unhappiness is not the test of unconstitutionality. There is in American constitutional law no right to die. There is, however, a constitutional right not to have one's life appropriated and one's body taken over by state-ordered machinery.

Thus the anti-totalitarian analysis explains far better than current doctrine can the actual right-to-die case law. It also suggests how the courts should respond to the recent controversies surrounding assisted suicide. Because there is no general right to die, laws criminalizing assisted suicide are properly upheld against right of privacy challenges.[49] But where the prohibition of assisted suicide has the effect of forcing someone to live a marionette's life—whether he is the puppet of medical technology or of a wasting, debilitating disease—the right of privacy should prevail.

48. *Id. See also Gardner,* 534 A.2d at 955–56; *Saikewicz,* 370 N.E.2d at 426 n.11.

49. *See, e.g.,* Vacco v. Quill, 521 U.S. 793 (1997); Washington v. Glucksberg, 521 U.S. 702 (1997).

The "fundamental right to marry," supposedly protected by current privacy doctrine, would have no protection under an anti-totalitarian right of privacy. A law limiting the relationships to which the state will give the imprimatur of lawful marriage denies status to some and at least an imagined felicity to others, but it effects no affirmative take-over of anyone's life. (By contrast, the anti-totalitarian principle would be implicated by a law preventing a married person from ever obtaining a divorce.) As a result, again in marked contrast to the situation prevailing on standard autonomy-based accounts of privacy, the anti-totalitarian principle is thrown into no confusion by laws barring polygamy, consanguineous marriage, and so on. Courts that speak of a fundamental right to marry typically forget to address the validity of such laws; the distinguishing thought, whether implicit or explicit, seems to be an insistence, by definitional fiat, that marriage just means the union of one man with one woman not too closely related by blood.

For better or worse, for richer or poorer, the American Constitution includes no right to marry. Nor should any such right be recognized under the heading of privacy. Justice William O. Douglas, writing for the Court in the decision that first articulated the contemporary right of privacy, referred to marriage as a relationship "intimate to the degree of being sacred"; marriage, he held, implicated "a right of privacy older that the Bill of Rights."[50] Constitutionalism as democracy does not recognize the idea of sacred rights or of immemorial rights pre-dating the Constitution itself. The only constitutional rights are those derived from the people's own acts of constitution-writing; the only legitimate argument for an unwritten right is that the right in question is necessary to the project of commitmentarian self-government itself. Marriage may be sacred, but the idea that it occupies a domain of "private life" unregulable by law is a fantasy. Law—whether religious or secular—defines marriage and the obligations attached thereto. Hence certain Supreme Court decisions in this area should be overruled. Say that a man is under a court-ordered obligation to support children that he fathered in a prior relationship but that are no longer in his custody. Say that he flouts this support obligation. There should be absolutely no constitutional difficulty if a state forbids this man to marry again until he makes good on his support obligations. The Court ruled otherwise some twenty years ago,[51] but from the perspective developed here, the case is wrongly decided.

50. *Griswold,* 381 U.S. at 486.

51. *E.g.,* Zablocki v. Redhail, 434 U.S. 374 (1978) (striking down a state statute providing that a person under a court child-support order "may not marry without a prior judicial determination that the support obligation has been met").

So too are the cases suggesting that procreation is a fundamental right beyond the reach of state regulation. A person told that he or she cannot have children in future is not forced into a particularized life or occupation of the state's choosing. If in the decades to come population growth should lead to a law setting limits on the number of children people can have, many would undoubtedly feel that the state was intruding unconscionably into their "personal" lives, or that the state was depriving them of a freedom crucial to their self-definition or happiness. But as indicated above, such a law would not violate an anti-totalitarian right of privacy.

This does not mean, of course, that government could arbitrarily or discriminatorily make certain persons unmarriageable or ineligible for childbearing. The equal protection clause does not disappear just because the right of privacy has no application to a given case. A state that deems black parents unfit to adopt white children violates the Fourteenth Amendment even though it does not violate the unwritten right of privacy. On the other hand, racial miscegenation laws are properly subject to both equal protection *and* privacy challenges. The purpose of America's miscegenation laws was, among other things, to control the genetic composition of ensuing generations in white supremacist fashion: to guarantee the creation of racially pure offspring. For this reason, the Supreme Court was correct to strike down such laws on both equal protection and privacy grounds.[52] These were eugenics laws, and eugenics, particularly racial eugenics, as this century knows too well, is a totalitarian project. As human control over the genome progresses, there will be increasing temptation on the part of state actors to indulge in human eugenic regulation. Every governmental foray into this field, even the most seemingly benign, must be met with the greatest caution.

I have used the word conscription to describe the kind of affirmative effect on a person's life that violates the anti-totalitarian right of privacy. Hence it seems important to say a word about the draft. I do not think that a wartime draft is necessarily unconstitutional, even though it would clearly take over and occupy individuals' lives in the way I have described. The reason is that constitutional rights are not secured by a doctrine that results in the nation itself being taken over by an occupying army, sweeping aside the Constitution altogether. This is not to embrace the idea, seemingly accepted by current doctrine, that constitutional rights are generally subject to a cost-benefit "compelling state interest" exception. Commitmentarian constitutionalism does not accept that idea, as was illustrated by the last chapter's discussion

52. Loving v. Virginia, 388 U.S. 1 (1967).

of strict equal protection scrutiny. Instead, the operative idea is a much narrower one: that constitutional rights should not be interpreted to be self-defeating. But for this reason, a peacetime draft, or indeed a draft effected to fight a war of aggression, might well be unconstitutional.

Homosexuality is a topic too complex to be treated adequately here. I will make only the following, insufficient remarks. The right of privacy has never been, and should not be understood as, a generalized right of sexual autonomy. It does not protect, as a principle of self-regarding acts might be supposed to protect (but cannot coherently protect), any and all acts of sex among consenting adults. To be sure, there has been an undoubted tendency in the Supreme Court's privacy decisions to gravitate around sex. The well-known decisions cover contraception, marriage, miscegenation, abortion, homosexuality—in other words, the conditions under which individuals may legally have sex and the consequences that follow upon it. Nothing in the privacy case law, or in the standard accounts thereof, says that the doctrine should focus in any special fashion on sex. Nevertheless, it has.

Part of the explanation may have to do with the association observed earlier between the American right of privacy and the idea of safeguarding "personhood" or "self-definition." Given the tendency of modern conceptions of personal identity to gravitate (as Foucault put it) "in ever narrowing circles" around sexuality, one might almost have predicted a similar tendency in the privacy case law. But there is something else to consider. Privacy in American constitutional law has never vindicated anything like a principle of sexual self-definition. Rather, it has applied itself to sex primarily where a prohibition of sex-related conduct has been a central plank in a set of institutions—not only legal, but economic, cultural, religious and political as well—whose aim has been to impose on individuals traditional, life-occupying, standardized, reproductive roles. This is most obvious in the decisions striking down anti-contraception and anti-abortion laws. In such cases, the real issue was not "sexual liberation"; it was whether the law could throw its coercive weight behind the social norms and practices forcing women into the reproductive roles with which they were and are so familiar. But this is why, when the right of privacy fully understands its own principles, the prohibition of homosexuality will fall.

Homosexuality laws seek to create heterosexuals. That is their point. Of course, law in such matters is only one small force in a much larger network of social forces; it is here, when the law throws its coercive force behind social norms, that constitutional analysis can appropriately take account of all the non-legal practices and discourses that so concerned both Mill and Foucault.

Anti-contraception and anti-abortion laws were exercises of totalitarian power against women in part because of the way they interacted and interlocked with an entire complex of social forces driving women into the home. In similar fashion, anti-homosexuality prohibitions throw state coercion behind our societies' creation of traditional masculine and feminine heterosexual forms of life. If a reader questions whether forcing heterosexuality on someone can count as a sufficiently determinate, particularized imposition in one's life to violate the anti-totalitarian principle that I have described, the question is a fair one, but it is almost certainly a heterosexual's question. If this reader will picture living in a society where heterosexuality is prohibited and loathed, and where as a result he is obliged to enter into a lifetime of homosexual relations if he is to have permitted sexual relations at all, he may find his question answered.

This is a good place to return to the subject of abortion, both because of the references to it in the preceding paragraphs and because, in response to those paragraphs, someone is bound to raise an objection that applies not only to homosexuality but also to abortion. The objection might be put as follows. "Anti-homosexuality laws do not *force* homosexuals into heterosexual relations. Homosexuals remain perfectly free, for example, to abstain from sex altogether if they so choose." Something similar is often said in defense of anti-abortion laws, and the anti-totalitarian account of *Roe v. Wade* is especially obliged to have a clear answer to this objection. The anti-totalitarian account, as I have said, holds that anti-abortion laws are unconstitutional because they force women to have children. But an opponent of *Roe* will say that such laws do not force anything on anyone. Putting aside cases of rape, he will say, women remain perfectly free to refrain from sex whenever they are unprepared to bear the children that might result. They also remain perfectly free to turn over any unwanted children they might have to an adoption service.

Call this the "force objection," because in essence it challenges the idea of force that I have been using throughout the foregoing discussion. On its face, the objection seems almost unanswerable. Isn't it just wrong to say that an anti-abortion law (other than in cases of rape, for which an exception could always be made) *"forces"* women to be mothers against their will, given that women could by their own choice avoid this result, either by refraining from sex or, if we are speaking of child-rearing as well as child-bearing, by surrendering their children to adoption?

But imagine a law mandating that certain men have to be bus drivers for the next eighteen years of their lives. This imaginary law contains a proviso:

the men in question can avoid this result, if they like, *simply by giving up sex or by relinquishing any children they happen to have to an adoption agency*. Now suppose that the state's lawyers come to court defending this law on the ground that it does not *force* anything on anyone. Every man to whom the law applies, the lawyers argue, remains "perfectly free" to avoid bus driving if he chooses. Hence no one is forced to do anything against his will. Would such an argument be taken seriously?

Certainly it shouldn't be. The force objection rests on a very poorly thought-through sense of what it means for the state to coerce. No law physically forces anyone to do anything. Even a criminal law leaves people with a choice—going to jail. When we say that a law "forces" someone to do something, we are not saying that the state has left the individual no choice at all. We are saying something about the nature of the choices left to the person if he refuses. And if we are concerned with totalitarian exercises of state power, then the kind of state force with which we should be most concerned is not nullified—it is not even diminished—if it imposes its terms "only" on those who "choose" not to give up sex or those who "choose" not to give up their children. On the contrary, the kind of normalizing, life-shaping state force that concerns us is made stronger, more dangerous, by the fact that it attaches its instrumentalizing devices to such basic human inclinations. Of course individuals would be unconstitutionally forced into an occupation if a law dictated that occupation to them on pain of giving up sex or relinquishing their children. Thus the force objection fails. An anti-abortion law does force motherhood on women in the constitutional sense, despite the "choices" it leaves open.

A very different objection to *Roe* concerns the status of the fetus. This question is much more complicated, and saying only a little about it is probably worse than saying nothing at all. Nevertheless, I will assume the risk and say a few words.

There can be no thought of trying to demonstrate by argument that a certain view of the fetus must be accepted by all "reasonable" minds. For many people, an embryo's humanity is an article of faith, and the argument presented here is neither intended nor remotely sufficient to shake anyone's faith. The question is not what a given individual may or may not think about the fetus. The question is how early in a woman's pregnancy the *state* may deem a developing fetus or embryo to be a human being, and the state labors here under obligations that individuals do not.

If a state sought to deem all post-conception abortion to be a killing of a human being, the state would not be able to rely on religious tenets, such as divine ensoulment, but would rather have to rest such a law on a proposition more like the following: a human being exists where there is nucleic genetic completion plus potentiality to develop into a full-grown person. There are good reasons to believe that this position is logically indefensible. I will briefly give these reasons, but in the end little will turn on this point, because I will concede in a moment, for purposes of discussion, that a life-begins-at-conception position is at least arguable.

The genetic-completion-plus-potentiality position equates a potential thing with the thing itself. No one would say that an acorn is a tree, and if an acorn in your hand is not a tree, it certainly does not become a tree the moment it is planted in the earth. Or again: if we can imagine butterflies having rights, it would not follow that a caterpillar had the same rights merely by virtue of the fact that the caterpillar is an earlier, genetically complete part of the butterfly's life cycle. Whether the caterpillar had the same rights would depend on what it was about butterflies that entitled them to the rights in question.

The difficulties of conflating potential things with the things into which they may develop are many. Here is one: recent developments in the technology of cloning suggest that the nuclei of many of our cells—or at the very least of some cells other than the zygote itself—also have the potential, when placed in the right environment, to develop into full-grown creatures. These other nuclei are just as genetically complete as that of a fertilized ovum. If they too have the potential to develop into full-grown persons, it would seem, on the genetic-completion-plus-potentiality view, that they too must be regarded as lives in being. When cloning science improves to the point where the cells on the skin of your arm can be made to grow into human beings, will we be obliged to say that you kill a human being whenever you scratch your elbow?

Perhaps someone will reply that a nucleus of a skin cell becomes a human being only when placed in an environment in which it actually (as opposed to potentially) has the potential to grow into a mature person. The notion here is that an implanted embryo has a kind of "actual potential" to continue along in the human life cycle that a clonable skin cell or its nucleus does not. But this idea of "actual potentiality" is very probably unintelligible. A potential can come *closer* to actuality (as a caterpillar, by stages, comes closer to being a butterfly), and hence we might well say that an acorn has a *greater* potential of becoming an oak after it is planted in the earth, meaning a greater likelihood of its achieving this potential. But the acorn does not obtain its potentiality only upon being planted in the earth. Its potential to grow into an oak does not become "actual" at that point, as opposed to merely having been a "potential potential" when it was dangling from a branch. The potential is there all along. If the proposition is that a fertilized ovum is an independent life in being (from the moment of conception) because it has genetic-completion-plus-potentiality, it is very difficult to distinguish between a fertilized ovum and a cell that can be cloned into a full-grown person.

Even the conceived zygote, fertilized in the natural way of things, cannot grow into maturity without a great deal being done to it. It must first be implanted in a uterus (or a machine simulating that environment). It must thereafter be warmed, fed, oxygenated, and so on. Its "actual potential" to develop into a person is just as contingent on its being placed and maintained in the right kind of environment as is the "potential potential" of the nucleus of a skin cell.

What is producing confusion here is a conflation of the seed with the developed thing. That which may one day develop into x is not x. Every attempt to say that the zygote cannot be logically or normatively distinguished from a child is doomed to confusion.

To be sure, there is no bright line demarcating the moment at which what was once an ovum turns into a person or human being. But the possibility of intermediate cases, to which no bright lines can be applied, is never sufficient to undermine a distinction. Just because day turns imperceptibly into night, it does not follow that day *is* night. An acorn is not an oak tree, notwithstanding the fact that there is no moment at which one can definitively say when it becomes an oak tree.

(It is just at this point of the analysis that the Court's current resolution of this problem—which takes viability to be a decisive turning point in the gestational process—begins to make a certain sense. For viability is the point at which the fetus attains a kind of independent being, and under current technology, viability coincides with extremely important organic developments in fetal ontogeny.[53] As everyone knows, however, the logic of viability is not stable. Future neonatal technology will someday undermine the concept of viability altogether.)

Nevertheless, despite everything that has been said so far, let me stipulate to the intelligibility of the life-begins-at-conception position. After all, contrary to what some philosophers seem to think, there is no constitutional requirement that states adopt the philosophically most rigorous position on any subject. The embryo's status is not merely a logical question. Nor is it even a merely factual question. It is also a moral question. If every fact of human embryology were known, all the way down to the most minute sub-

53. For more detail, see Jed Rubenfeld, *On the Legal Status of the Proposition that "Life Begins at Conception,"* 43 Stan. L. Rev. 599 (1991).

molecular penetralia, still people could and would disagree about when to regard the developing embryo or fetus as a human life in its own right. And contrary once again to conventional liberal philosophy, there has never been and never could be a constitutional bar prohibiting government from enacting into law a particular moral position.

But to repeat: the question to be resolved here is not what position individuals ought to take on this issue. The question is solely this: when may a *state* at the earliest deem an embryo or fetus to be a human being? Although a state may and must legislate morality, it cannot do so in such a way as to destroy a constitutional right.

This is a principle applicable throughout constitutional law. A state could not deem strong emotions to be "morally harmful" and on that basis ban political dissent. State legislators might deem it immoral for parents to expose their children to cannibalism, but a state could not on this ground deem certain high Christian services to be cannibalistic and therefore prohibit parents from taking their children to communion. If legalizing a particular moral position results in the eradication of a constitutional right, a state cannot enact that position into law.

Now once the right of privacy is reconceived as a right against the forced taking-over of lives, it becomes clear that, even though *individuals* may believe that human life or personhood begins at conception, a state cannot enact this moral belief into law. Doing so would, as we have seen, unconstitutionally force motherhood on women and thereby violate the anti-totalitarian right of privacy. At the earliest, a state may constitutionally deem a fetus to be a human life in being *only at a point far enough along in pregnancy so that women have a reasonable time to discover their pregnancy and to obtain an abortion if they choose.* Then no woman would be forced either to give up sex or her own children in order to avoid motherhood. So long as this requirement is satisfied (and the Court's current viability doctrine does satisfy this requirement), there is no constitutional violation if abortion is forbidden thereafter. So long as each woman has a meaningful opportunity *to make her own commitment to childbearing,* the state may hold her to that commitment thereafter.

But isn't it rather strained, someone might ask, to link anti-abortion laws and totalitarianism? What exactly is the connection between abortion and a people's continuing freedom to remake their constitutional order? There is a connection—in fact, a fairly direct one.

In the centuries of its governance, the legal and social regime domesticating women was also a regime that de-politicized them. How? Not only by formally denying to women equal rights of political participation, but also, in important part, by occupying so much of their lives with motherhood. Even female suffrage did not directly or immediately break up this regime. Changing labor conditions certainly played a role in doing so, but there can be little doubt that the legal availability of contraception and abortion placed for the first time in vast numbers of women's hands an unprecedented control over their own lives, which in turn has helped enable them to participate much more fully as economic and political actors. The regime of enforced domesticity for women was self-reproducing; a consequence of women's living so much of their lives in the roles of wives and mothers was to make it very difficult, perhaps impossible, for many men and women to reconceive the lives that women might lead. In other words, the regime of sex discrimination that lasted so long in our history, and that persists today, was in an important sense centrally concerned with producing women who not only were not, but would not struggle to be, authors of the laws that governed them. This result is surely unsurprising; people whose lives are subject to totalitarian control cannot be expected to be meaningfully self-governing.

Ultimately, however, the anti-totalitarian right of privacy reflects an imperative of individual freedom, a right not to be instrumentalized in a certain way. This right attaches to every citizen in a democratic society once democracy is understood on the model of writing. If democracy does not consist in effectuation of majority will, but is rather the temporally extended popular struggle for authorship of the nation's legal and political commitments, then a democratic society labors under a special obligation: to treat each of its citizens as ends, and not merely as means. This is a categorical imperative (it explains why the anti-totalitarian right of privacy can be violated even at the end of someone's life, when he is kept alive by state-ordered machinery, without regard to his status as ongoing participant in a democratic process), but it is not a categorical imperative in the Kantian sense of being derivable from a priori reason alone. It states a right held only by those recognized as citizens in a society pursuing self-government on the model of writing. A citizen whom the law treats solely as an instrument cannot be regarded as an author or even a co-author of the state in which he lives.

There is then, after all, a certain unwritten right to be let alone inherent in written constitutionalism. But to make sense of this phrase, we have to let go of the picture of a space of private life in which the state cannot enter, a duty-free zone beyond the reach of regulation. Law is all over our private lives. It is in our workplaces, in our homes, in our most intimate relationships. By the right to be let alone, therefore, we should understand just this: a right not to have the law script or conscript our lives.

The ultimate privatization of the modern era is that of time itself. The earth belongs to the living: what this really meant (and means) is that the present moment—and only the present moment—belongs to us. It is our private property.

But this means that the future is not ours. The future is foreign territory. It belongs to others. Dazzled by man's newfound freedom from past authority—temporal and spiritual—modernity's devotion to the present unknowingly forswore the future as well.

There was truth in Burke's observation that "[p]eople will not look forward to posterity who never look backward to their ancestors."[54] But Tocqueville captured this truth better. In a well-known passage, *Democracy in America* expresses the spirit of futurity, the utopian future-oriented perspective that modern democracy imagines for itself:

> Democratic peoples do not bother at all about the past, but they gladly start dreaming about the future, and in that direction their imagination knows no bounds, but spreads and grows beyond measure. . . . Democracy shuts the past to poetry but opens the future.

But later—knowingly or unknowingly, and with Tocqueville it is hard to know—he takes it all back:

> [N]ot only does democracy make men forget their ancestors, but it also clouds their view of their descendants. . . . Each man is forever thrown back on himself alone, and there is danger that he may be shut up in the solitude of his own heart.[55]

Tocqueville's poetry is too generous. This privatized man is not confined to the solitude of his heart. He has the whole earth to consume. He has economies to manage. He is not internalized. He is merely individualized and therefore de-politicized.

Contrary to their intentions, the present-tense temporality espoused by Jefferson and Rousseau ultimately disables man from thinking of himself politically. To think of ourselves politically requires reference not merely to a collective political entity, but to a *generation-spanning* political entity such as a nation. When each generation looks upon every other generation as it would upon a foreign nation, then there are no nations. There are only mar-

54. Edmund Burke, Reflections on the Revolution in France 33 (L.G. Mitchell ed., 1993) (1790).

55. 2 Alexis de Tocqueville, Democracy in America bk. I, ch. 17, at 485; bk.II, ch. 2, at 508 (J.P. Mayer ed. & George Lawrence trans., 1969) (1840).

kets. Everyone knows that the global market is a great engine of national disintegration. What is not always observed is the relation between the market and temporality. In the self-understanding of actors developing commercially exploitable technology, like the writers of our shortsighted computer codes, Jefferson's second declaration of independence is perfectly realized. For them, America's future looms on our horizon in precisely the same way that a nation in Asia does. It is just another *emerging market.*

Many will applaud the global market for breaking down national borders. And if global marketization were the dove of world peace, who could be against it? But the imperatives of the global marketplace are not the historical endpoint of Western democracy. They are one of democracy's most serious threats. As the East wholeheartedly embraces private enterprise, we will find that the great Western engine of individualism, the rights of private enterprise and of private consumer choice, will turn out in the end to be, just as Mill warned, the Chinese lady's shoe, threatening to make all peoples alike.

What is to be remembered is that all this privatization is in fact political. Not in the sense that the "personal is political," but in the sense that the market's relentlessly present-tense demolition of old products and old ways is itself the embodiment of temporally extended commitments of our own making. This state of affairs is not an end-state—of history or of national politics. It is only the end of the first book.

INDEX